Bloom's Major Literary Characters

King Arthur

Nick Adams

George F. Babbitt

Elizabeth Bennet

Leopold Bloom

Holden Caulfield

Sir John Falstaff

Huck Finn

Frankenstein

Jay Gatsby

Hamlet

Willy Loman

Macbeth

Hester Prynne

Raskolnikov and Svidrigailov

Satan

Bloom's Major Literary Characters

Holden Caulfield

Edited and with an introduction by
Harold Bloom
Sterling Professor of the Humanities
Yale University

CHELSEA HOUSE
P U B L I S H E R S
A Haights Cross Communications ✦ Company®
Philadelphia

Library of Congress Cataloging-in-Publication Data

Holden Caulfield / [compiled by] Harold Bloom.
    p. cm. — (Bloom's major literary characters)
  Includes bibliographical references and index.
  ISBN 0-7910-8174-5 (alk. paper)
  1. Salinger, J. D. (Jerome David), 1919- Catcher in the rye. 2. Salinger, J. D. (Jerome
David), 1919—-Characters—Holden Caulfield. 3. Caulfield, Holden (Fictitious character)
4. Runaway teenagers in literature. 5. Teenage boys in literature. I. Bloom, Harold. II.
Major literary characters.
  PS3537.A426C328 2004
  813'.54—dc22
                              2004025964

Contributing editor: Janyce Marson

Cover design by Keith Trego

Cover: © Royalty-Free/CORBIS

Layout by EJB Publishing Services

Contents

HAROLD BLOOM

The Analysis of Character

"Character," according to our dictionaries, still has as a primary meaning a graphic symbol, such as a letter of the alphabet. This meaning reflects the word's apparent origin in the ancient Greek character, a sharp stylus. *Charactēr* also meant the mark of the stylus' incisions. Recent fashions in literary criticism have reduced "character" in literature to a matter of marks upon a page. But our word "character" also has a very different meaning, matching that of the ancient Greek *ēthos*, "habitual way of life." Shall we say then that literary character is an imitation of human character, or is it just a grouping of marks? The issue is between a critic like Dr. Samuel Johnson, for whom words were as much like people as like things, and a critic like the late Roland Barthes, who told us that "the fact can only exist linguistically, as a term of discourse." Who is closer to our experience of reading literature, Johnson or Barthes? What difference does it make, if we side with one critic rather than the other?

Barthes is famous, like Foucault and other recent French theorists, for having added to Nietzsche's proclamation of the death of God a subsidiary demise, that of the literary author. If there are no authors, then there are no fictional personages, presumably because literature does not refer to a world outside language. Words indeed necessarily refer to other words in the first place, but the impact of words ultimately is drawn from a universe of fact. Stories, poems, and plays are recognizable as such because they are human utterances within traditions of utterances, and traditions, by achieving authority, become a kind of fact, or at least the sense of a fact. Our sense that literary characters, within the context of a fictive cosmos, indeed are fictional personages is also a kind of fact. The meaning and value of every character in a successful work of literary representation depend upon our ideas of persons in the factual reality of our lives.

Literary character is always an invention, and inventions generally are indebted to prior inventions. Shakespeare is the inventor of literary character as we know it; he reformed the universal human expectations for the verbal imitation of personality, and the reformation appears now to be permanent and uncannily inevitable. Remarkable as the Bible and Homer are at representing personages, their characters are relatively unchanging. They age within their stories, but their habitual modes of being do not develop. Jacob and Achilles unfold before us, but without metamorphoses. Lear and Macbeth, Hamlet and Othello severely modify themselves not only by their actions, but by their utterances, and most of all through *overhearing themselves*, whether they speak to themselves or to others. Pondering what they themselves have said, they will to change, and actually do change, sometimes extravagantly yet always persuasively. Or else they suffer change, without willing it, but in reaction not so much to their language as to their relation to that language.

I do not think it useful to say that Shakespeare successfully imitated elements in our characters. Rather, it could be argued that he compelled aspects of character to appear that previously were concealed, or not available to representation. This is not to say that Shakespeare is God, but to remind us that language is not God either. The mimesis of character in Shakespeare's dramas now seems to us normative, and indeed became the accepted mode almost immediately, as Ben Jonson shrewdly and somewhat grudgingly implied. And yet, Shakespearean representation has surprisingly little in common with the imitation of reality in Jonson or in Christopher Marlowe. The origins of Shakespeare's originality in the portrayal of men and women are to be found in the *Canterbury Tales* of Geoffrey Chaucer, insofar as they can be located anywhere before Shakespeare himself, Chaucer's savage and superb Pardoner overhears his own tale-telling, as well as his mocking rehearsal of his own spiel, and through this overhearing he is emboldened to forget himself, and enthusiastically urges all his fellow-pilgrims to come forward to be fleeced by him. His self-awareness, and apocalyptically rancid sense of spiritual fall, are preludes to the even grander abysses of the perverted will in Iago and in Edmund. What might be called the character trait of a negative charisma may be Chaucer's invention, but came to its perfection in Shakespearean mimesis.

The analysis of character is as much Shakespeare's invention as the representation of character is, since Iago and Edmund are adepts at analyzing both themselves and their victims. Hamlet, whose overwhelming charisma has many negative components, is certainly the most comprehensive of all literary characters, and so necessarily prophesies the labyrinthine complexities of the will in Iago and Edmund. Charisma, according to Max Weber, its first codifier, is primarily a natural endowment, and implies a primordial and idiosyncratic power over nature, and so finally over death. Hamlet's uncanniness is at its most suggestive in the scene of his long dying, where the audience, through the mediation of Horatio, itself is compelled to meditate upon suicide, if only because outliving the prince of Denmark scarcely seems an option.

Shakespearean representation has usurped not only our sense of literary character, but our sense of ourselves as characters, with Hamlet playing the part of the largest of these usurpations. Insofar as we have an idea of human disinterestedness, we tend to derive it from the Hamlet of Act V, whose quietism has about it a ghostly authority. Oscar Wilde, in his profound and profoundly witty dialogue, "The Decay of Lying," expressed a permanent insight when he insisted that art shaped every era, far more than any age formed art. Life imitates art, we imitate Shakespeare, because without Shakespeare we would perish for lack of images. Wilde's grandest audacity demystifies Shakespearean mimesis with a Shakespearean vivaciousness: "This unfortunate aphorism about art holding the mirror up to Nature is deliberately said by Hamlet in order to convince the bystanders of his absolute insanity in all art-matters." Of *Hamlet's* influence upon the ages Wilde remarked that: "The world has grown sad because a puppet was once melancholy." "Puppet" is Wilde's own deconstruction, a brilliant reminder that Shakespeare's artistry of illusion has so mastered reality as to have changed reality, evidently forever.

The analysis of character, as a critical pursuit, seems to me as much a Shakespearean invention as literary character was, since much of what we know about how to analyze character necessarily follows Shakespearean procedures. His hero-villains, from Richard III through Iago, Edmund, and Macbeth, are shrewd and endless questers into their own self-motivations. If we could bear to see Hamlet, in his unwearied negations, as another hero-villain, then we would judge him the supreme analyst of the darker recalcitrances in the selfhood. Freud followed the pre-Socratic Empedocles, in arguing that character is fate, a frightening doctrine that maintains the fear that there are no accidents, that overdetermination rules us all of our lives. Hamlet assumes the same, yet adds to this argument the terrible passivity he manifests in Act V. Throughout Shakespeare's tragedies, the most interesting personages seem doom-eager, reminding us again that a Shakespearean reading of Freud would be more illuminating than a Freudian exegesis of

Shakespeare. We learn more when we discover Hamlet in the Freudian Death Drive, than when we read *Beyond the Pleasure Principle* into *Hamlet*.

In Shakespearean comedy, character achieves its true literary apotheosis, which is the representation of the inner freedom that can be created by great wit alone. Rosalind and Falstaff, perhaps alone among Shakespeare's personages, match Hamlet in wit, though hardly in the metaphysics of consciousness. Whether in the comic or the modern mode, Shakespeare has set the standard of measurement in the balance between character and passion.

In Shakespeare the self is more dramatized than theatricalized, which is why a Shakespearean reading of Freud works out so well. Character-formation after the passing of the Oedipal stage takes the place of fetishistic fragmentings of the self. Critics who now call literary character into question, and who proclaim also the death of the author, invariably also regard all notions, literary and human, of a stable character as being mere reductions of deeper pre-Oedipal desires. It becomes clear that the fortunes of literary character rise and fall with the prestige of normative conceptions of the ego. Shakespeare's Iago, who wars against being, may be the first deconstructionist of the self, with his proclamation of "I am not what I am." This constitutes the necessary prologue to any view that would regard a fixed ego as a virtual abnormality. But deconstructions of the self are no more modern than Modernism is. Like literary modernism, the decentered ego came out of the Hellenistic culture of ancient Alexandria. The Gnostic heretics believed that the psyche, like the body, was a fallen entity, mechanically fashioned by the Demiurge or false creator. They held however that each of us possessed also a spark or pneuma, which was a fragment of the original Abyss or true, alien God. The soul or psyche within every one of us was thus at war with the self or pneuma, and only that sparklike self could be saved.

Shakespeare, following after Chaucer in this respect, was the first and remains still the greatest master of representing character both as a stable soul and a wavering self. There is a substance that endures in Shakespeare's figures, and there is also a quicksilver rendition of the unsettling sparks. Racine and Tolstoy, Balzac and Dickens, follow in Shakespeare's wake by giving us some sense of pre-Oedipal sparks or drives, and considerably more sense of post-Oedipal character and personality, stabilizations or sublimations of the fetish-seeking drives. Critics like Leo Bersani and René Girard argue eloquently against our taking this mimesis as the only proper work of literature. I would suggest that strong fictions of the self, from the Bible through Samuel Beckett, necessarily participate in both modes, the sublimation of desire, and the persistence of a primordial desire. The mystery of Hamlet or of Lear is intimately invested in the tangled mixture of the two modes of representation.

Psychic mobility is proposed by Bersani as the ideal to which deconstructions of the literary self may yet guide us. The ideal has its pathos, but the realities of literary representation seem to me very different, perhaps destructively so. When a novelist like D.H. Lawrence sought to reduce his characters to Eros and the Death Drive, he still had to persuade us of his authority at mimesis by lavishing upon the figures of *The Rainbow* and *Women in Love* all of the vivid stigmata of normative personality. Birkin and Ursula may represent antithetical and uncanny drives, but they develop and change as characters pondering their own pronouncements and reactions to self and others. The cost of a non-Shakespearean representation is enormous. Pynchon, in *The Crying of Lot 49* and *Gravity's Rainbow*, evades the burden of the normative by resorting to something like Christopher Marlowe's art of caricature in *The Jew of Malta*. Marlowe's Barabas is a marvelous rhetorician, yet he is a cartoon alongside the troublingly equivocal Shylock. Pynchon's personages are deliberate cartoons also, as flat as comic strips. Marlowe's achievement, and Pynchon's, are beyond dispute, yet they are like the prelude and the postlude to Shakespearean reality. They do not wish to engage with our hunger for the empirical world and so they enter the problematic cosmos of literary fantasy.

No writer, not even Shakespeare or Proust, alters the available stock that we agree to call reality, but Shakespeare, more than any other, does show us how much of reality we could encounter if only we retained adequate desire. The strong literary representation of character is already an analysis of character, and is part of the healing work of a literary culture, which implicitly seeks to cure violence through a normative mimesis of ego, *as if it were stable*, whether in actuality it is or is not. I do not believe that this is a social quest taken on by literary culture, but rather that we confront here the aesthetic essence of what makes a culture *literary*, rather than metaphysical or ethical or religious. A culture becomes literary when its conceptual modes have failed it, which means when religion, philosophy, and science have begun to lose their authority. If they cannot heal violence, then literature attempts to do so, which may be only a turning inside out of the critical arguments of Girard and Bersani.

I conclude by offering a particular instance or special case as a paradigm for the healing enterprise that is at once the representation and the analysis of literary character. Let us call it the aesthetics of being outraged, or rather of successfully representing the state of being outraged. W.C. Fields was one modern master of such representation, and Nathanael West was another, as was Faulkner before him. Here also the greatest master remains Shakespeare, whose Macbeth, himself a bloody outrage, yet retains our imaginative sympathy precisely because he grows increasingly outraged as he experiences the equivocation of the fiend that lies like truth. The double-natured promises and the prophecies of the weird sisters finally induce in Macbeth an apocalyptic version of the stage actor's anxiety at missing cues, the horror of a phantasmagoric stage fright of missing one's time, of always reacting too late. Macbeth, a veritable monster of solipsistic inwardness but no intellectual, counters his dilemma by fresh murders, that prolong him in time yet provoke him only to a perpetually freshened sense of being outraged, as all his expectations become still worse confounded. We are moved by Macbeth, however estrangedly, because his terrible inwardness is a paradigm for our own solipsism, but also because none of us can resist a strong and successful representation of the human in a state of being outraged.

The ultimate outrage is the necessity of dying, an outrage concealed in a multitude of masks, including the tyrannical ambitions of Macbeth. I suspect that our outrage at being outraged is the most difficult of all our affects for us to represent to ourselves, which is why we are so inclined to imaginative sympathy for a character who strongly conveys that affect to us. The Shrike of West's *Miss Lonelyhearts* or Faulkner's Joe Christmas of *Light in August* are crucial modern instances, but such figures can be located in many other works, since the ability to represent this extreme emotion is one of the tests that strong writers are driven to set for themselves.

However a reader seeks to reduce literary character to a question of marks on a page, she will come at last to the impasse constituted by the thought of death, her death, and before that to all the stations of being outraged that memorialize her own drive towards death. In reading, she quests for evidences that are strong representations, whether of her desire or her despair. Such questings constitute the necessary basis for the analysis of literary character, an enterprise that always will survive every vagary of critical fashion.

Editor's Note

My Introduction relates Salinger's protagonist to Huck Finn and his American literary descendants, including the heroes of Scott Fitzgerald, Hemingway, and Faulkner, all of them, like Holden, innocents in the tradition of Emerson's American Religion.

William T. Noon invokes a Catholic perspective, viewing Holden as a rebel who seeks Christ's love, while Levi A. Olan traces alienation from Huck Finn to Caulfield.

The psychology of Holden is judged by James Bryan to be far healthier in Caulfield the retrospective narrator than in the boy of the novel, after which Warren French defends Salinger from his exegetes.

Hemingway's strong influence upon *The Catcher in the Rye* is demonstrated by Sandra Whipple Spanier, while Edwin Haviland Miller reflects upon the book as an elegy for Holden's deceased brother, Allie.

In a feminist protest, Mary Suzanne Schriber disputes Holden's universalism, after which A. Robert Lee uncovers the aesthetic quester in Salinger's hero.

Joyce Rowe faults Salinger for too simplistic a protest against American materialism, while Paul Alexander sets Holden in his author's biographical context.

The formidable Anna Freud, favorite child of the Founder, is brought to bear, a touch disapprovingly, upon Holden by Robert Coles, after which Carl Freedman concludes this volume with an autobiographical reverie concerning a teacher of his own Caulfieldian youth.

HAROLD BLOOM

Introduction

As a literary character, Holden Caulfield has now demonstrated his durability and likely permanence. Fifty years of readership have not dimmed his poignance, his ability to represent the idealism and the refusal to be deceived that have marked the American tradition of representing adolescence. He holds his place in the sequence that goes from Huck Finn through Huck's descendants in Hemingway, Scott Fitzgerald, and Faulkner, on to the outraged protagonists of Philip Roth's moral fictions. What Toqueville called our "habits of the heart," the American balances between individualism and social concern, continue to find a crucial representative in Holden, whose appeal has survived the enormous changes in American sensibility over these last fifty years.

Holden's literary strength has little to do with his author's overt religious concerns, whether Buddhist or Christian. Haunted always by a brother's death, Holden evades the adolescent obsession with the sexual drive only to yield himself to the shadows of the Death Drive. His pathos is that of the survivor who can find no guidance in the art of survival. Teachers, parents, sages are unavailable to him, primarily because of his borderline sense that maturity and deathliness are the same state, an illusion of identity that in itself is deathly. The innocent and the beautiful, Yeats wrote, have no enemy except time, but poor Holden is too belated to make so confident a High Romantic assertion.

Holden essentially is a narrative voice, stemming directly from Fitzgerald's Nick Carraway, with Huck Finn hovering farther back. The largest difference is that Holden is desperate; even his humor balances on the verge of madness. Still, his desperation is vivacious; he is on the verge, but always with verve. All readers receive him into their affection, which may be the largest clue to his book's enduring charm. As a representation of a sixteen-year-old youth, the portrait of Holden achieves a timeless quality that is at variance with the novel's true status as a period piece, a vision of America in the aftermath of World War II. The timelessness of Salinger's hero has less to do with his refusal to mature than with his religious refusal of time. The American Religion, almost from its origins, has been closer to Gnosticism than to Christianity. Time in Christianity is an agent of redemption: the Incarnation breaks into time, and after that time becomes another form of God's mercy. But time, in Gnosticism, is the enemy, because time results from the Creation-Fall in which we were thrown out from our original fullness into this world of separations and angers. Holden is haunted by the characteristic Gnostic sense that what is best and oldest in him is no part of the Creation. Doubtless, Holden's religiosity is the result not so much of Salinger's interest in oriental esotericisms, but of Salinger's debt to Fitzgerald and Hemingway, whose protagonists tend to be pure embodiments of the American Religion. Freedom for Gatsby or for Jake Barnes, as for Huck Finn, comes only in solitude, and cannot be realized in the sexual life, which is shackled by time. Love is possible for Holden, but only for his dead brother, or for his ten-year-old sister, Phoebe. Holden, watching Phoebe in the rain, is in communion with Nick Carraway at Gatsby's funeral, and with Frederic Henry walking away after Catherine's death. In all these scenes, the rain constitutes an American Gnostic baptism, a rendering free through knowledge.

The innocence of Holden Caulfield, unlike that of Huck Finn, takes its informing context from the American Religion, that curious amalgam of Emersonian idealism and national messianism. Holden possesses neither a saving doctrine nor spiritual authorities to whom he can turn, yet his sensibility is wholly religious. Because of his inner isolation, and his lack of teachers, Holden courts the doom of the New Testament's Legion, the insane tomb-haunter infested by demons. Hence Holden's grim declaration, which is at once the darkest and the most significant sentence in his book: "If you want to know the truth, the guy I like best in the Bible, next to Jesus, was that lunatic and all, that lived in the tombs." *The Catcher in the Rye* essentially is a quest or romance in which Holden narrowly evades the madness of Legion, in order to survive as a wistful version of an alienated American Adam, dreaming of a Jesus-like role as a savior of children: "What I have to do, I have to catch everybody if they start to go over the cliff—" By catching himself, just in time, Holden at least has made a fresh beginning.

As a literary character, Holden hardly will sustain comparisons with figures in Shakespeare or Dickens, though such incongruous juxtapositions have been attempted. Holden's legitimate forbearers are located where we might expect them to be found, in Hemingway and in Fitzgerald, writers who may be said to have set the limits for Salinger's intense but narrow art. We can see Holden as a latter-day, potential version of Nick Carraway or Jake Barnes, or as a substitution for Hemingway's projections of himself in his final writings. Holden's capacity for sympathy with others is immense, and so is his aversion to everything that is inauthentic. This double capacity informs the eloquent pathos of his closing remarks:

> ... D.B. asked me what I thought about all this stuff I just finished telling you about. I didn't know what the hell to say. If you want to know the truth, I don't *know* what I think about it. I'm sorry I told so many people about it. About all I know is, I sort of *miss* everybody I told about. Even old Stradlater and Ackley, for instance. I think I even miss that goddam Maurice. It's funny. Don't ever tell anybody anything. If you do, you start missing everybody.

This affection of a narrator for his characters prophesies Holden's almost full return from alienation. Perhaps he will become his creator, Salinger; perhaps, like Huck Finn, he will light out for another territory. Either way, he will have the prospect of progressing from survival to freedom. His ability to move so many readers has something to do with how vulnerable and likeable he is, but perhaps more to do with the intimations he incarnates, which are religious, and which return us to that curious spirituality I call the American Religion. What shadows Holden always is his brother Allie's early death; what saves Holden is his love for his sister Phoebe. It is the mark of the American Religion that death is not acceptable to it. One thinks of the post-Christian faiths that originated in the United States, and that have survived: Mormonism, Christian Science, Seventh-Day Adventism, Jehovah's Witnesses. In common, they deny literal death, as though we could progress to godhood without the necessity of dying. At the root of these imaginings is an impulse that Holden profoundly shares: a passion for survival, at every cost. What is most American about Holden is the complex alliance between a desperation for survival, and a self-destructiveness that seems in love with death. Holden may not be a universal figure, but he is one of the most representative of Americans. In him we read some of our national paradoxes, central to our literature and to our still-emerging American spirituality.

Fables of our innocence are a recurrent element in American literature, and are a crucial component of the American Religion. If I were asked to nominate the most distinguished parable of that innocence in modern American fiction, I would choose Faulkner's *As I Lay Dying*, Nathaniel West's *Miss Lonelyhearts*, and Pynchon's *Crying of Lot 49*. Darl Bundren, Miss Lonelyhearts, and Oedipa Maas are all maddened by intimations of a primal goodness lost but still beckoning in America, and their quests for that original intensity of being remain purposive, however catastrophic. But these are all parables of the dark side, and need to be complemented by the more nostalgic fables of *The Sun Also Rises*, *The Great Gatsby*, and their younger and weaker brother, *The Catcher in the Rye*. Jake Barnes and Nick Carraway are necessarily wiser and graver than Holden Caulfield. But he participates in their nostalgia, in their affection for everyone whose stories they narrate. If Holden participates also in their purposefulness, that is because the lack of quest is as much the cost of confirmation in the American Religion as is the darker intensity of drive in the protagonists of Faulkner, West, and Pynchon.

WILLIAM T. NOON

Three Young Men in Rebellion

Ernest Pontifex, Stephen Dedalus, Holden Caulfield are three strong twentieth-century voices in revolt: What were they rebelling against? What were they trying to find?

It is now more than a hundred years since Father Newman told the undergraduates at the then newly conceived Catholic University of Dublin: "Literature is to man in some sort what autobiography is to the individual; it is his Life and Remains." Then Newman added: "On the whole, I think it will be found, and ever found as a matter of course, that Literature, as such, no matter of what nation, is the science or history, partly and at best of the natural man, partly of man in rebellion."[1] All art, then, in Newman's sense is self-revelation: world literature is nothing else than the autobiography of the human race. But some art is self-revealing in a special way, either announced and avowed confessions, or confessional fiction that in some sort gives the author's personal secret away. The autobiographical novel belongs in this latter class; as such it exercises a special hypnosis on those who read the imaginative record as true.

Three widely read novels of the twentieth century that are "in some sort" autobiography are stories of young men in rebellion: Samuel Butler's *The Way of All Flesh*, James Joyce's *A Portrait of the Artist as a Young Man*, and J.D. Salinger's *The Catcher in the Rye*. Enough has already been said to

From *Thought* 38, (1963): 559–577. © 1963 by Fordham University Press.

pinpoint each of these as in part autobiography. Every work of literature, poem, play, or novel, is in Newman's general sense autobiographical: the writer will always tell us about life as he himself knows it best from his own experience, interior or exterior, public or private. Some works—for instance, these three novels—are in a more special sense autobiographical: the writer looks back at the helterskelter of his own raw encounter with life, the conflicts that broke him, the crises that made him, and he tries to find a pattern. If his imagination is capable, he will in time find a meaning that he can put into words. The novel is always a story; the imagination is always active in telling it, the narrated experience is always much more controlled in the fiction than it can possibly be in the facts: poetry and truth, *Dichtung und Wahrheit*, as Goethe subtitled his own self-portrait. The narrator so far as he is an artist gives a form to his vision. Once fixed in words, this form is more or less enduring, an impersonal or inevitable quality of the personal narrative. For the sake of their illusion, most writers prefer in time to leave this selected form of theirs alone. They have other stories to tell us, or if they choose to tell the old story over, they prefer as a rule to do this in a different way. Stephen Dedalus, for example, came to interest James Joyce less and less as a voice or self-portrait: "He has," says Joyce, "a shape that can't be changed." George Eliot in one of her essays on fiction, "Looking Inward," tells us, "The haze is a necessary condition."[2] In another, "Looking Backward," she says that though "there have been many voluntary exiles in the world," she chooses to linger on in a half-visionary provincial England that one can only remember: "I belong to the 'Nation of London'."[3]

If one chooses mostly not to attend to the historical fidelity of these three narratives, he spares himself facing many thorny questions of facts, the interpretation of these facts, and their correspondence in detail with the truth that the three fictions maintain. What of these fictions? What is their truth? Why were these three young men of the novels—Ernest Pontifex, Stephen Dedalus, Holden Caulfield—in rebellion? What were they rebelling against? What were they trying to find? All three speak of evil; none just has an edge in his voice. Though each of the three, the *Catcher*, the *Portrait*, *The Way of All Flesh* tells a deeply personal story, subjective to a large extent, and written out of an enforced solitude of which each individual narrator feels obliged to speak, it would not be true to say of any one of them that the story is told to oneself alone. "That," says Jean-Paul Sartre, "would be the worst blow."[4] No, the stories are told to us, their readers. As Sartre also says, "Thus, reading is a pact of generosity between author and reader. Each one trusts the other; each one counts on the other, demands of the other as much as he demands of himself."[5] What demands do these three books make on us? How far do we trust their authors? How far do we share today the point of view that motivates the young man in each novel to make such disclosures to us as he does?

I

If we begin with Samuel Butler's *The Way of All Flesh*, that is not simply because this is a chronological convenience. Butler's is a twentieth-century novel, first published posthumously in 1903. In terms of twentieth-century canons of fiction, it is the least well informed, or least "well made" of the three. With the encouragement of his witty, crippled friend, Miss Savage, Butler worked intermittently at the first version of his story, 1880–1883, and, then, to meet her criticisms and with her aid carried the necessary rewriting to a point about half-way. There is a notable falling off in the style and tone of the last half of the story. Butler's remorse at his shabby treatment of Miss Savage overwhelmed him when she died, 1885, and he had no heart afterward to take up this manuscript again. For the purpose of comparing Ernest Pontifex's repudiation, or rebellion, in this novel with that of Stephen Dedalus in the *Portrait* and of Holden Caulfield in the *Catcher*, the revised section of *The Way of All Flesh* extends far enough, through Ernest's prep school days at Dr. Skinner's, Roughborough, into his happy but troubled life as a university student, Cambridge. We cannot be sure that Miss Savage recognized herself as the idealized prototype of Ernest's worldly, rich aunt, Alethea Pontifex. I expect that she did. Anyway Miss Savage did not like the idealized Alethea. She told Butler once, "You make her like that most odious of women, Mrs. John Stuart Mill."

Ernest Pontifex is only one of the two autobiographical voices that Butler makes use of to tell his story. There is the voice of Ernest himself, "our hero," as he is called most often, wryly, or "my unhappy hero," my "morbidly unheroic" hero, as he is called sometimes; but there is also the voice of the older blasé narrator—blasé, by Victorian norms—Edward Overton, who reflects throughout so knowledgeably on Ernest's folly as in good measure to turn Ernest's criticism of Victorian England into a self-criticism of Butler himself. Overton admits on one page of the novel, "I know that whether I like it or not I am portraying myself."

Ernest Pontifex's criticism is aimed at the entire Victorian establishment, "the toppling over," as he says, "of the whole system." Except that he is twenty-eight years old when he comes into his rich aunt's vast and unsuspected inheritance, we might call him the most affluent angry young man in all literary history. The system that Ernest dedicates himself to toppling over includes, first of all, the Established Church, but it also includes Roman Catholicism, whose sacramental rites and beliefs he sums up as "pure hanky-panky." The system comprises marriage, the family, a classical education—here, in particular the great Greek tragedians who are more grossly overrated, Ernest states with a Juvenalian flourish, than any other authors "with the exception perhaps" of David the Psalmist—the lying "High Priests of science," the music of Beethoven, Easter decorations in the churches, in fact, almost the whole status quo. Late in the novel, Ernest tells Overton that the cause of reform for which he is crusading is fated in time to win out: "The question of Christianity is virtually settled, or if not settled there is no lack of those engaged in settling it. The question of the day now is marriage and the family system." He admits that this is "a hornet's nest," but adds. "hornet's nests are exactly what I happen to like." In principle Ernest rejects the Victorian tradition as feeble and vicious; it has worn itself out. Further he aims scientifically to evolve, or forge, a new conscience that might give him imaginative power to tell good from evil in another way. Evelyn Waugh in our own days has been no less unsparing in his diagnosis of this Victorian compromise, but Waugh moves in from behind the Christian tradition and in favor of it in a way that Ernest Pontifex and his creator Samuel Butler would find unreal: untrue to their own experience and incoherent as a rational plan of their own lives.[6]

Ernest Pontifex's definition of his mission in life comes to him gradually; it is earned at the price of so much personal torment and bewilderment that the generous-minded reader may be inclined to imagine him, as does Overton, the victim of an inherently demoralizing system. The reader even may marvel that Samuel Butler, caught in the middle and having himself found the taste of this system so bitter, manages to tell Ernest's story with his wonted urbanity and wit. Overton agrees with Ernest's publisher on the last page of the novel that Ernest is indeed "in a very solitary position": "Mr. Pontifex is the exact likeness of Othello, but with a difference—he *hates* not wisely but too well."

The Way of All Flesh is more than the history of any single character. As designed, it is a family saga that begins with the simple-minded Paleham carpenter and organ-builder John Pontifex, runs through the succeeding generations of Pontifexes: George, successful London Philistine and publisher, Ernest's grandfather; Theobald, George's son and Ernest's father, a reluctant Anglican clergyman, trapped by the system, who soon gives up, however, goes over to the Establishment and all that this has to offer him, chilling and depressing as the wages are; and finally Ernest, who is presented as misunderstood and misused by his parents, malformed by his teachers, betrayed by his friends—notably by his fellow-curate, Mr. Pryer, a homosexual and a thief—ensnared by an unhappy but luckily invalid marriage to an alcoholic tramp of a wife. The friend whom he himself idealizes as hero is the rich, handsome, not overbright aristocrat Towneley, who had the good fortune to lose both his parents by drowning in a boating accident when he was only two years old. Providentially or melodramatically freed from marital nets, Ernest at the end sets his face resolutely against the evil of any marriage at all. He gives away his two children to be brought up by a stranger on barges. Butler's main point in this arrangement of incidents is to convince the reader that Ernest succeeds well in his children if not perfectly with himself in a recovery of the unconscious memory of the Pontifexes. In this way Butler would picture, not just diagram, his announced aim, that is, to free natural instinct from all the inhibiting pressures that Victorian smugness and self-consciousness had imposed on decent men of his race.

Butler's autobiographical novel is, then, a relentless total indictment of Victorian England; at the same time, it candidly dramatizes one man's search for a radically different new way of life. The book is by now a period-piece, but it is still one that is worth reading. We may or we may not subscribe to Ernest's devastating diagnosis; most now have other ideas about human decency and a remedy. In other hands Butler's diagnosis and remedy might have been handled so dourly as just to bore us today. Butler handles these on the whole wittily so that his book continues to provoke us to laughter rather than to either anger or applause. Modern minds appreciate the wit of Butler's strictures on the clerical and familial systems of his times; many now regard this wit as a trifle unfair, and most today are less enchanted than was Butler with the new system that his manifesto proclaims. Still most readers find themselves applauding Ernest part of the way. This is especially true of the chapters that are devoted to Ernest's odious schooldays at Roughborough, Dr. Skinner's prep school. Butler looks backward here through the haze to his own schooldays at Shrewsbury. "Our hero" is presented to us as one who "belonged to a debatable class between the sub-reputable and the upper disreputable, with perhaps rather more leaning to the latter." Dr. Skinner, a cleric as well as a headmaster, is "on the Liberal side, in politics," and the Protestant conservative in theology—though "his *Meditations on St. Jude*, such as they were, were cribbed," says Overton, "without acknowledgment." Ernest comes to the conclusion at Roughborough that "Latin and Greek are great humbug; the more people know of them the more odious they generally are." He wins the good-will of his school fellows on a Guy Fawkes day by the enthusiasm he shows in joining them to burn his own clergyman father, Theobald, in effigy an hour or so after the visiting Bishop has bestowed the sacrament of Confirmation on the boys of the school.

Later at Cambridge University Ernest "attended chapel," we are told, "as often as he was compelled to do so." Here he passes through a mild religious crisis so as briefly to give up "even his tobacco" for Christ. Theobald is "frightened out of his wits" when this mortification of his son is reported to him, for although Theobald is an ordained minister of Christ he is a man with "a common sense point of view," who believes, as Ernest soon does himself, "There should be moderation in all things, even in virtue." All the reputable clerics in this novel hate Rome as a matter of premise, more so even than they hate dissenters or atheists. Ernest is not buoyant about accepting priestly orders, but goes through with the rite, as had his father before him, to keep peace in the family and for want of anything better to do. With the connivance of his landlady, the amiable, accommodating Mrs. Jupp, he undertakes as a priest later, Bible under his arm, to convert a fellow lodger, Miss Snow, who is unable to hear him out owing to the unexpected arrival of a gentleman caller and customer, who turns out to be Towneley. Ernest leaves Miss Snow unconverted and goes almost at once, now without his Bible, to visit the room of another lady lodger, Miss Maitland. She is not a prostitute, as Ernest understandingly imagines; she is offended and appalled by Ernest's bold and unclerical advances, and in her fright calls in the police. Ernest is arrested and sentenced to six months in prison. So in disaster ends his clerical experiment in coming down to live among the poor. He decides while in prison that "he would be a clergyman no longer." Seeing this sensible decision on his part, we might take leave of Ernest Pontifex in his English jail, and for a spell take up with the Irishman Stephen Dedalus.

II

James Joyce's *A Portrait of the Artist as a Young Man* was first published forty-seven years ago, not in Ireland but in New York, 1916. This was a year in the First World War; in Dublin the year of the Easter Week rebellion. Joyce, then at Zurich in neutral Switzerland, was thirty-three, fifteen years younger than Butler had been when he gave up his rewriting of *The Way of All Flesh*. The haze was not so dense for Joyce, and he had not so far to look backward. The *Portrait* is also a most carefully rewritten or restyled novel, in fact an entirely recast one. He had begun it in its original form as *Stephen Hero* even before he went away from Ireland in 1904. He had carried this first form of the book forward to double the final, present length of the *Portrait*, and then gave it up still incomplete so as to start his story all over. Looking back, he himself called *Stephen Hero* "rubbish." But even as it stands, the *Portrait* might be justly styled in part an autobiographical revenge, for like Butler Joyce voices through his story the grievances that he still held against his home, his mother country and most of her people. His recollections of the System, if that is the right word here, are rather bitter ones, though the bitter tone is notably muted by comparison of the *Portrait* with what survives of the earlier *Stephen Hero* draft. The real life prototypes are at times so thinly veiled that any reader with even the most casual knowledge of James Joyce and his city is obliged to recognize some of them and to sense that the *Portrait* as a whole is the actual life story of a gifted young man's Catholic upbringing in Ireland at the turn of the century. The great danger is to read it as straight autobiography. The *Portrait* is a novel, a creative work of the capable imagination of Joyce. Sartre has said that it is the poet who creates the myth "while the prose-writer draws the portrait" of his times.[7] Joyce was himself much of a poet. In an as yet unedited and unpublished early notebook now at Cornell University, he defines a portrait as "not an identificative paper, but the curve of an emotion." Though *A Portrait of the Artist as a Young Man* is told in the third person, the entire story comes filtered to us through the consciousness of a persona, here the young man whose artistic dilemmas and moral strictures it re-presents. Stylistically it is the most subtle of the three novels in the interaction of its own images and the verbal miming of its own thought. It is a literary classic of our times. Already it shows us Joyce busy as a beaver working hard to rechannel the tradition of the novel and to dam up the deep and dark waters of the subconscious, or unconscious. Quite explicitly he proclaims a revolution of the word.

Rebellion, revolt, and resistance have for centuries found in Ireland a fertile soil in which to flourish. "The Croppy Boy," "Kelly the Boy from Killanne," "The Rising of the Moon," "Seaghan O'Duibhir an Gleanna," are a few only of the defiant rebel songs, set to traditional airs, that Joyce, a gifted singer as a young man, heard in the air all about him in his own Irish days:

> And though we part in sorrow
> Still Seaghan O'Duibhir a cara
> Our prayer is "God, save Ireland
> And pour blessings on her name.
> May her sons be true when needed,
> May they never fail as we did,"
> For Seaghan O'Duibhir an Gleanna
> We're worsted in the game.

Most of these are political rallying songs. James Joyce's disenchantment with Ireland extended so far as to make him despair of the turn taken by most of Ireland's revolutionary politics, of her better-left-unspoken Gaelic speech, and, as he saw it, of the fatal paralysis that left her prostrate at the portals to the realm of the spirit, "the realms of gold" that he himself most of all respected: art, the way of the artist, and in particular the power that the word of the artist, or literature, has to help a people know itself, judge itself truthfully, and face the chaos and possibilities that the contemplation of its own image might disclose. Thus the *Portrait* becomes an artist's, not a social reformer's story as is Butler's *Way*. Stephen Dedalus leaves Ireland at the end of the story, but he is defiantly hopeful: "I go to encounter for the millionth time the reality of experience and to forge in the smithy of my soul the uncreated conscience of my race." "Silence, exile, and cunning" are the "only arms" that he now finds at hand to defend himself in the unjust warfare that has been provoked, as he sees it, by his home, his fatherland, and his church. No one would dream from this ending that Dublin was then a city of classical song and the center of the Irish Renascence, Lady Gregory, the Abbey Theater, W. B. Yeats; nor might one infer readily, nor indeed at all that some few years earlier, 1886, Dom Columba Marmion, the distinguished Benedictine, a curate in Dundrum on the outskirts of Dublin, also left Ireland to enter a European cloister at Maredsous. Still one wonders sometimes: If those whose job it was to educate James Joyce had been themselves more creative spirits, would his Catholic faith have become so much unhinged? They might have opened their minds and hearts perhaps wider to what was going on in his.

Stephen Dedalus is as deeply convinced that the Church is to blame for the paralysis he finds all around him as had been Butler's Ernest Pontifex. Whereas Ernest blames mostly the Church of England, Stephen blames instead the Church of Rome. For the English Establishment, for Crown and Castle, for the Anglican Ascendancy in Ireland, Stephen has as much contempt as Ernest has for Victorian piety, but Stephen's own spiritual reaction has been conditioned by the Catholicism that as he sees it had made Ireland a land neither of scholars, artists, nor of saints.

The Stephen Dedalus story, at least as we have it in the *Portrait*, is that of a young man's growing up in Holy Ireland, his discovery of himself and of his vocation, his loss of innocence and his growth in experience, his flight to the continent of Europe. "You talk to me," he says, "of nationality, language, and religion. I shall try to fly by those nets." *The Adventures of Huckleberry Finn*, another subversive book, is the American novel with which the *Portrait* has been persistently compared. Huck's territory and Stephen's, the wilderness and the urban diaspora, are, however, different kinds of solitude for retreat. Hemingway's Nick Adams, "the town's full of bright boys," and Scott Fitzgerald's Nick Carraway, in *The Great Gatsby*, are American cousins of Stephen Dedalus as well as is Huck Finn. This theme of discovery, repudiation, and quest is age-old, as old as Homer. It sent the son of

Odysseus on his travels. Joyce calls the three opening Stephen Dedalus chapters of *Ulysses* his Telemachia.

The *Portrait* tells the Stephen story mainly in terms of the three Jesuit schools that Stephen, and Joyce himself, attended in Ireland: Clongowes Wood, an exclusive elementary boarding-school; Belvedere College, or high school, as we might say, Dublin; and, finally, University College, Dublin, the Catholic University that John Henry Newman founded for Ireland in the early 1850's, which had been rescued by the Jesuits from extinction in 1883 and carried on under their administration for the next troubled quarter-century until 1909. Although it might look at first sight as though Stephen is as hard on his Irish Jesuits as Ernest Pontifex is on his Anglican schoolteacher divines, this judgment would go beyond the evidence of the *Portrait* itself. Father Dolan, "Baldyhead Dolan," the prefect of studies, a priest of the Dr. Skinner type, beats Stephen at Clongowes for having broken his glasses, but Father Arnall, Stephen's own class teacher, is remembered as "very gentle," and Father Conmee; the Clongowes Rector, as a "kind-looking" man, who treats Stephen's protest decently. Long after this, in *Finnegans Wake*, Joyce alludes' to *The Way of All Flesh* as "a butler's life ... strabismal [or, wall-eyed, cross-eyed, and abysmal] apologia."[8] Jesuit readers of the *Portrait*, more likely than others, are apt to take note of Stephen's appraisal of those Irish Jesuits who in the fiction at least show themselves eager at Belvedere to welcome the sixteen year old Stephen as a novice into their own priestly ranks: "Whatever he had heard or read of the craft of Jesuits," writes Joyce, "he [Stephen] had put aside as not borne out by his own experience. His masters, even when they had not attracted him, had seemed to him always intelligent and serious priests."

The central conflict that the *Portrait* dramatizes is that of Stephen's vocation. Shall he be an artist or shall he be a priest? This conflict is actually resolved in the fourth, or Belvedere, section of the novel, after the crisis of Stephen's high school retreat. Stephen is intellectually tempted by the prospect of a priestly vocation. His imagination, however, is powerless to view this otherwise than as "the pale service of the altar," "cerements shaken from the body of death," and in the half-vision, half-actuality of seeing the bird-like girl "in midstream, alone and still, gazing out to sea," he makes up his mind not to be a priest but an artist, and to follow this vision of "mortal beauty," "profane joy," wherever it might lead him, even unto "the gates of all the ways of error and glory." Unlike Ernest Pontifex, Stephen never commits himself to a priestly service in which he has no heart: "I will not serve that in which I no longer believe, whether it call itself my home, my fatherland, or my church." Still the *Portrait* nowhere inveighs against the family system that brings down in retrospect Ernest's strictures. In fact, tried as it is, Stephen's sense of solidarity with his family is very strong. Stephen's father, Simon Dedalus, is a drunkard, but on the whole he is shown as an amiable drunkard, who flirts with the barmaids and knows how to sing. Stephen's mother is a rather ineffectual lady, but always a lady, a gentle lady, even when she and her impoverished brood of children are obliged, after many auctions and house-movings, to live on the wrong side of the tracks as the novel comes to a close.

For the most part its tone is serene; at times it is very comic. It would not be easy to find in modern fiction a more amusing and still realistic scene than the famous Christmas-dinner in the first section, when Stephen comes home from Clongowes Wood during his family's affluent days to celebrate with them the birthday of the Prince of Peace. The Dedalus family and their invited guests quarrel violently about the rights and wrongs of Kitty O'Shea's divorce and the consequent repudiation of Charles Stewart Parnell, "uncrowned king of Ireland": the dinner breaks up with door-slammings, shouts, curses, clenched fists and crashes, upturned chairs and rolling napkin-rings—a first-class Irish brawl. The much frightened little boy Stephen "sobbed loudly and bitterly." As Joyce closes the incident, "Stephen, raising his terror stricken face saw that his father's eyes were full of tears." Whereas the wealthy, leisured aristocrat Towneley is Ernest's hero in *The Way of All Flesh*, so an idealized Parnell, blameless and broken, is Stephen's hero in the *Portrait*. Neither Stephen nor James Joyce ever forgave Ireland for throwing Parnell to the wolves. Stephen cannot follow Parnell in person, and he cannot serve God as priest at the altar. He has no call to the drawing-room. What can he do? He can be, he thinks, an artist. In this way he will be saving Parnell and all his people, "race of clodhoppers" that he calls them, for the world of art: "I tried to love God, he [Stephen] said at length. It seems now that I failed."

Fortunately it is not any man's business to judge. of Stephen's, or Joyce's, failure before God. Joyce himself succeeded admirably as artist; as he grew older, he edged far away from his symbolic identification with Stephen Dedalus. In *Ulysses*, the good man is Leopold Bloom: as Joyce told his friend Frank Budgen while *Ulysses* was still in the making, "As the day wears on Bloom should overshadow them all."[9] And in *Finnegans Wake*, he is Everyman, Humphrey Chimpden Earwicker, H.C.E., "Here Comes Everybody," in a story where Everybody is Somebody Else. Stephen Dedalus did not become a priest at the altar, and neither did Joyce. When Stephen says in the *Portrait* that he will become instead "a priest of the eternal imagination," his metaphor is meaningful, but he is talking about something else than the rite of priestly consecration. This metaphor should not be pushed too far in Stephen's case, and in Joyce's own it is one that has tended to obscure the two Vocations between which he made an election; he himself chose not altar but art. It is a choice that haunted him most of his life.

Before leaving Stephen Dedalus for Holden Caulfield, I should like to quote briefly and gratefully from Thornton Wilder. In a letter to me Mr. Wilder wrote: "The book on which *Finnegans Wake* is built is not Vico's but the Missal and Offices [of the Catholic Church. At no page are we far from this supporting material.... Certainly James Joyce was outside 'faith', but not as Voltaire or Montaigne were. The growing boy had seen an interpretation of existence of vast grandeur and could never forget it; he had seen the order of rites in which that interpretation was made accessible and he could never forget them, and as he grew older they returned to him as the only language he could use. To honor and treasure the forms without possessing the faith that animates them is a despairful condition."

III

J.D. Salinger's *The Catcher in the Rye*, published first back in 1951, when Salinger was thirty-two, is today a widely read story, almost a modern testament, of a young man's search for vocation. William Golding's *Lord of the Flies* has challenged but I think not yet anyway taken over Salinger's rostrum as spokesman for American youth. *The Catcher in the Rye* is the least convenient of the three novels to talk about as spiritual autobiography. Until *Time* magazine with its staff of researchers published its cover story in September, 1961, most readers could find out little about Salinger, and there is much that is still obscure. He is inscrutable as a public personage and has great reserve in talking personal sense about himself. In form the *Catcher* is an extended confidential monologue of seventeen year old Holden Caulfield. At the start, Holden, a New York boy—like Salinger—says that he is not going to tell his whole autobiography, "what my lousy childhood was like ... all that David Copperfield kind of crap," and he adds, "my parents would have about two hemorrhages apiece if I told anything personal about them." Consequently he presents his parents for the most part in shadow, but he ends up telling his readers, or listeners, several rather searching things about them, and in a torrent of confidences he tells many most personal things about himself.

At the risk of appearing to be unsystematic and of snarling my own pattern of the three young men in rebellion, I should say that I do not believe Salinger's *The Catcher* belongs to the same stream as do Butler's *The Way* and Joyce's *Portrait*. For one thing it does not announce itself as autobiographical. Or if it does, it pretends to be Holden Caulfield's story, not the author's own. Further, the other two are both mainly in the stream of the novel of social protest, an individual in rebellion against a system that he thinks is wrong. George Moore's *Confessions of a Young Man*, Somerset Maugham's *Of Human Bondage*, and Henry Adams' *The Education of Henry Adams*, are all also in that stream of personal and social protest; not all, to be sure, are novels, but all are more or less confessional, and all tell a personal story much as a novelist might tell it who wanted to quarrel with a past that made him what he is. Salinger's *The Catcher in the Rye* is mostly in another different stream, one that goes back to *What Maisie Knew*, of Henry James, and back of that, perhaps, to Herman Melville's *Billy Budd*: a vision of personal evil that is heartbreaking for the young person of the novel, and a vision that transfixes the reader forever and ever. Heartbreak is not, just the same as protest, nor do we react to grief in the same way as to a grievance or a quarrel. How disorienting is the personal discovery of evil in ourselves or in the lives of those whom we have come to love! Salinger's *Catcher* is like Golding's *Lord* in its revelation, of the personal horror of the evil that stalks the world in our times, the heavy presence of the past. Salinger's vision is, however, less dark and appalling than is Golding's. Holden Caulfield is much saddened and depressed by what he sees. But the title of his story recalls, a happy song, and at the end it is suggested that all is going to work out all right for this much troubled and confused young man.

Holden Caulfield's story in the *Catcher* is a record of the weekend that he spent on his own in New York City the preceding year. On the last page we learn that he is telling it in a hospital, where he is under a psychoanalyst's care. "Don't ever tell anybody anything. If you do, you start missing everybody" are the words with which Holden ends his tale. The last page hints that he will get well. Except for the priority of Thomas Hardy, this book might have been called *The Return of the Native*.

This record of the native's return starts at Pencey, an expensive boarding-school for boys. One gathers that Salinger is helping himself to some of his own prep school memories of Valley Forge Military Academy when he constructs Holden's impressions of Pencey. Holden has already received word that he is being "kicked out" of Pencey for "flunking four subjects"; his parents in New York are being notified that he should not come back after the Christmas holidays scheduled to start the next. Wednesday. Late Saturday night, acting on an impulse, Holden leaves Pencey, rides up to New York by train, but does not at first go home. Instead he stops alone at a hotel. The rest of the story narrates his adventures on his own in the city. Near the end he watches two truckmen unloading a Christmas tree; one of them keeps swearing at the other, "Hold it *up*, for Chrissake!"

Mostly Holden's adventures are the bewildered experiences of his various encounters: for example, his chance breakfast meeting with the two nuns at a lunch counter in Grand Central Station; the meeting in his hotel room with the hardened young prostitute and with Maurice, the elevator-boy who serves as her pimp; the meeting with Sally Hayes, teen-age city girl, whom he takes on a date to see the Lunts and afterwards to skate at Rockefeller Plaza; the two meetings with former teachers at schools that he had flunked out of before he went to Pencey; two most important meetings with his little sister Phoebe, whom he visits first late at night in the family apartment, and later takes on a walk to the zoo. No young man in literature is more lonely, depressed, more often than is Holden Caulfield; none is more gregarious! "If a body *meet* a body, need a body cry?" It depends to be sure on how the meeting goes.

Throughout most of the novel, Holden is running away. He runs away from Pencey soon after the start of the story; he runs away from Sally Hayes, whom he leaves stranded in the Plaza bar; he runs away from the prostitute, or at least obliges her, pride injured, to run away from him; he is running away "to go out West" when the unexpected appearance of "old Phoebe," bags packed to run away with him, effects a change of mind that is really a change of heart for him as the fable closes. On one page Holden says, "I never seem to have anything that if I lost it I'd care too much." But at the end he cares.

Holden Caulfield passes through many crises, but a religious crisis is never one of them. Several times he says his prayers, but he explains, "I can't always pray when I feel like it. In the first place, I'm sort of an atheist." The problem of a religious vocation never rises for himself. When he meets the two nuns at the Grand Central lunch-counter, he is much interested to hear that one of them, with "a big nose and iron glasses and a helluva kind face," is an English teacher. English is the one subject at Pencey that Holden never failed. Earlier back at Pencey, he recalls: "What really knocks me out is a book that, when you're all done reading it, you wish that the author that wrote it was a terrific friend of yours and you could call him up on the phone whenever you felt like it.... You take that book *Of Human Bondage*, by Somerset Maugham.... It's a pretty good book and all, but I wouldn't want to call Somerset Maugham up. I don't know. He just isn't, the kind of a guy I'd want to call up, that's all. I'd rather call old Thomas Hardy up. I like that Eustacia Vye." Talking to the two nuns in Grand Central, Holden remembers Eustacia Vye, and wonders: "She wasn't too sexy or anything, but even so you can't help wondering what a nun maybe thinks about when she reads about old Eustacia." Later when his sister Phoebe challenges him to name just one thing that he "likes a lot," he thinks of the two nuns; later still, on Monday, when the whole week-end has fizzled out, he keeps looking to see if maybe somewhere in the city they aren't still around.

Holden's parents do not mean much to him. His father, a wealthy corporation lawyer, plays almost no part in his story nor in his life. Once, says Holden, his father was a Catholic, but quit. His mother plays only a minor role: Holden feels sorry for her because she is grieving about his younger brother's death and because she has frequent splitting headaches, and will certainly have another when she receives the letter from Pencey announcing his dismissal. Holden admires his successful older brother and loves his little sister. There is not much system to the family as he knows it. He nowhere feels a desire to burn any of them in effigy, the idea would offend him, and he nowhere thinks of forging a conscience for them, or indeed for anyone else.

What is he running away from? from himself? Maybe. But that is not how he sees it nor what he says. He is running away from *phoniness*. One commentator has counted the number of times that Holden uses the word "phony" or some derivative of it: forty-four.[10] In the intermission with Sally at the play of the Lunts, he listens to the conversation of the theater crowd in the lobby: "You never saw so many phonies in all your life, everybody smoking their ears off and talking about the play so that everybody could hear and know how sharp they were.... I was all set to puke when it was time to go sit down again." *Phoniness* covers all the signs of hypocrisy, cant, fraud, and selfish insincerity with which Holden is obliged to collide.

It does not occur to Holden to work out a program for toppling over this phony status quo, and it is not in him to nurse unforgiveness toward the phonies, or frauds, that make him sick. I have never counted the number of times that Holden says he feels sorry or sad for all these phony people. I expect he says this or its equivalent far oftener than forty-four times. He tells us early in his story that he "felt sorry as hell" for Mr. Spencer, his teacher at Pencey; he feels depressed about the three single girls from Seattle whom he met in a bar when they tell him that they are getting up early Sunday morning to see the first Radio City Music Hall show; all of a sudden on his date he feels "sort of sorry" for Sally Hayes; and when Phoebe, his sister, asks him in alarm why did he "get the ax again" at school, "It made me sort of sad, the way she said it." Mr. Antolini, his favorite former teacher, a homosexual like Mr. Pryer in Butler's *The Way*, turns out to be much mistaken in sizing Holden up: "You're wrong about that hating business," Antolini tells him. But Holden hates nobody all week-end; he calls Maurice, the elevator-boy and pimp, a "dirty moron" and dreams of how nice it would be to "plug him," but in a way he feels sorry even for him. Blasphemous at first as some of his plain censures may sound, his voice nowhere expresses bitterness—only, at the most, concern. Habit mellows even that. Phoebe comes closer to the truth when she tells her brother, "You don't like anything that's happening.... Name something that you'd like to *be*."

That is a shrewd challenge from "little old Phoebe." What is Holden Caulfield's vocation? It isn't at all like Ernest Pontifex's, to be a radical, solitary reformer of society; it certainly isn't the split vocation between priesthood or the imagination, altar or art, that causes the tension in Stephen Dedalus' life. What is it? What does Holden want to be? The answer lies in the title of his story: he wants to be "the catcher in the rye." Earlier on this sad Sunday, he had seen a little boy with his parents walking home from church. The little boy was singing: "If a body catch a body, coming through the rye." Late that night, to meet Phoebe's challenge, Holden tells her all about it. She corrects him: "It's 'if a body *meets* a body coming through the rye' ... a poem by Robert Burns." Holden answers: "I thought it was, 'If a body *catch* a body'. Anyway, I keep picturing all these kids playing ... in this big field of rye.... And I'm standing on the edge of some crazy cliff. What I have to do, I have to catch everybody if they start to go over the cliff.... I have to come out from somewhere and catch them. That's all I'd do all day. I'd just be the catcher in the rye." A little later, the Caulfield parents come home late to their apartment from a party. Holden steals out unnoticed, but as he goes he thinks: "I didn't give much of a damn anymore if they *caught* me. I really didn't. I figured if they caught me, they caught me. I almost wished they did." But of course they don't!

Some of Salinger's readers, Mary McCarthy, Maxwell Geismar, have claimed that Holden is himself a phony. There are to be sure the nice phonies, and then there are the others who are not so nice. Leslie Fiedler sees the climax of the *Catcher* as an instance of the Orestes-Iphigenia story "that Salinger all along has been trying to rewrite," and is a bit put out by what he sees, the "downgrading" in the tone of the legend.[11] Another brother in *Franny and Zooey*, published in 1961, tells his sister, an older girl than Phoebe: "What'll happen when you start your ... revolution?, I can't bear to think, about it.... If you're going to go to war against the System, just do your shooting like a nice, intelligent girl because, the enemy's *there*."[12] It's you: you and your shadow! That is where the revolution matters, that is where the reform starts, and that is where the work of art begins. Many mixed-up young men and women of our times appear not to find all this just a horrifying joke.

Mary McCarthy's characteristically contrary reading of the *Catcher* and Leslie Fiedler's rather eccentric comparisons blur the sense of Salinger's parable. Unknowingly, perhaps, he well illustrates Tertullian's famous dictum that the *anima* is *naturaliter Christiana*, that is, the soul craves to find and to give a satisfying love. Holden might have just given this love to Phoebe and then as la token of something larger accepted the fractional return she was capable of. But he is at once too old and too young to be aware here of his

opportunity so to pull together a whole mixed-up life. Except for Phoebe and
the nuns, all the rest are against Christ, as Holden himself realizes, and he is
against the *againsters* without knowing the positive and actual values of the
faith that might save him, "catch" him from going over the cliff where he
hangs. Holden is too old to respond fully to Phoebe's love, or to Christ's,
which is back of it, because already he has been too deeply wounded by his
own defensive worldly sophistication. He is too young to respond because a
person needs a harder core to his love, if he is to survive in the adult world,
than that of just being a "catcher in the rye." But even if Holden is lost, he is
not lost at the end as was Ernest to England or Stephen to Ireland. He will,
one senses in the end, come through: he will, it seems, save his soul.

In his long autobiographical poem *The Prelude*, Wordsworth speaks of
the power that books have had in shaping his life. He calls one of the earliest
a "slender abstract of the Arabian tales," and in his famous dream he tells
how "the Arab of the Bedouin tribes" "cast a backward look" as he carried to
safety two precious books, the stone and the shell, science and poetry, so that
neither might be lost under "the fleet waters of a drowning world." Like the
Bedouins, we cast our own backward looks on the slender abstracts of the
times. Our so-called "rebellious" young novelists, John Knowles in *A
Separate Peace*, Michel de Saint Pierre in *The New Aristocrats*, many others
care enough about their own times to look back from where they are.
Forging a conscience or toppling one, hammering out or counterfeiting, the
artist makes himself responsible even as a young man for the illusions that
shape his own and others' history, rebel voices in the air that we call our
collective "Life and Remains."

NOTES

1. *The Idea of a University*, Discourse IX, "Duties of the Church towards
Knowledge," n. 6.

2. "Looking Inward," *Theophrastus Such*, *Works*, Library ed. (Edinburgh. 1901).
X.14.

3. *Ibid.*, 30.

4. *What Is Literature?*, tr. Bernard Fechtman (London, 1950), p. 29.

5. *Ibid.*, p. 39.

6. Cf. Richard Watson, "A Handful of Dust: Critique of Victorianism," *Modern
Fiction Studies*, VII (Winter, 1961–62), 327–337.

7. *What Is Literature?*, p. 23, n. 4.

8. *Finnegans Wake* (New York, 1947), p. 189.

9. *James Joyce and the Making of "Ulysses"* (New York, 1934), p. 116.

10. Edward P.J. Corbett, "Raise High the Barriers, Censors," *America*, CIV (7
January 1961), 443.

11. "Salinger's Saints," *Partisan Review*, XXIX (Winter, 1962), 130.

12. *Franny and Zooey* (Boston, 1961), pp. 160–161.

LEVI A. OLAN

The Voice of the Lonesome: Alienation from Huck Finn to Holden Caulfield

Malcolm Cowley in his introduction to Van Wyck Brooks's *The Ordeal of Mark Twain* tells us that it was planned as the first in a trilogy of studies of American writers. The project grew out of Brooks's critical judgment in 1921 that "for a half century the American writer has gone down to defeat." He concluded that the cause for this decline lay in the unformed emotional nature of American society which he described as "sealed against that experience from which all literature derives its values." He found another source in the lack of imaginative awareness of the writers themselves. To change this situation he planned three studies of American writers, the first of which depicted a talented writer who stayed in this country and yielded to the environment. The second one was to be a writer who escaped by living abroad; the third, a writer who stayed in the American environment and mastered it. The names of each type in this study turned out to be Twain, James, and Emerson.

Brooks's method in each of these is that of clinical biography in which he relates the conscious and unconscious experiences of the author to the nature of his literary work. In the case of Twain, the representative of writers who conformed to the "iron hand of convention," he found an unconscious artistic talent which was ensnared by strong Philistine forces of his environment. Indeed, he is described as a dual personality who had an

From *Southwest Review* XLVIII, No. 2 (Spring 1963): 143–150. © 1963 by *Southwest Review*.

obsession with the subject. Brooks, unlike Twain, had already heard of Freud, and he loads his sentences with the symbols of the psychiatrist. Thus, he tells us that Twain suffered a "dissociation of consciousness," that he had conflicting wishes, one to be an artist which was repressed, the other to win approval which was dominant. "The individual had given way to the type ... his will ... opposed to his essential instinct." He discovers in Twain a "frustrated spirit, a victim of arrested development," and calling upon the authority of the psychologist, Brooks finds that he had been "balked," he had been "divided," he had even been "turned against himself." The "poet, the artist in him, consequently, had withered into the cynic and the whole man had become a spiritual valetudinarian."

The clinical method in literary criticism is popular in our time and valuable as well. The biographical data does help us better to understand the writings of men, and in the instance of the *Ordeal* there is ample testimony to justify its consideration. The "Gilded Age" which Twain so caustically delineated was the witch who held him in her narcotic spell. He was a promising artist whom the currents of a nation, raucously driven toward success and status, sucked in and dried out. Brooks's book did not go unchallenged; the debate ranged for a decade at least with Bernard DeVoto leading the assault. Without passing judgment there is warrant for the view that the *Ordeal* is an important piece of literary criticism which in its day opened the door for a better understanding of American culture.

Having praised a virtue we must now turn to a serious shortcoming. The positive value of the clinical method has embedded within it a grave defect which in the case of Brooks is crucial. The merit of relating biography to literature may blind us to, or, at least prejudice us against, the worth of a specific piece of writing. This is particularly relevant to the work of Twain, whose posing and childish self-adulation tend to antagonize us against all of his writings. It is probably true that the major part of his literary productivity is of a low grade. But let us suppose that we did not know who the author of *Huckleberry Finn* is, and were therefore free to assess it on its own merit; our judgment would be uncluttered by emotional responses to the vagaries of the author's behavior. The foibles and frivolities of Dreiser, Lewis, or Dylan Thomas are vital statistics of literary history, but they are not determinative factors in the basic creative work of these men.

Mark Twain wrote only one genuinely artistic book, *The Adventures of Huckleberry Finn*, although there are parts of other stories which are in the same class with it. Whether it deserves the place reserved for "The Great American Novel," as some aver, or whether it may even rank as one of the best novels in world literature, as others claim, we will leave to those who enjoy the game. The significance of *Huckleberry Finn*, Leslie Fiedler suggests, is its "improbable" ancestry of Camus's *The Stranger* and all the existentialist heroes who dominate our own period of literature. It precedes Kafka's *The Trial* by almost half a century, and is one of the earliest expressions in fiction of modern man's alienation. The story employs "lonesome" as its favorite adjective and reveals what amounts to an obsession with death. It begins with Huck's confession, "I felt so lonesome I most wished I was dead." The droning of bugs and flies "makes it seem so lonesome and like everybody's dead and gone ... it makes a body wish he was dead too, and done with it all."

Much has been said concerning Twain's pessimism; indeed, Brooks opens his study with a chapter entitled "Mark Twain's Despair." He introduces it with a quotation from a marginal note of one of Twain's books: "What a man sees in the human race is merely himself in the deep and honest privacy of his own heart. Byron despised the race because he despised himself. I feel as Byron did, and for the same reason." This gloomy view of human nature increased in intensity as he endured the disappointments and tragedies of life, and ended up in two major attempts at expressing his disillusion formally. The first was a sophomoric piece lied "What is Man?" This embodied a mechanistic view, an unconscious imitation of Watsonian Behaviorism, wherein man is a machine because he has no innate ideas. It finds that there really is no difference between the selfish and the unselfish, and finally that man is not responsible for either the good or the evil he does, in fact he is not responsible at all. If anyone is to blame it is God. Much of this sounds like a village agnostic or a poor attempt to mimic Robert Ingersoll.

Twain was not a formal thinker, and his voluminous efforts at this sort of thinking are puerile. He did a little better with his misanthropy in *The Mysterious Stranger*, where he allowed his intuition to guide him. Satan's final devastating statement comes closer to a mature expression of despair. "There is no God, no universe, no human race, no earthly life, no heaven, no hell. It is all a dream—a grotesque and foolish dream. Nothing exists but you. And you are but a *thought* ... wandering forlorn among the empty eternities!" This has the ring of Prospero:

> *The cloud-clapped towers, the gorgeous palaces,*
> *The solemn temples, the great globe itself,*
> *Yea, all which it inherit, shall dissolve ...*
> > *... We are such stuff*
> *As dreams are made on ...*

At his best, however, Twain's conscious attempts to express his dark despair were flat and unconvincing. When Hannibal becomes Eseldorf the natural artist has given way to a contrived, and childish, expression. Twain's Achilles heel was the illusion that he was a thinker. In *Huckleberry Finn* he responded to the human situation as a total being, an artist who apprehends by a mysterious talent and creates uninhibited by either logic or purpose. Fiedler suggests that Twain was intelligent when he did not know he was thinking.

The modern version of Huck Finn, separated from him by fourscore years, is Holden Caulfield. For both adaptation to the world is worse than hell, a condition they unhappily prefer. Both are strange and alien to their world, not unlike the disoriented figures of much of modern literature. Huck's sole purpose is to stay alive and all moral codes are essentially derived from this major premise. He lies, he steals, he deceives—but never, like Tom Sawyer, for glory. His every move is aimed at outwitting all the forces, both good and evil, which would destroy his life. He sees little value in Widow Douglas' preachment on his helping other people and never thinking about himself, since the only advantage is for other people. He dreads civilization as represented by parents, school, clothing, Sunday School, and all the other structural institutions of society. In the end he must "light out for the territory ahead of the rest, because Aunt Sally she's going to adopt me and sivilize me, and I can't stand it. I been there before." Threatened with an eternity in hell if he violates the code of Hannibal, he chooses the fiery nether world, convinced that he could not exist by Hannibal's rules. Indeed, the basic crisis of the book lies in the tension between what he knows he ought to do and what he is aware he must do.

In the most decisive incident of the novel, Huck is torn between what is right and what lies beyond good and evil. To protect the runaway slave Jim is wrong: this absolute he accepts without questioning its morality. He has no theories about freedom, and he is not an abolitionist; he is outraged when somebody like Tom, with his upbringing, joins in the conspiracy to outwit the law. He does not believe in the equality of the races, and when asked if anybody was killed in an accident replies, "No'm, killed a nigger." What he does for Jim is part of staying alive, and he is willing to go to hell for him, just as he is for cussing, smoking, or scrunching a little. Huck is not about to change the world, and whether Jim is enslaved or free is not for him to decide. When he reaches the terrible moment before he tears up the letter to Miss Watson, the ultimate persuader is a recollection "how Jim would always call me honey, pet me, do everything he could think of for me."

The world for Huck was bounded by the females of Hannibal, who represent civilization and its stifling, crushing codes, and by his father, who was the incarnation of all the stupidity, brutality, cowardice, dishonesty, and meanness of the river-folk. He can go back to neither and survive, finding only a temporary home with Jim on the raft, a society different from anything which exists on earth. Here is the perfect order, one in which he gives up nothing of himself, and in Jim he has a mother, father, playmate, and beloved. It is, as Fiedler says, "an impossible society," in which even the breach of black and white is healed by love. This is a family against all families, engaged in a transitory risk-laden experience of the moment. But this is possible only on a river raft, as Huck so well tells us. "There weren't no home like a raft after all." When the Duke and the Dauphin intrude with their comic-tragic deceit and violence, he complains: "It did seem so good to be free again and all by ourselves on the big river and nobody to bother us ... it seems all I could do to keep from crying." But Huck and Jim must separate, and the prospect ahead is a sad loneliness from which he cannot be saved. When, in the end, he lights out, he accepts his fate to be "without regrets what he was from the start, neither son nor brother—but a stranger an outcast, a boy Ishmael."

Twain, in one of the most remarkable endings of any book, says: "... and so there aint nothing more to write about, and I'm rotten glad of it, because if I'd 'a' knowed what a trouble it was to make a book, I wouldn't 'a' tackled it, and aint a-going to no more." Aside from its candor and its summation of what most artists feel after the agony of creation, it also reveals the unconscious realization that Huck could not be taken into adult living. To have moved him from the river to Hartford, Connecticut was beyond the artistic resources of the author. Huck must never grow up lest the world he inhabits cease to be a childhood myth. He has no place to which he can return or to which he can point with any hope. His is a life of escape, not knowing what he is escaping from, only that he is escaping into nothing. Running is an end in itself. So there is no place on earth which can be a home and where he can realize his purpose. There is, as Fiedler says, "no utopia." Twain had begun with the shining American dream of "The New Jerusalem," the promise of a land of justice, honor, and hope for man. The truth however, lay in Dawson Landing with its deceit, violence, and hopeless resignation. The modern heirs of Twain's world of disillusion are many, and they dominate the cultural marketplace.

The Victorian Humpty-Dumpty had a big fall and all the king's horses and all the king's men can't put him together again. In 1877 Lewis Morgan could write: "Democracy in government, brotherhood society, equality in right and privilege, and universal education foreshadow the next higher place of society to which experience, intelligence, and knowledge are steadily tending." It was the era of confidence and decorum. The problem of liberty and authority was resolved by sanctifying a mad scramble in the economic field and a disciplined behavior in the social realm. A rugged individualism, unrestrained by governmental authority, was balanced by a code of moral conduct which emphasized restraint and conformity. Parents, especially the father, were God's surrogate in the home. Sex was unmentionable in public, and suspect in private. No decent person was an atheist publicly, no matter what he thought secretly. The reigning philosophy was Hegelian Idealism, where the absolute was real and rational and the prevailing moral code the product of the highest reason. Culturally, there was a dash of romantic escapism, a flurry of exotic adventures, a tendency toward the solid and somewhat showy. There was one unifying factor in all of the Victorian era: man had a sense of belonging to an orderly and decorous universe in which the best of all possible worlds was just around the corner.

How outlandish and bizarre all of this sounds now! Who today dare recite Tennyson, counseling men, "Do your best, whether winning or losing it ... Let a man contend for his life's prize, be it what it will." We are more at home with Yeats:

> *Things fall apart; the center cannot hold;*
> *Mere anarchy is loosed upon the world,*
> *The blood-dimmed tide is loosed, and everywhere*
> *The ceremony of innocence is drowned.*

Just prior to his death, H.G. Wells found that "hitherto events have been held together by a certain logical consistency as the heavenly bodies have been held together by a golden cord of gravitation. Now it is as if the cord had vanished, and everything is driven anyhow, anywhere, at a steadily increasing velocity ... there is no way out, or around, or through the impasse. It is the end." It is the end! This prophecy of doom is by a writer who, in the first decades of this century, was confident that science and education would usher in the heavenly kingdom.

Popularly, and somewhat superficially, the modern mood of despair is ascribed to the collapse of the high hopes of the nineteenth century into the horror of two world wars, gas chambers, continuing international chaos, and the presence of enough megaton destructive power to annihilate all life. More subtle and more pervasive have been the effects of the new sciences which tend to root out man's confidence in the business of living. What is dimly understood is the revolution which technology brought into the nature of our civilization. We seem to be living in the presence of an impersonal power which controls a highly sensitized productive machine whose decisions affect our daily well-being. We are left with the feeling that something is going on behind our backs. Furthermore, there is a temporary character about our lives; people are ever on the move, ever joining new groups and belonging to none. The family, which ever nurtured us and gave our existence a center of gravity, is steadily losing its influence. The new cosmology has snatched from us the comfortable firmament and substituted a universe with no center in which everything is in motion, all positions are relative, and distance is measured by light years. In the meantime, the globe we inhabit is growing small and we are running out of room. We are confronted with a vast emptiness which staggers our imagination and reduces life to a tiny affair; yet the finite size of the earth is where we live and where technological progress must occur. Psychology, since Freud, reveals man to be a creature of conflict in the depths of his unconscious. His conscious behavior, as well as his life of reason, are at the mercy of these submerged forces. The slogan today is "adjustment," hardly ever a matter of right. Anthropology and sociology unveil a variety of moral patterns, and raise in our minds the troubling question: Can there be amoral law amidst social relativism?

The effect of these pervasive changes upon the human condition constitutes the material with which the modern artist works. He is the first to confront us with the unsavory truth primarily because that is his reason for being. Joseph Conrad counseled the creative writer: "In the destructive element immerse. That is the way." The immersion is almost total. A dark cloud of despair hangs threateningly over the race of men, whose moral will appears to be in a state of shock. Jules Romain, writing it seems for our age, dedicated his "Men of Good Will" to those "who have lost all desire to do away with themselves, to those who come home from work with lowered heads and heavy shoulders and find each evening as sorrowful as the night before; to those who are rich and bored; to those who are poor and full of bitterness," Modern man, as he arises from most contemporary literature, is an "Outsider," a "Stranger," an "Exile on Earth." A world drained of all values and subject to blind, amoral forces looms before him as an alien and an enemy. It is Joyce's *Ulysses*, Mann's *Joseph in Egypt*, and Camus's *Oedipus*. The great weight of the characters created by our leading novelists is an expression of bitter disillusionment and sad disenchantment.

The influence of Kafka upon the literature of our era is a subject of many professional discussions. What is pertinent is that his name has come to symbolize our age because his writing clearly reveals its mood. His work discloses two basic themes: the operation of a superhuman justice, incomprehensible and even absurd, condemning man to think of himself as "indicted though free"; and the futility of all effort, a frustrating condition which is ultimately accepted. If man is suddenly transformed into a cockroach, it is an incident which needs no explanation. It begins with punishment, the desert of which is ignored; and the other members of the house learn to live with their son turned into vermin. Men are judged by a power unknown and unapproachable, and for them to "mend their ways" cannot alter the judgment in any respect. We live in a world in which we die all wrong. Interest in Kafka's writings was intensified during World War II, and for some time thereafter. The reports of cruelty and degeneracy in the concentration camps bear a frightfully remarkable resemblance to the world of the novelist's characters. There was little difference, if any, between the imaginative story and the reports of the journalists.

The line of succession is easily recognizable. Sartre's *Nausea* and Camus's *Stranger* in France are of this genre, as is Hermann Hesse's *Steppenwolf*, whose chief character confesses aberration and loneliness by giving himself without restraint to sensuality and irrationality. It is the wolf in man that must be released. There is that forgotten novel of Paul Bowles, *Let It Come Down*, in which a character pleads: "If only existence could be cut down to the pen point of here and now, with no echoes reverberating from the past, no tinglings of expectation from time not yet arrived." D.H. Lawrence, besides announcing the ecclesiastical dictum that in the flesh, in woman, we know "God the Father, the Inscrutable, the Unknowable," also observed that men touch reality when they follow Persephone to the "sightless realm where darkness is married to the dark."

In the brief, almost meteoric, life of Thomas Wolfe there is incarnated the mood of our era. He shifted between a settled loneliness and an aimless wandering. Between *Look Homeward, Angel* and *You Can't Go Home Again* there is unveiled man's anxiety arising from an uncontrollable urge to return, to regress to his beginnings, and a bitter realization that he cannot do it. "This is man," Wolfe cries, "for the most part a foul, wretched, abominable creature, a packet of decay ... yes, this is man, and it is impossible to say the worst of him."

That Hemingway and Faulkner are blood brothers with all these is evident in their writings. Hemingway's characters generally are like the driven leaf, blown violently and fiercely to no accepted end. It is in Faulkner that modern pessimism becomes cosmic chaos. Like Kafka's invisible force, there is a "stage manager" who strikes the set while man is still playing before an audience and "dragging on synthetic and spurious shadows and shapes of the next one." He is given the honorific title of "Cosmic Joker." A character who hints at suicide is told:

> You won't do it under these conditions ... (it is strange) that a man who is conceived by accident and whose every breath is a fresh cast with dice already loaded against him, will not face the final

main which he knows beforehand he has assuredly to face without essaying expedients ranging all the way from violence to petty chicanery ... No man does that after the first fury of despair or remorse or bereavement, he does it only when he has realized that even the despair or remorse or bereavement is not particularly important to the dark diceman.

Imagination permits us to arrange a visit by Huck Finn to Holden Caulfield in his New York apartment. Dialogue between them is impossible in almost every area of young people's interests. The very English language itself has a foreign sound to each of them. Indeed, they could readily appear one to the other as coming from different worlds. The fact is that the age of Huck Finn, removed from us chronologically by only eighty years, is in the nature of its civilization millennia away. There is, however, one quality of life which Huck and Holden share, though they may not know how to verbalize it to each other. They are both of them alien to their respective worlds; they find no place in it for any real self to exist. The organizations of men stifle them and often appear destructive and even ludicrous. Huck, at least, can go back to a raft on the river and escape the tragicomic play of people along the shore. Holden has nowhere to go except, as Paul Tillich has said, to experience the void. The literature from Twain to Salinger discloses an intensification of man's isolation in the universe to a point where today he is discovered paralyzed in nothingness. These writers in varying forms give a common answer to the old question, "What is man?" If it is not the sole function of art to answer the question which the Psalmist asked, it is certainly a major one. The academic disciplines also deal with the nature of man— biology, psychology, anthropology, philosophy, and theology. In the main, they arrive at answers through the process of reason and experience. The artist alone responds to man's life by way of a unique instrument fashioned of thought, feeling, and a third ingredient we must vaguely describe as talent. The artist speaks the truth even as does the prophet of God; this is his vocation. The modern artist has been thundering the truth about ourselves for several decades, yet most of us have ears that hear not. Thus Picasso on canvas, Schoenberg in music, Auden in poetry, Williams on the stage, all join in a chorus of despair as they view modern man.

It is suggested by Decherd Turner that the "poet cannot offer salvation ... he can only lead man to it, to make him aware of its necessity." For those who accede to this description of the role of the artist in society, Twain and our modern writers who follow after him have fulfilled their mission with greater, or lesser talent. The theologians who in large part declare in ecclesiastical terms that man is innately corrupt, and that he was never meant for this world, offer salvation by a leap of faith. Whether this is salvation for Huck Finn and Holden Caulfield is not our present concern. There is even some doubt as to whether there is any salvation for man at all. Perhaps the artist can be induced to extend his reach and, like the prophet old, see a vision and tell us about it.

JAMES BRYAN

The Psychological Structure of
The Catcher in the Rye

Standing by the "crazy cannon" on Thomsen Hill one sunless afternoon, listening to the cheers from a football game below, "the two teams bashing each other all over the place," Holden Caulfield tries to "feel some kind of a good-by" to the prep school he has just flunked out of:

> I was lucky. All of a sudden I thought of something that helped make me know I was getting the hell out. I suddenly remembered this time, in around October, that I and Robert Tichener and Paul Campbell were chucking a football around, in front of the academic building. They were nice guys, especially Tichener. It was just before dinner and it was getting pretty dark out, but we kept chucking the ball around anyway. It kept getting darker and darker, and we could hardly *see* the ball any more, but we didn't want to stop doing what we were doing. Finally we had to. This teacher that taught biology, Mr. Zambesi, stuck his head out of this window in the academic building and told us to go back to the dorm and get ready for dinner. If I get a chance to remember that kind of stuff, I can get a good-by when I need one.[1]

A careful look at this first scene in the novel provides clues for interpretation, by no means crucial in themselves, but illustrative of a pattern of scene

From *PMLA* 89, no. 5 (October 1974): 1065–74. © 1974 by The Modern Language Association of America.

construction and suggestive imagery which does yield meaning. Appropriate is this adolescent's sense of his "darkling plain" where, if an extravagant metaphor be allowed, "ignorant football teams clash by afternoon." In a pattern repeated throughout the novel, he thinks back to a time when he and two "nice guys" passed a football around, shared rather than fought over it, though even then the idyllic state seemed doomed. Holden is poised between two worlds, one he cannot return to and the other he fears to enter, while the image of a football conflict is probably an ironic commentary on Holden's adolescence, football's being a civilized ritualization of human aggression.

What is forcing Holden's crisis? Everything in the idyllic scene points to the encroachment of time—the season, the time of day, even such verbal echoes from his friends' names as "ticking," "bell," and "pall." Accrual of this sort of evidence will justify what may seem overinterpretation here, especially of the significance of a biology teacher's ending the boys' innocent pleasures—their idyll already sentenced by time, darkness. More than anything else Holden fears the biological imperatives of adulthood—sex, senescence, and death—which are delicately foreshadowed in the innocent October scene by the unwelcome call to dinner.

Much of the *Catcher* criticism has testified to Holden's acute moral and esthetic perceptions—his eye for beauty as well as "phoniness"—but the significance of his immaturity in intensifying these perceptions has not been sufficiently stressed nor explained. Precisely because this sixteen-year-old acts "like I'm about thirteen" and even "like I was only about twelve," he is hypersensitive to the exploitations and insensitivity of the postpubescent world and to the fragile innocence of children. A central rhythm of the narrative has Holden confronting adult callousness and retreating reflexively into thoughts and fantasies about children, childlike Jane Gallaghers, and especially his ten-year-old sister, Phoebe. These juxtapositions render both worlds more intensely and at the same time qualify Holden's judgments by showing that they are emotionally—or, as we shall see, neurotically—induced.

While a fair number of critics have referred to Holden's "neurosis," none has accepted Salinger's invitation—proffered in the form of several key references to psychoanalysis—to participate in a full-fledged psychoanalytical reading. The narrative, after all, was written in a mental hospital with Holden under the care of a "psychoanalyst guy." One problem is that Holden tells us very little about "what my lousy childhood was like" or the event that may have brought on the trauma behind all of his problems: the death of a younger brother when Holden was thirteen. We know little more than that the family has been generally disrupted since and that Holden has not come to grips with life as he should have. Allie's death takes place outside the province of the narrative, but a valuable psychological study might still be made of the progression of Holden's breakdown—how he provokes fights in which he will be beaten, makes sexual advances he cannot carry through, and unconsciously alienates himself from many of the people he encounters. As a step toward psychological understanding, I shall consider certain manifestations of Holden's disturbances. An examination of the structure, scene construction, and suggestive imagery reveals a pattern of aggression and regression, largely sexual, which is suggested in the Pencey Prep section, acted out in the central part of the novel, and brought to a curious climax in the Phoebe chapters.

I

One implication of the novel's main motif, that which polarizes childlike and adult responses, concerns the dilemma of impossible alternatives. Here characters suggest human conditions that Holden either cannot or must not make his own. In the novel's first paragraph Holden tells us that his brother D.B. has "prostituted" his writing talents by going to Hollywood—a failure implicitly contrasted throughout with the purity of Allie, the brother who died before the temptations of adulthood. Holden's first encounter is with Spencer, the old teacher who fills his mind with thoughts of age and death, while his last is with Phoebe, his emblem of unattainable childhood beauty. Stradlater and Ackley are antithetically placed to represent what Holden fears he may become if he is either sexually appropriative or repressed. Because the novel is built around these impossible alternatives, because Holden's world provides no one he can truly emulate, the many critics who read *Catcher* as a sweeping indictment of society have virtually drowned out those who attack Holden's immaturity. One feels the justice of this, yet the novel's resolution, like all of Salinger's mature fiction, transcends sociological indictment in affirming individual responsibility. When Holden answers for his own life as he verges toward some rather dreadful appropriation of his own, he begins to come to terms at once with himself and society.

At the outset of traditional quest narratives, the hero often receives sage advice from a wise old man or crone. The best old Spencer can do is to wish Holden a depressing "good luck," just as another agent of education, a woman "around a hundred years old," will do in the penultimate chapter. Spencer's plaintive "I'm trying to *help* you, if I can" and the old woman's irrelevant chatter near the end bracket the bulk of the narrative in which Holden seeks answers from without. And in both scenes the human resources that do see him through are dramatized in his compassion for the two old people.

Though the Spencer chapter serves notice that Holden has flunked the administrative requirements of education, we learn immediately that he draws sustenance from art. He returns to his room to reread in Isak Dinesen's *Out of Africa* that chronicle of sensitivity surrounded by primitive id forces. At this point he is interrupted by eighteen-year-old Robert Ackley, a grotesque possibility of what Holden may become if his manhood is similarly thwarted. Unleavened sensitivity will not be enough as we see Holden vacillating through five chapters between Ackley and Ward Stradlater, the equally unacceptable model of male aggressiveness. Stradlater's vitality is dramatized in his "Year Book" handsomeness, "damn good build," and superior strength, while Ackley's impotence is reflected in acned, unsightly looks, general enervation, and repulsive habits. Stradlater is slovenly too—Holden calls him a "secret slob"—but he elicits some admiration where Ackley is only pathetic.

Stradlater's date for the evening is Jane Gallagher, a girl with whom Holden has had a summer romance. That relationship was characterized by Jane's habit of keeping her kings in the back row when they played checkers—later on, Holden says specifically that their lovemaking never went beyond the handholding stage. In Holden's request that Stradlater ask Jane if she still keeps her kings in the back row, one critic sees Holden signaling warnings about her "sexy" date.[2] Holden tells us in another chapter that Jane was the kind of girl you never wanted to "kid too much." "I think I really like it best," he goes on to say,

> when you can kid the pants off a girl when the opportunity arises, but it's a funny thing. The girls I like best are the ones I never feel much like kidding. Sometimes I think they'd *like* it if you kidded them—in fact, *I know* they would—but it's hard to get started, once you've known them a pretty long time and never kidded them. (p. 101)

On an action level, of course, Jane did keep her checker kings in the back row and Holden is indeed talking about kidding. But such double entendres as "kidding the pants off a girl" reveal not only Holden's sexual preoccupations but the elaborate coding his mind has set up against recognizing such preoccupations for what they are. In the early parts of the novel, Salinger may be training the reader to see through Holden's words in these rather apparent ways, thus to prepare for the most subtle and crucial coding of all in the Phoebe section.

Stradlater's strength and sexuality cause Holden to discountenance his own. This night, for example, Stradlater uses Holden's "Vitalis" hair tonic and borrows his "hound's-tooth" jacket, leaving Holden "so nervous I nearly went crazy" as he thinks of this "sexy bastard" with Jane. Conversely, Holden this same night endures Ackley's droning narrative of his sexual exploits with a final comment, "He was a virgin if I ever saw one. I doubt if he ever even gave anybody a feel." Not until Holden faces the Ackley and Stradlater in himself will he be able to do the purgative writing that is of course the form of the novel itself. They are almost like doppelgangers; one will interrupt him when he reads to escape while the other rejects the composition he ghostwrites because it is escapist. Even when he attacks the cocksure Stradlater after the latter's date with Jane, Holden's brief blood initiation is, as we shall see, a needful battle against himself. Right after the fight, getting no consolation from that other polar figure, Ackley, Holden leaves Pencey Prep.

The five Stradlater and Ackley chapters make for closely woven, dramatized exposition of Holden's psychological quandary which prepares for the loose, episodic middle section of the novel where Holden goes questing after experience and wisdom. Rejecting the alternatives implicit in Stradlater and Ackley, Holden wants his life to be vital without appropriation, innocent without retrogression. In the Phoebe section where the novel tightens up again, we shall see that Holden nearly becomes *both* appropriative and retrogressive and that it is precisely Holden's awareness of this that points the way to maturity.

Immediately after arriving in New York and checking into a hotel room, Holden is treated to a fresh installment of the Ackley–Stradlater antithesis. Through one window across an airshaft he sees a transvestite dress himself and mince before a mirror, while in the window above a couple squirt water "out of their mouths at each other." Holden confesses at this point that "In my *mind*, I'm probably the biggest sex maniac you ever saw" and that he might enjoy such "crumby stuff" as squirting water in a girl's face. Characteristically, he decides to call his chaste Jane, thinks better of it, and phones Faith Cavendish, a stripper recommended to Holden as one who "didn't mind doing it once in a while." Her ritual objections to the late-hour call dispensed with, she suggests a meeting the next day. Holden declines, however, and "damn near" gives his "kid sister Phoebe a buzz," justifying the switch by describing Phoebe's charms at length. Later in a bar he is flanked on his left by "this funny-looking guy" nervously reciting to his date "every single goddam play" of a football game he had seen, and on the other side by a suave young man giving a beautiful girl "a feel under the table," over her embarrassed objections, "at the same time telling her all about some guy in his dorm that had ... nearly committed suicide." All around him Holden sees distorted reflections of his own spasmodic aggression and withdrawal. And in the last instance cited we get an early hint of one of the most dangerous manifestations of his neurosis: his association of sex with death.

When he retreats in a panic to Grand Central Station, for example, he begins to read a discarded magazine to "make me stop thinking" about Antolini's apparent homosexual advances. One article convinces him that his hormones are "lousy" and another that he would "be dead in a couple of months" from cancer. What seems burlesque here ("That magazine was some little cheerer upper") becomes urgent in Holden's response to an obscene legend he sees shortly after in Phoebe's school:

> Somebody'd written "Fuck you" on the wall. It drove me damn near crazy. I thought how Phoebe and all the other little kids would see it, and how they'd wonder what the hell it meant, and then finally some dirty kid would tell them—all cockeyed, naturally—what it meant.... I figured it was some perverty bum that'd sneaked in the school late at night to take a leak or something and then wrote it on the wall. I kept picturing myself catching him at it, and how I'd smash his head on the stone steps till he was good and goddam dead and bloody. But I knew, too, I wouldn't have the guts to do it. I knew that. That made me even more depressed. I hardly even had the guts to rub it off the wall with my *hand*, if you want to know the truth. I was afraid some teacher would catch me rubbing it off and would think *I'd* written it. But I rubbed it out anyway, finally. (pp. 260–61)

As we shall see, Holden is more repelled by the "obscenity" of the sexual act itself than by the obscene word. And his fear of being identified with the sort of "pervert" who planted it in Phoebe's school is reiterated when, in one more withdrawal, he goes to the mummy tomb in the museum and again finds the legend. At this point he decides,

> You can't ever find a place that's nice and peaceful, because there isn't any. You may *think* there is, but once you get there, when you're not looking, somebody'll sneak up and write "Fuck you" right under your nose. Try it sometime. I think, even, if I ever die, and they stick me in a cemetery, and I have a tombstone and all, it'll say "Holden Caulfield" on it, and then what year I was born and what year I died, and right under that it'll say "Fuck you." I'm positive, in fact. (p. 264)

It is not enough to leave it that Holden's sickness has brought about this odd commingling of lovemaking and dying in his mind. Looking back at Holden's ostensibly random comments on various fascinations and aversions, one sees a subtle but coherent psychological pattern taking shape. Early in the novel we learn of his interest in Egyptian mummification and his particular fascination—mentioned again in the tomb scene—that the process ensured that "their faces wouldn't rot or anything." After watching the "perverts" squirt water in each other's faces, Holden reflects that

> if you don't really like a girl, you shouldn't horse around with her at all, and if you do like her, then you're supposed to like her face, and if you like her face, you ought to be careful about doing crumby stuff to it, like squirting water all over it. (p. 81)

If there are sexual inhibitions reflected in Holden's curious concern with the "preservation of faces," they must also be implicit in his general and constant longing for a state of changelessness. He laments, for instance, that though his beloved museum never changed, he did:

> The best thing, though, in that museum was that everything always stayed right where it was. Nobody'd move. You could go there a hundred thousand times, and that Eskimo would still be just finished catching those two fish, the birds would still be on their way south.... Nobody'd be different. The only thing that would be different would be *you*. Not that you'd be so much older or anything. It wouldn't be that, exactly. You'd just be different, that's all. You'd have an overcoat on this time.... Or you'd heard your mother and father having a terrific fight in the bathroom.... I can't explain what I mean. And even if I could, I'm not sure I'd feel like it. (pp. 157–58)

Readers experienced in the strategies of unreliable narration will suspect that Holden probably does somehow "explain" and that there must be a reason why he's not sure he'd "feel like it" if he could. One notices, as a possible clue, that the museum is associated here and elsewhere with Phoebe.

> I kept thinking about old Phoebe going to that museum on Saturdays the way I used to. I thought how she'd see the same stuff I used to see, and how *she'd* be different every time she saw it. It didn't exactly depress me to think about it, but it didn't make me feel gay as hell, either. Certain things they should stay the way

they are.... I know that's impossible, but it's too bad anyway. (p. 158)

Indeed, Holden's feelings about Phoebe may explain much that is puzzling in his narrative.

II

The expository sections of the novel dramatize Holden's problems as essentially sexual and moral. Yet most critical readings of the novel's ending either ignore these things or imply their absence by declaring that the resolution is "blunted" or else "humanly satisfying" while "artistically weak." Those critics who attest to a harmonious resolution generally do so on philosophical grounds, the effect being a divorce of theme from Holden's human situation. To deny a fused sexual and moral resolution of some sort in the closing emotional crescendo of the Phoebe section would, it seems to me, impugn the integrity of the novel.

I am suggesting that the urgency of Holden's compulsions, his messianic desire to guard innocence against adult corruption, for example, comes of a frantic need to save his sister from himself. It may be Phoebe's face that Holden unconsciously fears may be desecrated; hence the desire to protect Phoebe's face that compels his fascination with mummification. And it may be Phoebe who provokes his longing for stasis because he fears that she may be changed—perhaps at his own hand. Holden's association of sex with death surely points to some sexual guilt—possibly the fear that he or Phoebe or both may "die" if repressed desires are acted out.

I do not mean to imply that Holden's desires, if they are what I suggest, drive him inexorably to Phoebe's bed. The psychoanalytical axiom may here apply that a sister is often the first replacement of the mother as love object, and that normal maturation guides the boy from sister to other women. At this point in his life, Holden's sexuality is swaying precariously between reversion and maturation—a condition structurally dramatized throughout and alluded to in this early description:

I was sixteen then, and I'm seventeen now, and sometimes I act like I'm about thirteen. It's really ironical, because I'm six foot two and a half and I have gray hair. I really do. The one side of my head—the right side—is full of millions of gray hairs. I've had them ever since I was a kid. And yet I still act sometimes like I was only about twelve. Everybody says that, especially my father. It's partly true, too, but it isn't *all* true.... Sometimes I act

a lot older than I am—I really do—but people never notice it.
(p. 13)

The narrator's overall perspective is thus mapped out: his present age representing some measure of maturity, and thirteen and twelve the vacillation that normally comes at puberty and that is so much more painful when it occurs as late as sixteen. This vacillation is somehow resolved in a climax beginning in Phoebe's bedroom (or rather the bedroom of D.B., the corrupt brother, where she sleeps) and ending at the carrousel after Holden has refused to let her run away with him. However one interprets the ending, it comes as a surprise which is dramatically appropriate precisely because it shocks Holden. Hence, also, the aptness of providing only scattered hints of things to come through the quest section, hints which, in my presentation, will necessarily seem tentative.

One notes in passing, for example, Holden's sudden infatuation with Bernice, one of the prosaic Seattle girls, while they are dancing. "You really can dance," he tells her. "I have a kid sister that's only in the goddam fourth grade. You're about as good as she is, and she can dance better than anybody living or dead." A possible association might be made of the name of the young prostitute, "Sunny," with "Phoebe."[3] Certainly Sunny's childlike aspects are emphasized throughout the episode:

> She was a pretty spooky kid. Even with that little bitty voice she had, she could sort of scare you a little bit. If she'd been a big old prostitute, with a lot of makeup on her face and all, she wouldn't have been half as spooky. (p. 127)

Holden has to beg off with the excuse that "I was a little premature in my calculations." His beating at the hands of Maurice, her pimp, suggests psychic punishment as well, particularly when Holden imagines that he's dying and pretends "I had a bullet in my gut."

More can be made of an assertion Holden is constrained to repeat that Phoebe is "too affectionate." After retreating from making the date with Faith, he describes Phoebe at length and tells the reader,

> She's all right. You'd like her. The only trouble is, she's a little too affectionate sometimes. She's very emotional, for a child. She really is. (p. 89)

Later, when Holden awakens Phoebe and "She put her arms around my neck and all," he blurts out:

She's very affectionate. I mean she's quite affectionate, for a child.
Sometimes she's even *too* affectionate. I sort of gave her a kiss. (p.
209)

One begins to recognize the brilliant stratagem of imprecise adolescent
qualifiers such as "sort of," "I mean," "and all," and the nervous repetition of
"affectionate" which dramatize Holden's confusion of restraint and desire.
This confusion develops in the first passage as language moves from firm
declaration to qualification; in the second, Phoebe's presence provokes even
more qualified language.

Then, there is the curious matter of "Little Shirley Beans," the record
Holden buys for Phoebe:

It was about a little kid that wouldn't go out of the house because
two of her front teeth were out and she was ashamed to.... I knew
it would knock old Phoebe out.... It was a very old, terrific record
that this colored girl singer, Estelle Fletcher, made about twenty
years ago. She sings it very Dixieland and whorehouse, and it
doesn't sound at all mushy. If a white girl was singing it, she'd
make it sound *cute* as hell, but old Estelle Fletcher knew what the
hell she was doing, and it was one of the best records I ever heard.
(p. 149)

The significance of the record is underscored by Holden's anxiousness to
give it to Phoebe and his inordinate dismay when he breaks it:

Then something terrible happened just as I got in the park. I
dropped old Phoebe's record. It broke into about fifty pieces.... I
damn near cried, it made me feel so terrible, but all I did was, I
took the pieces out of the envelope and put them in my coat
pocket. (p. 199)

One wonders if the accident wasn't psychically determined. If the Shirley
Beans affair were a subject of dream analysis, the missing teeth, the shame,
and the translation through "whorehouse" jazz by a singer who "knew what
the hell she was doing" would conventionally suggest the loss of virginity.
Hence, Holden's unconscious forces would dictate the destruction of this
"record" as well as its purchase. In the same vein is the information Holden
passes on, as he sneaks into the apartment to see Phoebe, that the maid
wouldn't hear "because she had only one eardrum. She had this brother that
stuck a straw down her ear when she was a kid, she once told me."

At one point Holden hears a child singing the song that becomes the anthem of his savior fantasies: "If a body catch a body coming through the rye." Yet in the next paragraph he buys the "Little Shirley Beans" record—the pairing symbolically dramatizes his conflict of protecting and of violating. His thoughts turn to the Olivier *Hamlet* he and Phoebe had watched and he singles out this highly suggestive scene:

> The best part in the whole picture was when old Ophelia's brother—the one that gets in the duel with Hamlet at the very end—was going away and his father was giving him a lot of advice. While the father kept giving him a lot of advice, old Ophelia was sort of horsing around with her brother, taking his dagger out of the holster, and teasing him and all while he was trying to look interested in the bull his father was shooting. That was nice. I got a big bang out of that. But you don't see that kind of stuff much. The only thing old Phoebe liked was when Hamlet patted this dog on the head. (pp. 152–53)

In all of these early clues, one notices that the nearer Holden's desires come to surfacing, the more hesitant his language and behavior become. When the dreadful suggestions have the protective coloration of, say, the art of "Little Shirley Beans" or *Hamlet*, he is not so uneasy: "That was nice. I got a big bang out of that."

After a series of abortive adventures with women, Holden rather desperately seeks the counsel of a former classmate who was regarded as the dormitory's resident expert on sexual matters. Luce is too pompous to help, but his cutting assessments are probably accurate. He tells Holden that his "mind is immature" and recommends psychoanalysis, as he had done the last time they had talked. Holden's self-diagnosis at this point—that his "trouble" is an inability to get "sexy—I mean really sexy—with a girl I don't like a lot"—raises questions when one recalls his fraternal affection for Jane Gallagher and the relatively sexy episodes with the likes of Sally Hayes and "a terrible phony named Anne Louise Sherman." A probable answer, as we shall see, lies in his confused feelings about Phoebe.

All chances for normal sexual expression or even sexual understanding now depleted, Holden gets drunk and goes to Central Park to find "where the ducks go in winter." One critic reads this episode, filled as it is with thoughts of death, as Holden's "dark night of the soul," after which the boy begins to gain in psychic strength (Strauch, p. 109). It ought to be pointed out that Holden's breakdown occurs after the events of the narrative. His desperation in the park is certainly one extreme of his vacillation, the withdrawing extreme which is imaged by coldness and thoughts of death. Finally, he decides to see Phoebe, "in case I died and all," more explicitly associating Phoebe with death.

Holden makes his way into the apartment furtively—ostensibly to keep his parents from learning that he had flunked out of school. Yet his guilt seems obsessive. "I really should've been a crook," he says after telling the elevator operator that he was visiting the "Dicksteins" who live next door, that he has to wait for them in their hallway because he has a "bad leg," causing him to limp "like a bastard." Though his mother "has ears like a goddam bloodhound," his parents are out and he enters Phoebe's room undetected.

Phoebe is asleep:

> She had her mouth way open. It's funny. You take adults, they look lousy when they're asleep and they have their mouths way open, but kids don't. Kids look all right. They can even have spit all over the pillow and they still look all right. (p. 207)

Suddenly Holden feels "swell" as he notices such things as Phoebe's discarded clothing arranged neatly on a chair. Throughout the Phoebe section, double entendres and sexually suggestive images and gestures multiply, most flowing naturally from Holden's mind while others, once the coding is perceived, become mechanical pointers to the psychological plot.

When Holden awakens Phoebe and is embarrassed by her overaffection, she eagerly tells him about the play in which she is "Benedict Arnold":

> "It starts out when I'm dying. This ghost comes in on Christmas Eve and asks me if I'm ashamed and everything.... Are you coming to it?" (p. 210)

When the Benedict Arnold image recurs at the end, we shall see that the role of "traitor" is precisely the one she must play if her brother is to weather his crisis. Phoebe then tells him about *The Doctor*, a movie she has seen "at the Lister Foundation" about

> "this doctor ... that sticks a blanket over this child's face that's a cripple and can't walk ... and makes her suffocate. Then they make him go to jail for life imprisonment, but this child that he stuck the blanket over its head comes to visit him all the time and thanks him for what he did. He was a mercy killer." (p. 211)

This suggestive plot points to a horrible psychological possibility for Holden. He may "kill" Phoebe, pay his penalty agreeably, and even receive the gratitude of his victim. If interpretation here seems hard to justify, especially the implications of *Phoebe's* having suggested all this to Holden, consider the climax of the chapter in which Phoebe puts "the goddam pillow over her head" and refuses to come out. "She does that quite frequently," Holden reassures us—and then takes it all back: "She's a true madman sometimes." However innocent, Phoebe's responses to Holden's secret needs become the catalyst for both his breakdown and recovery.

Through the next chapter Phoebe hears Holden out on his "categorical aversions," in Salinger's phrase, to all the "phoniness" that has soured his world. The conversation begins in a curious manner:

> Then, just for the hell of it, I gave her a pinch on the behind. It was sticking way out in the breeze, the way she was laying on her side. She has hardly any behind. I didn't do it hard, but she tried to hit my hand anyway, but she missed.
>
>   Then all of a sudden, she said, "Oh, why did you *do* it?" She meant why did I get the ax again. It made me sort of sad, the way she said it. (p. 217)

Holden spells out his dissatisfactions at length—and indeed he cites valid and depressing instances of human failings—until Phoebe challenges him several times, "You don't like *any*thing that's happening." "Name one thing," she demands. "One thing? One thing I like?" Holden replies. "Okay." At this point he finds he can't "concentrate too hot."

> She was in a cockeyed position way the hell over the other side of the bed. She was about a thousand miles away. (p. 220)

He can't concentrate, I suggest, because the truth is too close.

> About all I could think of were those two nuns that went around collecting dough in those beat-up old straw baskets. Especially the one with the glasses with those iron rims. And this boy I knew at Elkton Hills. (p. 220)

Repression has transferred the true thing he "likes a lot" to a nun, an inviolable "sister," who, we remember, had embarrassed Holden by talking about *Romeo and Juliet*, "that play [that] gets pretty sexy in parts." It may also be significant that *Romeo and Juliet* involves forbidden love that ends tragically—especially significant in connection with the other "thing" Holden thinks about, James Castle, the boy who had killed himself wearing Holden's turtleneck sweater.

None of this will do for Phoebe and she repeats the challenge:

> "I like Allie," I said. "And I like doing what I'm doing right now. Sitting here with you, and talking, and thinking about stuff, and—" (p. 222)

When she objects that "Allie's dead," Holden tries to explain but gives up:

> "Anyway, I like it now," I said. "I mean right now. Sitting here with you and just chewing the fat and horsing—" (p. 223)

Her insistence drives him to the loveliest—and most sinister—fantasy in the novel:

> "You know that song 'If a body catch a body comin' through the rye'? I'd like—"
> "It's 'If a body *meet* a body coming through the rye!'" old Phoebe said. (p. 224)

Holden proceeds to conjure up the daydream of himself as catcher in the rye, the protector of childhood innocence. As Phoebe implies, however, the song is about romance, not romanticism. Because he has to, Holden has substituted a messianic motive for the true, erotic one.

In the next chapter Holden and Phoebe seem to be acting out a mock romance, much the way Seymour Glass does with the little girl in "A Perfect Day for Bananafish." The episode is at once movingly tender and ominous. Holden finds Phoebe "sitting smack in the middle of the bed, outside the covers, with her legs folded like one of those Yogi guys"—an image one critic interprets as making her an emblem of "the still, contemplative center of life" (Strauch, p. 43). This may be valid for one level of Holden's mind. When he immediately asks her to dance, however, and "She practically jumped off the bed, and then waited while I took my shoes off," his excessive justifications point to guilt:

> I don't like people that dance with little kids.... Usually they keep yanking the kid's dress up in the back by mistake, and the kid can't dance worth a damn *any*way, and it looks terrible, but I don't do it out in public with Phoebe or anything. We just horse around in

the house. It's different with her anyway, because she can *dance*. She can follow anything you do. I mean if you hold her in close as hell so that it doesn't matter that your legs are so much longer. She stays right with you. (p. 227)

After the dance, Phoebe "jumped back in bed and got under the covers" and Holden "sat down next to her on the bed again ... sort of out of breath." "'Feel my forehead,' she said all of a sudden." Phoebe claims she has learned to induce fever psychosomatically so that

> "your whole forehead gets so hot you can burn somebody's hand."
> That killed me. I pulled my hand away from her forehead, like I was in terrific danger. "Thanks for *tell*ing me," I said.
> "Oh, I wouldn't've burned *your* hand. I'd've stopped before it got too—*Shhh!*" Then, quick as hell, she sat way the hell up in bed. (p. 229)

The parents have returned and the scene that follows—Holden gathering up his shoes and hiding in the closet as the mother interrogates Phoebe about the (cigarette) "smoke" in the bedroom and asks "were you warm enough?"—is reminiscent of nothing so much as that mainstay of French farce, the lover hiding in the closet or under the bed as the girl ironically "explains" to husband or parent. More important are the implications of Phoebe's "heat." Though she cannot really induce it, her innocent compliance in the whole sexual charade does place Holden "in terrific danger."

When the mother leaves, Holden emerges from his hiding place and borrows money from Phoebe. Phoebe insists that he take all of her money and Holden "all of a sudden" begins to cry:

> I couldn't help it. I did it so nobody could hear me, but I did it. It scared hell out of old Phoebe when I started doing it, and she came over and tried to make me stop, but once you get started, you can't just stop on a goddam dime. I was still sitting on the edge of the bed when I did it, and she put her old arm around my neck, and I put my arm around her, too, but I still couldn't stop for a long time. I thought I was going to choke to death or something. Boy, I scared hell out of poor old Phoebe. The damn window was open and everything, and I could feel her shivering and all, because all she had on was her pajamas. I tried to make her get back in bed, but she wouldn't go. (p. 233)

Holden's breakdown, his visiting of his own suffering on the child, the chill air, and the innocence of their intimacy in this moving scene signal his growing, frightening awareness of the other sort of intimacy. From now until he sees Phoebe again, Holden is in full flight. Nonetheless, their parting is filled with suggestions of a sort one might expect after a casual, normal sexual encounter. (The emphases in the following passage are my own.)

> Then I *finished buttoning* my coat and all. I told her I'd *keep in touch* with her. She told me *I could sleep with her* if I wanted to, but I said no, that I'd better beat it.... Then I took my hunting hat out of my coat pocket and *gave it to her*. She likes those kind of crazy hats. She didn't want to take it, but *I made her*. I'll bet she *slept with it* on. She really likes those kinds of hats. Then I told her again I'd *give her a buzz* if I got a chance, and then I left. (p. 233)

It is almost as if Holden is acknowledging the real content of the sexual charade and escaping while he can. It would also seem that realization, however vague, is equated with deed as Holden immediately indicates that he wanted to be punished:

> It was a helluva lot easier getting out of the house than it was getting in, for some reason. For one thing, I didn't give much of a damn any more if they caught me. I really didn't. I figured if they caught me, they caught me. I almost wished they did, in a way. (pp. 233–34)

Holden leaves Phoebe to spend the night with Mr. Antolini, a former teacher who during the course of the evening offers sound if stilted assessments of Holden's future which become particularly relevant in the epilogue. Antolini has been drinking, however, and disrupts the peace he has provided (Holden feels sleepy for the first time) by awakening the boy with tentative homosexual advances. Certainly Holden is victimized ("I was shaking like a madman.... I think I was more depressed than I ever was in my life"), but the encounter may torment him most for its parallels to his own unconscious designs on a child. Now one begins to see the significance of Holden's unfounded suspicions about Jane Gallagher's stepfather and his murderous rage at the "perverty bum" who wrote the obscenity on Phoebe's school wall—inordinate reactions pointing to fears about himself.

At this point Holden's neurosis verges on madness. Each time he crosses a street, he imagines he will "disappear" and "never get to the other side of the street." I do not take this so much as a symbolic manifestation of "identity crisis" and of his fear that he "may never reach maturity"—although both are implicit—but rather as a literal, psychologically valid description of the boy's breakdown. He retreats into wild fantasies of running away forever, living in a cabin near, but not in, the woods ("I'd want it to be sunny as hell all the time"), and feigning deaf-muteness, all to escape the confusion about to engulf him. Phoebe betrays these plans—the first ironic level of the Benedict Arnold motif—by joining in his escape. When she appears, bag in hand and the hunting cap on her head, Holden reacts wildly:

> "I'm going with you. Can I? Okay?"
> "What?" I said. I almost fell over when she said that. I swear to God I did. I got sort of dizzy and I thought I was going to pass out or something again.
>
> . . . .
>
> I thought I was going to pass out cold. I mean I didn't mean to tell her to shut up and all, but I thought I was going to pass out again.
>
> . . . .
>
> I was almost all set to hit her. I thought I was going to smack her for a second. I really did....
> "I thought you were supposed to be Benedict Arnold in that play and all," I said. I said it very nasty. "Wuddaya want to do? Not be in the play, for God's sake?" That made her cry even harder. I was glad. All of a sudden I wanted her to cry till her eyes practically dropped out. I almost hated her. I think I hated her most because she wouldn't be in that play any more if she went away with me. (pp. 267–68)

These near-hysterical responses can be understood, it seems to me, only in the context that Phoebe is the very thing he is fleeing. He somehow realizes that she *must* be his "Benedict Arnold."

Holden's fury at Phoebe having set the climax in motion, Salinger now employs a delicate spatial strategy. Phoebe returns the hat, turns her back on Holden, announces that she has no intention of running away with him, and runs "right the hell across the street, without even looking to see if any cars were coming." Positioning here signifies the end of their relation as possible lovers, but love remains. Holden does not go after her, knowing she'll follow him "on the *other* goddam side of the street. She wouldn't look over at me at all, but I could tell she was probably watching me out of the corner of her crazy eye to see where I was going and all. Anyway, we kept walking that way all the way to the zoo." They are still apart as they watch the sea lions being fed, Holden standing "right behind her."

> I didn't put my hands on her shoulders again or anything because if I had she really would've beat it on me. Kids are funny. You have to watch what you're doing.
>   She wouldn't walk right next to me when we left the sea lions, but she didn't walk too far away. She sort of walked on one side of the sidewalk and I walked on the other side.
> . . . .
> Old Phoebe still wouldn't talk to me or anything, but she was sort of walking next to me now. I took a hold of the belt at the back of her coat, just for the hell of it, but she wouldn't let me. She said, "Keep your hands to yourself, if you don't mind." (pp. 271–72)

Holden promises not to run away and they rejoin as brother and sister in the presence of the carrousel—miraculously open in winter. Phoebe wants to ride and Holden finds a mature, new perspective:

> All the kids kept trying to grab for the gold ring, and so was old Phoebe, and I was sort of afraid she'd fall off the goddam horse, but I didn't say anything or do anything. The thing with kids is, if they want to grab for the gold ring, you have to let them do it, and not say anything. If they fall off, they fall off, but it's bad if you say anything to them. (pp. 273–74)

The substitution of a gold ring for the traditional brass one may point to Phoebe's future as a woman. In any event, Holden has renounced his designs on Phoebe and thus abrogated his messianic role. Another Salinger story has young de Daumier-Smith relinquish his sexual designs on a nun with the announcement, "I am giving Sister Irma her freedom to follow her destiny. Everyone is a nun." One need not search for literary sources to recognize that the carrousel finally represents everyone's sacred, inviolable human destiny.

III

Readers now dubious about this paper's clinical approach ("aesthetic pathology," Salinger has called it) may wonder why I have thus far neglected to make a masculine symbol of Holden's long-peaked hunting cap—which he purchased, one recalls, after losing the fencing team's foils in a subway. This rather mechanical symbol does partake of the boy's masculinity or sexuality. But more than that, it becomes the most reliable symbolic designation of Holden's psychic condition through the novel. Ackley points out that it is a deer hunter's hat while Holden maintains that "This is a people shooting hat.... I shoot people in this hat." When one remembers that hunters wear red hats to keep from being shot and that Holden usually wears his backwards in the manner of a baseball catcher, the symbol embraces Holden's aggressive and withdrawing tendencies as well as the outlandish daydreams of becoming the messiah in the rye.

Holden's masculinity is plainly involved in such instances as when he has to retrieve the hat from under a bed after the fight with Stradlater and when it is entrusted to Phoebe's bed, but the symbol becomes more encompassing when she "restores" the hat in the climactic carrousel scene.

> Then all of a sudden she gave me a kiss. Then she held her hand out, and said, "It's raining. It's starting to rain."
> "I know."
> Then what she did—it damn near killed me—she reached in my coat pocket and took out my red hunting hat and put it on my head.
> . . . .
> My hunting hat really gave me quite a lot of protection, in a way, but I got soaked anyway. I didn't care, though. I felt so damn happy all of a sudden, the way old Phoebe kept going around and around. I was damn near bawling, I felt so damn happy, if you want to know the truth. I don't know why. It was just that she looked so damn *nice*, the way she kept going around and around, in her blue coat and all. God, I wish you could have been there. (pp. 274–75)

At its deepest level, the hat symbolizes something like Holden's basic human resources—his birthright, that lucky caul of protective courage, humor, compassion, honesty, and love—all of which are the real subject matter of the novel.

As the symbolic hat gives Holden "quite a lot of protection, in a way" and he gets "soaked anyway," those human resources do not prevent emotional collapse. In the epilogue we learn that Holden went West "after I went home, and ... got sick and all"—not for the traditional opportunity there but for psychotherapy. This would be a bleak ending were it not for the fact that Holden has authored this structured narrative, just as Antolini predicted he might:

"you'll find that you're not the first person who was ever confused and frightened and even sickened by human behavior. You're by no means alone on that score, you'll be excited and *stimulated* to know. Many, many men have been just as troubled morally and spiritually as you are right now. Happily, some of them kept records of their troubles. You'll learn from them—if you want to. Just as someday, if you have something to offer, someone will learn something from you. It's a beautiful reciprocal arrangement. And it isn't education. It's history. It's poetry." (p. 246)

The richness of spirit in this novel, especially of the vision, the compassion, and the humor of the narrator reveal a psyche far healthier than that of the boy who endured the events of the narrative. Through the telling of his story, Holden has given shape to, and thus achieved control of, his troubled past.

NOTES

1. J.D. Salinger, *The Catcher in the Rye* (Boston: Little, 1951), pp. 7–8. Page numbers from this edition will be cited in the text.

2. Carl F. Strauch, "Kings in the Back Row: Meaning through Structure—A Reading of Salinger's *The Catcher in the Rye*," in *Wisconsin Studies in Contemporary Literature*, 2 (Winter 1961), 5–30; rpt. in *If You Really Want to Know: A Catcher Casebook* (Belmont, Calif.: Wadsworth, 1962), p. 104.

3. Salinger may be echoing Phoebus rather than Phoebe, the personification of the moon; but he also may have in mind an antithesis between "Sunny" and Phoebe, the cool and chaste.

WARREN FRENCH

The Artist as a Very Nervous Young Man

I A Gathering of Exegetes

So much has already been written about *The Catcher in the Rye* that it might appear unlikely that there is anything left to say. Although the novel was not accorded as immediate scholarly attention as James Gould Cozzens' *By Love Possessed*, it has, since 1954, been the subject of probably more critical pronouncements than any other postwar novel.

Despite readers' enthusiastic response to *Catcher*, the critical chorus has generally been discordant. One thing, in fact, that has tended to detract from Salinger's reputation is that only a few of his ardent admirers have been heard from in print. Henry Anatole Grunwald's *Salinger: A Critical and Personal Portrait* (1962) anthologizes most of these comparatively few "appreciations" in two sections entitled "Between Miracle and Suicide" and "The Phoenix." Perhaps the most impressive is Dan Wakefield's "Salinger and the Search for Love," originally prepared for *New World Writing* (Number 14). Wakefield speaks for most Salinger *aficionados* when he says that the author "speaks for all who have not lost hope or even if they have lost hope, have not lost interest— in the search for love and morality in the present-day world" and that Salinger is "the only new writer to emerge in America since the second world war who is writing on what has been the grandest theme of literature: the relationship of man to God, or the lack of God" (Grunwald, 178, 186).

From *J.D. Salinger*. Boston: G.K. Hall & Co. (1976): 102–29. © 1976 by G.K. Hall & Co.

Even more sweeping is Martin Green's claim reproduced from his book *A Mirror for Anglo-Saxons* (1960), that Salinger is a cultural "image-maker," who provides in Holden Caulfield a kind of heroic figure to whom we all look up and in whom "Wellesley and Harvard undergraduates can recognize themselves transfigured, more intensely alive, more honest, more passionate, more courageous" (Grunwald, 253). Similar sentiments are expressed in an essay written by an undergraduate, Christopher Parker, for the anthology. Although Parker admits that most young men who read *Catcher*, "don't think about it enough—what's really behind it all," he says that we "can all identify ourselves" with Holden's plight (Grunwald, 258, 254).

A somewhat more sober approach is taken in the essay that signaled the beginning of academic attention to *Catcher*—Arthur Heiserman and James E. Miller, Jr.'s, "J.D. Salinger: Some Crazy Cliff," written as one of a series of "revaluations" for *Western Humanities Review* in 1956. The two authors attempt to place the novel in the mainstream of American and world fiction by showing its relationship to the "tradition of the quest," a preoccupation of the rising school of myth critics. The article especially endears itself to admirers of the book because of the authors' conclusion that "it is not Holden who should be examined for a sickness of the mind, but the world in which he sojourned and found himself an alien" (Grunwald, 205).

Most critics have not, however, been swayed by such passionate rhetoric. The first influential naysayer was Ernest Jones, Freud's student and biographer, who, in his review of the novel for the *Nation* (September 1, 1951, 176), provided an enduring catchphrase when he described *Catcher* as "a case history of all of us." The book, Jones says, is "not at all something rich and strange, but what every sensitive 16-year-old since Rousseau has felt, and of course what each of us is certain he has felt." The novel, as a result, although "lively in its parts," is "as a whole ... predictable and boring." While Jones appears to be judging *Catcher* as a psychoanalytical document rather than as a work of art, his observation that Holden "mistakes whatever is spontaneous in his behavior for madness" is vital to an understanding that Holden is not a romantic rebel in the American transcendental tradition.

A far less justifiable conclusion is reached in the first discussion of *Catcher* in a book about contemporary American literature, John W. Aldridge's *In Search of Heresy* (1956). Seizing upon the comparison between Huck Finn and Holden, which has been carefully and thoughtfully explored by many writers (see essays by Charles Kaplan, Edgar Branch, and Alvin R. Wells listed in the bibliography), Aldridge argues that whereas Huck's innocence is "a compound of frontier ignorance, juvenile delinquency, and penny-dreadful heroism," Holden's is "a compound of urban intelligence, juvenile contempt, and *New Yorker* sentimentalism" (129–30). Arguing further that Holden never recognizes the phoniness that he objects to as "what one part of humanity *is*," Aldridge—who apparently has no concept of the moral complexity of urban life—reaches the conclusion to which many other critics have objected: that Holden "remains at the end what he was at the beginning—cynical, defiant, and blind" (131). Ihab Hassan dismisses these charges in *Radical Innocence* (1961), but he points out that among the novel's "real failings" are Holden's refusal "to draw any conclusions from his experience" and Salinger's failure to modify Holden's point of view by any other (275).

Maxwell Geismar in *American Moderns from Rebellion to Conformity* (1958) also takes Salinger to task for the lack of conclusions in the novel, which he describes as "the *New Yorker* school of ambiguous finality at its best" written by an "Exurbanite Radical Party of One." Acknowledging that *Catcher* protests "against both the academic and social conformity of its period," Geismar asks, "What does it argue *for*?" Its real achievement, he thinks, "is that it manages so gracefully to evade just those central questions which it raises" (198). Still more disturbed about Salinger's lack of concern with "issues" is Barbara Giles, whose "The Lonely War of J.D. Salinger" (*Mainstream*, February, 1959) is the only discussion of Salinger's work I can locate in a journal of leftist opinion. She asks: "Is it a superior virtue to dream of rescuing imaginary children from a mythical danger instead of saving 'innocent guys'—real ones—from legalized death because the crusader can't be certain that his sword is untarnished by a fleck of exhibitionism?" (7).

Two other critics link Salinger with Jack Kerouac in expressing the suspicion that Holden's lack of meaningful rebellion is symptomatic of a decline in American frontier traditions. Leslie Fiedler in *Love and Death in the American Novel* (1960) comments that "whether on the upper-middle-brow level of Salinger or the Bohemian-kitsch level of Kerouac, such writers echo not the tragic *Huckleberry Finn*, but the sentimental book with which it is intertwined" (271). More barbed than Fiedler's truncheons are the words wielded to like effect by Kingsley Widmer, who, in "The American Road" (*University of Kansas City Review*, June, 1960) points out that in both *Catcher* and *On the Road*, "we find much the same messianic yearnings" of heroes "who repeatedly get bailed out before fully engaging their own experience and the consequences." Although earlier the "road" had been "the way of honor ... and initiation ... of the archetypal American hero," Holden does not really "break into freedom," but only "ritualistically *plays* at the big–boy's kind of freedom just to neutralize and dispel it for easier adjustment" (307, 313–14).

Another group of ill-disposed critics has sought to account for the popularity of *Catcher*. Frank Kermode, in "Fit Audience" (*Spectator*, May 30, 1958), argues that Holden's "attitudes to religion, authority, art, sex, and so on are what smart people would like other people to have, but cannot have themselves because of superior understanding." Thus he believes that Salinger's success "springs from his having, with perfect understanding supplied their demand for this kind of satisfaction" (705). His charges are augmented by Alfred Kazin's observation in a *Harper's* special supplement on "Writing in America" (October, 1959, p. 130) that Salinger lacks strength because "he identifies himself too fussily with the spiritual aches and pains of his characters" and exemplifies the writer who is "reduced to ... the 'mystery of personality' instead of the drama of our social existence." Writing the next month about "The Salinger Industry" in the *Nation* (November 14, 1959, pp., 360–63), George Steiner (author of the widely acclaimed *Tolstoy or Dostoevsky?* and *The Death of Tragedy*) stridently appointed himself to command of the anti-Salinger forces by charging that the novelist's "semi-literate maunderings of the adolescent mind" flattered "the very ignorance and shallowness of his young readers." Salinger, Steiner continued, depicted as "positive virtues": "formal ignorance, political apathy, and a vague *tristesse*." The "industry" that had promoted Salinger to the ranks of the great writers, Steiner attributed to American academic critics who cannot write "with plainness or understatement," who are under "undue pressure to publish," and who, therefore, do not carry out the critic's proper task of distinguishing "what is great from what is competent."

Part of Steiner's essay and other examples of recent sniping at Salinger may be found in that section of Grunwald's *Salinger* titled "Magician, Clubman, or Guru." It contains, for example, David Leitch's attribution in "The Salinger Myth" of the novelist's influence to the prevalence of the type of person "young, or obsessed with youth" and "profoundly conscious of being set apart from the run-of-the-mill human beings he sees around him," who considers "communication with outsiders ... not only useless but impossible," and "apt, if attempted, to cause unpleasant situations" (Grunwald, 70–71).

Despite the vast amount of writing about *The Catcher in the Rye*, there have been remarkably few articles that have attempted simply to analyze the novel without excessively praising the author or picking a quarrel with him. Frederick Gwynn and Joseph Blotner in *The Fiction of J.D. Salinger* (1958; largely reprinted in Grunwald, *Salinger*), the first monograph about the novelist, analyze many short stories in detail, but spend little time on the novel. They do draw a forced comparison between Holden and Jesus; but this attempt to climb on the critically fashionable bandwagon with those who find a passion legend in every tale of individual tribulation obliges the collaborator to confuse compassionate forgiveness with adolescent nostalgia. The discussion closes with the unwarranted statement that the novel's conclusion is "just as artistically weak—and as humanly satisfying—as that of *Huckleberry Finn*," probably because to round off their parallel Holden would have to be "crucified," as Jim Casy is in *The Grapes of Wrath*.

The most useful article written about *Catcher* is Donald Costello's "The Language of *The Catcher in the Rye*," which Grunwald naively treats as an example of the lengths to which "earnest scholarship can go." Costello identifies the specific ingredients of the "type of informal, colloquial teenage American speech" used in the novel, to which many critics had paid vague tributes. He also catalogues and provides specific examples of the devices Salinger uses to characterize Holden individually (ending sentences with "and all," "I really did," "if you want to know truth and"), and also as a typical teen-ager of his time (crude language, slang, trite figures of speech, use of nouns as adjectives, adverbs) (Grunwald, *Salinger*, pp. 266–76).

The only really objective analysis of *Catcher* and the most ambitious discussion of the novel written thus far is Carl F. Strauch's "Kings in the Back Row: Meaning through Structure" (*Wisconsin Studies in Contemporary Literature*, Winter, 1961). Arguing from the premise that "structure is meaning," Strauch points out that "except in scattered and fragmentary flashes, it has thus far escaped attention that Salinger sharply accentuates the portrayal of Holden with a symbolic structure of language, motif, episode, and character" (6). He attempts to rectify this situation by an explanation of "the interlocking metaphorical structure" of the novel, which allows us to perceive that "Salinger has employed neurotic deterioration, symbolic death, spiritual awakening, and psychological self-cure as the inspiration and burden of an elaborate pattern" (7).

Although Strauch's theory that "Holden psychologically dies only to be reborn into the world of Phoebe's innocence and love" and then effects "his own psychological regeneration" leads to subtle insights into Holden's language ("slob" for the public world, "literate" for his private world) and into the imagery of the novel, it leads also to the untenable conclusion that the end of the novel is "blunted ... because we cannot say what society will do to impose adjustment upon a body who has effected his own secret cure" (27). The trouble with this conclusion is that, if Holden has really effected his own cure, society will not be able to "impose" anything upon him; for he will have prepared himself to meet its demands. The "end of the novel could not then be "blunted," for Holden's subsequent career would be too obvious to be depicted. Strauch strains too hard to make the novel conform to a single narrative pattern. He does not, therefore, either elucidate the complex interweaving of several narrative strands in the novel or discern how the conclusion provides a complete and satisfactory resolution of these strands.

II THE CATCHER IN THE RYE—SEARCH FOR TRANQUILLITY

To determine the exact relationship to an overall pattern of each detail in the novel would require a book as long as the novel itself. It is possible, however, to provide a more complete structural analysis of *The Catcher in the Rye* than has previously appeared by outlining the three main patterns that must be considered in interpreting the work.

Although *Catcher* is richly and elaborately embellished, it is basically the account of the breakdown of a sixteen-year-old boy. The novel does not attempt to trace the whole history of this catastrophe from its origins, but concentrates on the events of its critical stage. Salinger tries hard to make clear just what he is doing when he has Holden comment that "all that David Copperfield kind of crap" bores him and that he is going to tell only "about this madman stuff" that happened just before he got "pretty run-down" (3).*

Even though Holden acknowledges being attended by a psychoanalyst at the end of the book, his breakdown is clearly not just—or even principally—mental. He is physically ill. He has grown six and a half inches in a year and "practically got T.B." (8). He also admits that he is "skinny" and has not kept to the diet that he should to gain weight (140). He is passing through the most physically difficult period of adolescence when only the most sympathetic care can enable the body to cope with the changes it is undergoing.

Holden's condition is complicated, however, by emotional problems. His mother is ill and nervous, and his father is so busy being successful he never discusses things with his son (140). Holden is thus without the kind of parental guidance an adolescent urgently needs during this crucial period. The school to which he has been packed off fails to take the place of his parents. Holden's complaint is not that Pencey Prep-like schools in European novels such as Sybille Bedford's *A Legacy* or even the monstrous American military academy in Calder Willingham's *End As a Man*—is overbearing or destructive of individuality, but rather that "they don't do any damn more molding at Pencey than they do at any other school" (4). While the administrators entertain prospective donors, the kind of cliques of hoodlums that drive James Castle to suicide operate unchecked. Although Holden is trying to cling to an unrealistically rigid Victorian moral code, he also lacks what David Riesman calls the "psychological gyroscope" that keeps the "inner-directed" personality on course. (To classify Holden in the terms provided by *The Lonely Crowd*, he is an inner-directed" personality in an "other-directed" society—an unhappy phenomenon so common today that it alone could account for many persons' identification with Holden.

Holden also has the intellectual problem of preparing himself for a vocation, because he rejects the kind of career for which his schooling is preparing him and as yet he can conceive of no realistic substitute for it. His emotional and intellectual problems do not, however, cause his breakdown; rather his rundown physical condition magnifies the pain these problems cause him. The boy is struggling, without enlightened assistance, against greater odds than he can fight for himself; and his "quest" during the critical period described in the book is not really for some metaphysical "grail" but simply for a "nice" (he uses the word himself at the end of his adventures, p. 275) refuge from the "phony" world that threatens to engulf him.

Those who find the book nothing more than a satirical attack upon the "phoniness" that irritates Holden's condition are probably as disturbed as the boy himself; for—as Marc Rosenberg points out—Holden suffers because of an undisciplined hypersensitivity.[1] The most common complaint that cooler and supposedly wiser heads like Ernest Havemann[2] level at the novel is that Holden is himself guilty of all the things that make him call other "phony." As Christopher Parker admits, the charge is absolutely true.[3] In the opening chapters of the novel, Salinger strains to make it clear that Holden does precisely what he objects to other people's doing. He displays the vain irresponsibility that he criticizes in "secret slob" Stradlater (35) when he loses the fencing team's equipment (6). He stands in another's light as he complains Ackley does (40, 28). He lectures Ackley in the same way that he objects to the history teacher's lecturing him (32, 16–17). Like Ackley, he will do what others want only when he is shouted at (32, 63). Like Luce, he will discuss only what he feels like talking about (188, 71). He is especially guilty of overgeneralizing. Although he complains that everybody—especially his father—"think something's all true" when it's only partly true, he ends the very paragraph in which he makes this charge with his own generalization that "people never notice anything" (13). Elsewhere he comments   to cite only a few examples—"people never believe you" (48), women always leave bags in the aisle (70), "all those Ivy League bastards look alike" (112).

There is no point in multiplying examples; Holden obviously fails to see that his criticisms apply to himself. If, however, we think that his failure to practice what he preaches invalidates his criticisms, we fall into an *argumentum ad hominem*—we cannot justify our shortcomings by pointing the finger of scorn at our critics, especially if we do not wish to admit that we are as sick as they are. Like many sensitive but immature people, Holden is not yet well enough in control of his faculties to see the application of his strictures to himself. As Ihab Hassan warns, there is as great a danger "in taking Holden at his word as in totally discounting his claim."[4] Despite Martin Green's claims, Salinger is not offering Holden to the world as an example of what it should be.[5] If those who think that Holden could pull

himself together if he would just "try" are as insensitive as the people who
fail Holden in the novel, those who make a martyr of Holden are victims of
the same immature hypersensitivity that he is. Both make the mistake of
supposing that the novel is what Ernest Jones calls "a case history of all of
us." It is not; there are adolescents like those Holden says are "as sensitive as
a goddam toilet seat" (72); there are those who are driven to suicide by their
real or imagined tormentors (like James Castle or Seymour Glass); and there
are sensitive ones who are saved by a stronger sense of "inner direction" than
Holden possesses. The popularity of the novel suggests, however, that fully
literate youth in our society finds it especially easy to identify with Holden.

Many people who read too much of themselves into the novel do not
seem to realize that Holden is not seeking admiration, but the understanding
that will help him through a difficult period. (When Phoebe does
dramatically show admiration for him by insisting upon running away with
him, he realizes that he cannot accept the responsibility of hero-worship.)
He is not—like most restless rebels in American literature (Leatherstocking,
Ahab, Carol Kennicott, Arrowsmith, Clyde Griffiths, Danny in *Tortilla Flat*,
Dean Moriarity, Henry Miller in *Tropic of Cancer*, even Nick Carraway, until
he is disillusioned)—seeking to run away from a monotonous, humdrum life,
but to run toward some kind of tranquil sanctuary. It has not even been
generally observed that Holden does not even consider "running away" from
urban society until very near the end of the book, and that he leaves school
early and goes to New York City so that he can hibernate in a cheap hotel
room and "go home all rested up and feeling swell" (66). He cannot carry out
this plan, however, because he cannot stand being alone; he feels like "giving
somebody a buzz" as soon as he hits town. If he were not constantly seeking
company, he might have to think about his situation and his experiences, but
he is not yet ready to accept this demanding intellectual responsibility.

He needs sympathy, and he has not been able to find it at school. His
history instructor lectures him about things he already knows, but he cannot
answer the one question that Holden plaintively asks—"Everybody goes
through phases and all, don't they?" (21). His schoolmates aggravate his
condition: Ackley will move only if yelled at; Stradlater is not interested in a
person's "lousy childhood," but only "very sexy stuff" (42). Both give Holden
"a royal pain" by running down the few accomplishments that may give other
people some vitally needed self-confidence (37). When Holden yells, "*Sleep
tight, ya morons!*" as he leaves Pencey (68), he probably does not fully
understand his own motives, but he senses that those he leaves behind are
sleeping morons because they are too obsessed with their own nose drops,
pimples, and good looks even to be interested in trying to figure out what
may really be troubling a boy who they know is flunking out. (Holden, of

course, does not try to figure out what their problems are, but he is at least sometimes aware that he does not know all about people. His immediate problem, furthermore, is more urgent than theirs.)

Holden fares no better in New York City. Readers who tend to idealize him should notice that his failures generally result from his own desperate impetuousness. When he first fails to arrange a rendezvous with the "available" Faith Cavendish, he acknowledges that he "fouled that up" (86). Although he finds one of the girls from Seattle whom he meets in the Lavender Room of his hotel to be a marvelous dancer, he snobbishly rejects all of them because "they don't know any better" than to drink Tom Collinses in the middle of December (97) or to go to Radio City Music Hall (98), where he subsequently goes himself. He irritates a touchy taxi driver with questions about the ducks in Central Park (107–8), and he leaves a night club because he doesn't want to be "bored to death" by an old flame of his brother's and her naval officer escort (114).

Although it is "against his principles," he allows Maurice, an elevator operator, to send a prostitute to his room (119). Feeling "much more depressed than sexy," he attempts to engage the unwilling girl in conversation (123). When he refuses to pay an extra five dollars that she and the pimp try to bilk him of, he is beaten up, although his plaint is only that "it'd be different" if they had asked for ten dollars to begin with (134). His old girl friend, Sally Hayes, actually proves no more understanding than the prostitute. Sally has evidently made her adjustment to the sophisticated life Holden hates. When he asks her if she hates school, she replies that "it's a terrific *bore*," but she doesn't "exactly *hate* it" (169). When he pleads with her, to run away to the woods with him, she tries to "reason" with him by pointing out that his idea is "fantastic" and that there will be "oodles of marvelous places to go" if they get married after he finishes college (172). When he tells her that she gives him "a royal pain," she leaves in tears, and Holden rationalizes that he probably would not have taken her with him anyway (173–74). Obviously, from the way Sally attempts to change the subject from hating school and phonies, she cannot possibly help Holden because her own adjustment is still too precarious. Although she agrees that Holden is in "*lousy* shape," she cannot provide the understanding he needs.

Turning to a more mature ex-schoolmate, now a student at Columbia, Holden draws another blank. Carl Luce avoids discussion of the questions that most disturb Holden and finally coldly advises that the boy see a psychiatrist. A prototype of Lane Coutell in "Franny," Luce is described by Holden as one of those intellectuals who "don't like to have an intellectual conversation with you unless they're running the whole thing" (191). There is no aid for the bewildered in such monomaniacal monologues.

Finally, in the often-discussed scene in the Antolini apartment, Holden turns to a still older person, a respected teacher. Although Antolini does not mind being disturbed late at night and offers Holden a refuge, even this well-intentioned man fails as abysmally as the others to provide what the boy needs. After lecturing Holden at great length about not dying nobly for a cause, but living humbly for it—especially by applying one's self in school— Antolini wakes the boy who has at last gone to sleep by stroking him on the head. Much comment has been made about the soundness of Antolini's advice, which some critics think would have saved Holden, and also about Antolini's real intentions toward the boy, who jumps to the conclusion that the man who has appeared to be his last refuge from a "phony" world is making a homosexual advance toward him.

As far as the second matter goes, Salinger does not provide enough evidence to confirm or deny Holden's assumption. Although the teacher's calling Holden "handsome" and saying that he has been sitting "admiring" him arouse suspicion, his specific intentions are really beside the point. What matters is that he is guilty of a seriously faulty judgment, for, if he had perceived the depth of the boy's disturbance, he would have done nothing that might puzzle or upset him. By the time Holden reaches Antolini's, he is nearly at the breaking point. He not only yawns rudely in the man's face, but he contradicts himself several times. He says, for example, that an instructor at Pencey Prep "was intelligent and all, but you could tell he didn't have too much brains" (240). He also insists that "there were a couple of [classes] I didn't attend once in a while ... but I didn't cut any" (242). If Antolini were really sensitive to another's condition, he would have noted these danger signals and left the boy strictly alone until the crisis had past; but, boozed up and enraptured by the sound of his own rhetoric, the "instructor" rattles on. Whatever his sexual propensities, his insensitivity drives the boy from his last refuge.

Antolini's behavior also casts doubt on the wisdom of his advice. Many writers have praised what he tells Holden because they agree with it; but this doesn't mean that Salinger does. Holden keeps the card upon which Antolini writes Stekel's advice about living humbly for a cause, but he may do this simply out of politeness or sentiment. Certainly when, a little later, he passes through his crisis, he does not recall the advice. What he wants from Antolini at the time he visits him is not more advice, but some kind of a gesture. Antolini makes a gesture all right, but an unfortunate one. Holden has come for understanding and receives instead the kind of lecture that Polonius delivers to Laertes in *Hamlet* before the son leaves home. And we know exactly what Holden thinks about this advice, for earlier in the book he has referred to the speech specifically as "the bull his father was shooting" (153).

While it is dangerous to interpret an earlier work in the light of a later, we should at least recall, in considering Salinger's concept of Antolini, that many of the novelist's later works have been devoted to the celebration of Seymour Glass, who does not live humbly, but dies conspicuously, "dazzled to death by his own scruples."[6]

Certainly, whatever the value of Antolini's advice, Holden's last hope in the world of his peers and elders has failed him; he can turn only—as he has in moments of reverie throughout the book—to the unchanging dead, to the memory of his brother Allie, and it is Allie whom he addresses as his physical breakdown approaches its crisis. Walking along the street alone, Holden pleads with Allie not to let him "disappear." Holden survives, and only after this crisis has passed—as he is sitting on a bench somewhere in the Sixties, breathless and sweating (257)—does he decide that he will run away, pretend to be a deaf mute, and hide his children. Society has failed him.

This decision climaxes the story of the disturbed boy's search for understanding. All of his requests for assistance have failed; he can now be redeemed only by an unsolicited gesture. This is made by his little sister Phoebe, who—when she learns that he plans to run away—insists on accompanying him. In the meantime, Holden has discovered obscene words scribbled not only in Phoebe's school, but in the almost sacred balls of the Museum of Natural History, and he has realized that "you can't ever find a place that's nice and peaceful, because there isn't any" (264). He has resigned himself to the phoniness of the world; and as far as he himself is concerned, he can simply renounce it. When Phoebe insists on running away with him, however, he realizes that he cannot take the responsibility for her, because he will be depriving her of too many of the opportunities open to her. He is most angry because if she runs away with him, she won't be in the school play (274).

He decides that he must go home, not for his own sake, but for Phoebe's; and lest the skeptical reader misinterpret his intention, he emphasizes, "I really did go home afterwards" (274). He manages, too, to reconcile Phoebe to accepting his decision, not by pounding her ear, but by leaving her alone until she is willing to respond to him. Having made and also elicited a gesture of submission, Holden is rewarded at last with the peace that he has sought, in the sight of Phoebe going around and around on the carousel. He does not understand why the sight makes him so happy; "it was just that she looked so damn *nice*" (275). Eventually, of course, the carousel will stop and Holden and Phoebe will have to return to the world that is "going somewhere"; but since there is no place that is permanently "nice and peaceful" in this world, these few minutes of aimless joy are the best that life affords.

This resolution of Holden's quest for physical tranquillity does not bring us to the end of the book, however, but only to the end of the penultimate chapter in which the climax of this strand of the narrative occurs and Phoebe's spontaneous gesture of affection produces a happier ending than might have been anticipated. Is the last brief chapter that closes the "frame" around Holden's account of his experience simply a tacked-on recital of "what came afterwards" in the tradition of the nineteenth-century novel? If the novel were only the story of the overstrained Holden's search for something "nice" in a phony world, it would end with his admiring Phoebe riding the carousel.

III The Catcher in the Rye—The Growth of Compassion

Another story, however, is intertwined with that of Holden's physical breakdown—the story of the breaking down of Holden's self-centeredness and his gradual acceptance of the world that has rejected him. Actually there is less development in this subplot than the other, because as the book opens Holden is already well on the road to countering his own phoniness with a kind of undiscriminating, universal love. As much as he detests some things about Ackley, he admits that he has to feel sorry for him (51). He also admits that whenever he is given a present, he ends up feeling sad (67). On the train to New York, instead of brooding over his own injuries, he concocts a tale that will make the mother of one of the "ratty" boys at Pencey Prep think well of her son (74). Unlike Ackley and Stradlater, he is not eager to minimize other youths' accomplishments.

In New York, the more he is hurt, the sorrier he feels for others. Even though he does not like the girl whose presence makes him leave the night club, he feels "sort of sorry for her, in a way" (113). He is still a virgin, because whenever he has tried to "make out" with girls and has been told to stop, he has stopped because he gets to "feeling sorry for them" (121). He even feels sorry for Jesus because the disciples let him down. Significantly, Holden supposes that the disciples proved a disappointment because Jesus had to pick them "*at random*" and "didn't have time to go around analyzing everybody" (130–31). While waiting for Sally Hayes, Holden supposes that most girls will get married to "dopey," "boring" men, but he admits that he has to be careful about "calling certain guys bores," because he doesn't understand them (that is, he doesn't have time to go around analyzing them.) He recalls one boring roommate who was a terrific whistler and wonders if "maybe they're secretly all terrific whistlers or something" (160–61). During his interview with Antolini, Holden also admits that he doesn't "hate too many guys" and that, when he does hate people, "it doesn't last too long." If he doesn't see people for a while, he "sort of" misses them (243). Antolini—like the history teacher at Pencey Prep—is not ready, however, to follow up this line of discussion which particularly concerns Holden. Antolini sits silent for a while and then—although Holden wishes he would postpone the discussion until morning—plunges again into what he has on *his* mind.

The climax of the story of the internal development that accompanies Holden's external breakdown occurs only a few minutes before his climactic decision to run away. Awakening from a nap on a bench in Grand Central Station, he thinks over what happened in Antolini's apartment and wonders if "just maybe" he was wrong in thinking that Antolini "was making a flitty pass." Maybe Antolini "just liked to pat guys on the head when they're asleep." Asking himself, "how can you tell about that stuff for sure?," he replies, "You can't" (253). This answer leads directly to the conclusion of the book, in which Holden reports that he has begun to "miss" everybody he has written about, even those that he has "hated" most—Stradlater, Ackley, and worst of all; Maurice, the dishonest and brutal elevator operator. In the light of what Holden told Antolini, his "missing" them indicates that he no longer "hates" them, because they, too, need understanding. Even Maurice, who has hurt him most seriously, is a pathetic figure, who—if Holden's prediction is true—will in a few years be "one of those scraggy guys that come up to you on the street and ask for a dime for coffee" (135). Recalling his own sufferings, Holden develops a profound sense of the human condition lying behind the injunction that we must all love each other.

The brief concluding chapter in which this point is made does not seem too well integrated into the novel because the idea of universal compassion—as Salinger handles it—is not too convincingly presented. Having recognized that the "nice" world of his dreams does not really exist, Holden seems unwilling to make any distinctions within the "phony" world. The implication of Holden's last statement grouping Ackley and Maurice with the less offensive people that Holden has met is that one is either phony or not; and since all are phony, all must be accepted equally. When one asks why comparative judgments may not be made, one finds—in the passage about Jesus and the disciples—only the somewhat lazy-minded explanation that one doesn't have time "to go around analyzing everybody." Holden's curious notion that Jesus picked the disciples at random can only reflect his own thinking about the way he would undertake such a task. Holden's impatience with taking the necessary time to make proper judgments also explains his advice at the end of the book, "don't ever tell anybody anything," for then one begins missing people (277). Since value judgments are complex and difficult to make, the best thing to do is to avoid them altogether. Holden's brand of "universal sympathy" seems less attractive when seen as the kind of two-valued "either ... or" thinking which is the refuge of lazy minds. It is to this flabby aspect of Holden's thought that R.G.G. Price objects in *Punch* when he implies that Americans have a hard surface and a soft core.[7] With his swearing and swaggering, Holden exhibits a hard surface; but his refusal to make judgments—to speculate about motives—is indicative of a soft, sentimental core—and soft cores rot easily.

The trouble with this kind of sentimentality has been pointed out by William Wiegand in "J.D. Salinger: Seventy-Eight Bananas," and it is evident that Holden is an even more perfect exemplar than Seymour Glass of banana-fish fever. People must learn to make distinctions not because they should consistently follow some set of ethical principles, but simply because they are incapable of absorbing and retaining every experience. As Wiegand points out, Holden's trouble is that "he has no capacity to purge his sensations. He is blown up like a balloon, or like a bananafish, with his memories. Thus with the good things he remembers ... he retains the bad things as well—until nothing is either good or bad after a point, but simply retained and cherished as a part of himself, submerging him with the sheer weight of accumulated burden."[8]

If the individual is submerged in this flux of undifferentiated experience, he can never hope to make his way toward any goal. The purpose of education should not be—as Antolini suggests in the novel—to give the individual an idea "what kind of thoughts [his] particular size mind should be wearing" (247), but to provide the individual with the tools for discriminating between experiences. As long as Holden has no wish to discriminate, he cannot possibly derive anything from attending classes. The reason he cannot tell the psychiatrist whether or not he is going to "apply" himself when he returns to school is that he still does not know *why* he is going to school or why he might wish to apply himself. He will continue to excel only in classes—like English composition—that may offer him a chance to express himself uncritically. The trouble with compassion is that, although without it one cannot be a decent human being, it cannot by itself provide a person with the means of making himself useful—as Holden learns when one of his most beautiful illusions is blasted. Being simply a saint requires no education.

IV THE CATCHER IN THE RYE—ARTIST IN EMBRYO

Mention of Holden's lack of occupation brings us at last to the question of his "growing up" not physically (which is causing him pain) or emotionally (as he is doing when he rails, against the kind of preconceived biases that make Catholics, intellectuals, bridge-players, and Book-of-the-Month Club members league snobbishly together [p. 170]), but intellectually. A principal reason why Holden, is having special difficulty while he is undergoing the physical changes leading to maturity and why he inclines towards a flabby sentimentality is that he does not wish to grow up because he sees no role for himself in the adult world.

What he considers especially "phony" is revealed in his conversation with Sally Hayes after he tells her, "I hate living in New York and all" (169). The "all" turns out to include such accouterments of urban life as "taxicabs, and Madison Avenue buses ... and being introduced to phony guys that call the Lunts angels, and going up and down in elevators when you just want to go outside, and guys fitting your pants all the time at Brooks...." He associates this life with his successful lawyer-father, who flies to California instead of attending Phoebe's play (210). Part of Holden's hatred of school stems from his unarticulated feeling that, if he ever finishes prep school, he may have to enter a hated Ivy League college and then take his place in the "rat-race." That in time he will is evident from the fact that he is no rebel. Whatever Holden wants, he does not wish to overthrow society. His question about everybody "going through phases" and even his undiscriminating love are evidences that he does not wish to be different from other people. As Hugh MacLean points out in "Conservatism in Modern American Fiction," Holden is a conservative[9]—partly because he accepts uncritically certain prejudices of his class and partly because he does not have the nerve to be anything else.

Examples of his unconscious acceptance of the prejudices of the urban upper-middle class are found in his criticism of the girls from Seattle who "didn't know any better" than to drink Tom Collinses in December (97), in his refusal to wear his beloved red hunting cap into the hotel because he doesn't want "to look like a screwball or something" (79), in his acknowledgment that he rooms with Stradlater because they both have good luggage (142), in his statement that he never says "crude things" to girls (178), and, most important of all, in his constantly displaying the trait of describing whatever is spontaneous in his behavior as "mad," because "everybody"—by which Holden means his father—has told him that he acts as if he were "only about twelve." (13).

His fear of asserting himself is much more strongly emphasized in the book than are his middle-class prejudices. He admits to Phoebe, for example, that "he was too yellow not to join a secret fraternity at school (217). He also didn't have "the guts to exact justice from the boy who stole his gloves (116). "If you want to stay alive," he observes on another occasion, you've got to say "stuff" like "glad to've met you" to people you aren't glad to have met (114). He is afraid that Sally Hayes will tell her father what Holden has called her

(173). Also in the famous statement, which some people have tried to fling back into Salinger's face, about calling up the author of a book that "knocks you out," Holden says, "you wish that the author *was a terrific friend of yours* and you could call him up on the phone whenever you felt like it" (25, italics mine). Holden does not even think about calling up authors he does not know; he is not pushy.

Holden rejects not only rebellion, but also suicide. He is too "yellow" even to follow Seymour Glass and Teddy into the oblivion that will end his troubles. The one time he contemplates suicide he fears that he might not be covered up right away and he doesn't want "a bunch of stupid rubbernecks" looking at him when he is "all gory" (136).

If one neither wishes to change and grow up, to run away, or to end it all, there remains only the conservative alternative of wishing that things would remain static and trying to keep them that way. This Holden adopts. "Certain things they should stay the way they are," he says in one of the few positive statements of belief he makes (158). Immediately before making this statement he has expressed his tremendous admiration for the lifelike exhibits in the New York Museum of Natural History, because "the best thing ... in that museum was that everything always stayed right where it was." He observes sadly that on successive visits to the museum, "the only thing that would be different would be *you*" (157–58).

This desire to keep things exactly as they are inspires what is probably the most often quoted passage in the novel—the one which provides its title—in which Holden confesses to Phoebe his desire to be a "catcher in the rye" who would stand on the edge of "some crazy cliff" and catch the little kids "if they start to go over" (224). Although this "crazy cliff" may be identified in many ways, it is most obviously the border between the carefree innocence of childhood and the phony adult world that Holden himself does not wish to enter. His only ambition is the completely unrealistic one of keeping children from growing up.

Some readers—like John Aldridge—think that the book ends with Holden clinging to this forlorn hope. The climax of this strand of the narrative occurs, however, a little after those of the other two, in the same twenty-fifth chapter in which all of the intertwined histories are resolved. Many have objected to the vulgar language of *Catcher*, especially to the use of the word that Holden finds scrawled on the schoolroom and museum walls. The word is not employed, however—as stupid people. suppose artists use words—so that the writer can see how much he can get away with, but because it is demanded by the structure of the story. Salinger's very point is that we cannot pretend that the word is not there by refusing to look at it, for it *is* written even on the walls of the buildings where small children go to be educated.

The word is there, so that Holden—in an attempt to play the role that he has envisioned for himself as a "catcher in the rye"—may attempt to erase it. Its use is essential to Salinger's point. We must know what the word is to understand why Holden, in addition to erasing it the first time he sees it, has a fantasy of catching the person who wrote it on the wall and smashing "his head on the stone steps till he was good and goddam dead and bloody." Holden's dream of playing protector of the innocent leads to his climactic recognition of his own incapacity. Abandoning his fantasy, he says sadly, "I knew, too, I wouldn't have the guts to do it ... I hardly even had the guts to rub it off the wall with my *hand*, if you want to know the truth. I was afraid some teacher would catch me rubbing it off and would think I'd written it" (261).

Yet he does erase the words; he finds them again, however, scratched into the wall. Then he recognizes sadly that "if you had a million years to do it in, you couldn't rub out even half" of the dirty symbols of the phony adult world that lead little children to the edge of "some crazy cliff" (262). After seeing the third of these signs Holden has a bowel movement (a rather literal symbol of catharsis) and then faints (265). Although he thinks that he could have killed himself, he hasn't. Rather he feels "better" after passing out. We need not look far for the symbolism of this passage. Holden himself has fallen over the "crazy cliff," but he is not destroyed—rather he feels better for being purged of the fantasies that tortured him.

That he has been changed is obvious from a passage near the end of the twenty-fifth chapter. After Holden puts Phoebe on the carousel, all the kids—including her—keep "trying to grab for the gold ring. "The thing with kids is," he observes, "if they want to grab for the gold ring, you have to let them do it, and not say anything. If they fall off, they fall off, but it's bad if you say anything to them" (273–74). This statement has a double significance. First, it shows that Holden no longer sees himself as a catcher in the rye. People will imitate others and grab for the gold ring, and "if they fall off, they fall off." He has resigned himself to the realities of human behavior. Second, the statement answers Antolini, who spoke of "a special kind of fall, a horrible kind" (243). He tried to talk Holden out of suffering this fall; but Holden finally finds the words with which he should have answered Antolini when he says that if kids "want to grab for the gold ring, you have to let them do it.... It's bad if you say anything to them." One must learn about life for himself. While academicians who are sympathetic with Antolini's viewpoint may think that his advice could have saved Holden, Holden could have taken the advice only if he had been a different person, heading for a different goal, in a differently structured book. *The Catcher in the Rye* is the story of a man who is not going to be saved by lectures.

His dreams of being a catcher shattered, is Holden left totally at loose ends? I think not. There are clues throughout the book that there is something he could be if he wished. In the description of his train trip to New York, Holden says that he had the woman to whom he was speaking "in a trance" and that he could "go on lying for hours" (73, 76). His "lies," of course, are pleasant fictions that he is inventing to delight his audience. In another place, Holden says self-mockingly, "All I need's an audience. I'm an exhibitionist" (38). He is closer to the truth than he realizes. He also unemphatically discloses that he is a good dancer (93) and a good golfer (100), and he insists on Phoebe's participating in the school play.

His attitude toward the movies is especially ambivalent. His judgment that his brother D.B. is "prostituting" himself in Hollywood (4), for example, shows Holden does "hate the movies like poison" (38). Yet he also gets "a kick out of imitating them" (38), as he does on several unlikely occasions: after the elevator operator beats him up (136) and after Carl Luce abandons him in the bar (194–95).

His mixed feelings are shown by his remark that the movie at the Radio City Music Hall was "so putrid I couldn't take my eyes off it" (179). He displays similar ambivalence towards other exhibitions: bleeding after Stradlater has beaten him, he finds that the gore "partly scares" and "partly fascinates" him (59); watching the "perverts" in the hotel where he is staying, he observes that "the trouble was, that kind of junk is sort of fascinating to watch, even if you don't want it to be" (87).

His ambiguous feelings about movies and other forms of public exhibitionism are a serious matter, because he had already been invited to appear in a movie short about golfing (100). He refused, because he thought that anybody who hated the movies as he did would be a "phony" if he appeared in one. Was his refusal, however, that simply motivated? He has much to say about the "phoniness" of celebrated performers. He says that if he were a piano player like "Old Ernie" at the night club he visits, he'd "play it in the goddam closet." Ernie's success has made him a snob, so that he doesn't even know "any more when he's playing right or not" (110). Holden has similar objections to the very perfection of the Lunts' acting. "They didn't act like people and they didn't act like actors," he explains. "They acted more like they knew they were celebrities and all. I mean they were good, but they were *too* good" (164). The only public performer who actually pleases him is the drummer at the Radio City Music Hall, who doesn't get to play much, but—when he does—"does it so nice and sweet, with this nervous expression on his face" (179).

Holden's feeling that the Lunts are "too good" and his admiration of the drummer's "nervous expression" show that Holden can identify with the drummer and not with the Lunts because the boy knows that he would be worried about any performance of his own. He could be "good" himself, but he refuses to do any "trick stuff" while dancing, for he hates guys that do "a lot of show-off tricky stuff on the dance floor." This could be modesty, but it could also be stage-fright. Holden has reason to be nervous, for in his present gawky state, he often fluffs major gestures. He has made himself an outcast at school by losing the fencing team's equipment. His defiant shout upon leaving Pencey is spoiled by his falling downstairs after tripping over peanut shells (68). Trying to act sophisticated when greeting the prostitute, he falls over a suitcase (123). He inadvertently blows smoke into the face of the nuns he admires (147). He doesn't know why he even "started all that stuff" about running off with Sally Hayes (134). He gets drunk and breaks the treasured record that he has bought as a gift for Phoebe (199).

These falls are not designed simply to add "comic relief" to the novel. They are exactly what is to be expected of a boy in Holden's physical and emotional condition. He is too disturbed during this time of crisis to have full control over himself. When he has regained his composure and comes to terms with the "phony" world, he may overcome his hatred of these things that entertain people, as he has his hatred of people themselves. And when he achieves better control over his body and feelings, he may prove to be quite a performer himself.

Perhaps it is not at all ironic that the novel ends near Hollywood, for Holden may find—like his brother D.B.—that he is really at home in the movie capital. *The Catcher in the Rye* proves upon close scrutiny to be the story of an ex-would-be-catcher-in-the-rye. It might more appropriately be titled "A Portrait of the Artist as a Very Nervous Young Man." That the novel is about a young man with an artistic bent is not surprising. Artists are likely—whatever subject they choose—to end up contemplating the problems of being an artist. The tracing of Holden's intellectual development, although the least emphasized part of the book, is the most successful; for, while even the good artist—without other training—has no special insight into the problems of physical or emotional growth, the one thing he may know is the problems of becoming an artist.

This analysis by no means exhausts the possibilities of the intricate pattern of *The Catcher in the Rye*, for every episode—probably every sentence—could be shown to play a specific part in completing the overall design. What I have tried to show is that the novel does not need to be interpreted in terms of any outside conventions or traditions. Rather the significance of any detail may be shown to be in some way related to illuminating the physical, emotional, or intellectual crises that the hypersensitive Holden Caulfield passes through during the brief but terrifying period when he begins to discover that he is not a carefree, childish animal, but a unique human being.

V HOLDEN ABROAD

Although its idiom and situations are characteristically American, *Catcher* has by no means been confined to an American audience. In an age of nuclear terror, adolescents everywhere—despite cultural differences—are perplexed by the same problems.

The novel was published in England within a month after its American release and has been almost as popular there as at home. First issued as a hard bound, it has been included in the paperbound Penguin series, and David Leitch reports that 180,000 copies of the latter edition were sold in two years.[10] The first British reviewers took the novel even less seriously than most American ones. The *Times Literary Supplement* (September 7, 1951, p. 561) found that "the endless stream of blasphemy and obscenity ... palls after the first chapter," and R.D. Charques writing in *Spectator* (August 18, 1951, p. 224) expressed the general sentiment when he wrote that "the tale is rather too formless to do quite the sort of thing it was evidently intended to do." One of the most perceptive criticisms to appear on either side of the Atlantic, however, was contributed to *Punch* by R.G.G. Price:

> The weakness of the novel is its sentimentality. The boy is looking for something and the reader is rightly left as doubtful as the boy what it is. It may be a cause, an attitude, a security. The Search, while the basis for some of the greatest of allegories, is also too often an occasion for self-pity and a sensuous enjoyment of failure ... I suspect that this sentimentality is in character, that the author has not invented it but approves of it. This may be merely the reaction of a corrupt European, who prefers a soft surface and a hard core.[11]

The formidable task of translating *Catcher*'s distinctive idiom has also been undertaken in a dozen countries, mostly in northern Europe, although Salinger's novel was not as rapidly translated into other languages as such other prominent American works as Herman Wouk's *The Caine Mutiny*. Since the title is based upon Holden's misconstruction of a line in an English song lyric, it has given great trouble to translators who have had little success in arriving at literal equivalents. Some of the foreign titles, however, especially the Japanese and the original Dutch (if the words are taken in the sense in which jazz musicians use them) capture the spirit of the book remarkably well.

According to the United Nations Economic and Social Council's annual *Index Translationum, Catcher* appeared in three foreign-language editions in 1952, the year after its publication in this country. The Italian translation by Jacopo Darca was called *Vita da Uomo* (A Man's Life); the Japanese translation by Fuoko Hashimoto, *Kikenna Nenrei* (Dangerous Time of Life); and the Norwegian translation by Åke Fen, *Hver Tar Sin—Så Får Vi Andre Ingen* (Every Man for Himself, and the Devil Take the Hindmost).[12] The other Scandinavian nations had their own editions the next year (1953): in Sweden, *Räddaren I Nöden* (The Rescuer in Time of Need), translated by Birgitta Hammar; and in Denmark, *Forbandede Ungdom* (Outcast Youth), translated by Vibeke Schram, who in 1955 was also responsible for the first recorded translation of *Nine Stories*. A French edition also appeared in 1953, *L'Attrape-coeurs* (The Catcher of Hearts), translated by Jean Baptiste Rossi. The next year (1954) a German translation by Irene Muehlon—who has also translated such British celebrities as Churchill, Maugham, and Orwell— appeared in Zurich and Constance, Switzerland, and in Stuttgart, West Germany, bearing the uninformative title *Der Mann im Roggen* (The Man in the Rye). There was also in 1954 a Dutch edition, *Eenzame Zwerftocht* (Lonesome Ramble)—later changed to *Puber* (Puberty)—translated by Henk de Graaff.

The novel entitled *Ani, New York W-khol Ha-Shear* (Myself, New York; and All the Rest) appeared in Israel in 1956 in a translation by Avraham Danieli. In 1958, the first translation in a Communist country—Yugoslavia— was listed by UNESCO. Nikola Krsic's version bore the apparently literal title *Lovac u Zhito*. Donald Fiene has also located later editions in Czechoslovakia (*Kdo Chytá v Zhitu*, translated with a literal rendition of the title by Rudolf Pellar and with a critical afterword by Igor Hájek) and Russia (*Nad Propastyu vo rzhi*—"Above the Cliff in the Ryefield," translated by Rita Wright-Kovaleva). Both of these versions first appeared in magazines in 1960. Fiene also reports translations of the work made in 1961 in Finland, Estonia, Argentina, and Poland.

This is not the time or place to attempt a survey of the reception of *Catcher* abroad, but some report of what has happened in West Germany, the non-English-speaking country where the novel has attracted the most critical attention; provides useful insights into the problem of translation and the international reception of contemporary American fiction. German reviewers received the book—which by 1954 was internationally known— even more enthusiastically than English and American. The distinguished novelist Hermann Hesse himself reviewed *Catcher* for *Die Weltwoche* (December 24, 1953) and said: "Whether one reads this novel as the individual history of a temperamental adolescent boy or as a symbol for a whole nation and people, one is led by the author down the beautiful path from unfamiliarity to understanding, from distaste to love. In a problematical world and time, literary art can achieve nothing higher."[13] *Bücher Kommentare* (a quarterly collection of book reviews the much resembles the unfortunately suspended *United States Quarterly Book Review*) carries in its first issue for 1954 another favorable review by Annemarie Weber, who—after succinctly describing the book—compares it to the work of Hesse himself. She writes that, besides Hesse, "none has yet so well described the dangers of this 'bitter age' from the inside. [*The Catcher in the Rye*] is a nerve-wracking appeal not to fail to see the still helpless child behind the often quite unsympathetic mask, an appeal to perceive the dangers which threaten the tendency toward Good and Nobility in the first crisis of life." Miss Weber thinks that this novel, which deals with "a soul capable of very distinguished love," "fits into the picture" of the United States "a new and significant piece."

The German response to *Catcher* is of particular interest since the first scholarly article in a language other than English to be devoted entirely to an explication of the book is Hans Bungert's "Isolation und Kommunikationsversuche des Jugendlichen" (youth's isolation and search for communication) in *Die Neueren Sprachen* (May, 1960).[14] After noting that Salinger takes the place, for post-World War II American youth, of the whole group of novelists who appeared after World I, Bungert explains that Holden's disturbance is "characteristic to a certain extent of his age group," but that general considerations from the teachings of the developmental psychologists provide nothing more than a starting point for the study of the novel, since Holden's personality "sharply cuts him off from his contemporaries."

Bungert also points out that Holden's terrible isolation is "intensified by the time of the action: in the days before Christmas, the holiday of men united by love," and he perceives that Holden "gives up his suicidal intentions without outside help because of his artistic sensitivities." Most of the action, Bungert explains, is devoted to Holden's "search for communication," which is frustrated because "Sally Hayes is too narrow-minded and superficial, Stradlater is too gross and bored, Carl Luce too egocentric and self-seeking." He agrees with American critics that the high point of the novel is Holden's achieving "a community of feeling" with Phoebe, which leads him to recognize at last that his "wish for the preservation of the unsullied purity and beauty" of children is "as unfulfillable and just as illusory as a return to his own lost childhood."

Despite this enthusiastic and perceptive German reception, the German-language edition of the novel has not fared well enough to justify the kind of inexpensive paperbound reprint that is as popular there as here. Some of the reasons for this are suggested by my good friend, Hans Ulherr, an English teacher in the secondary schools of Bavaria, who is familiar with American adolescents and their idiom. He comments that just within the first few pages of the translated book, the distinctive flavor is lost when the last word of "David Copperfield *crap*" becomes *Zeug*, meaning just "stuff." "My parents would have about two hemorrhages apiece" becomes "my parents would have fits," and the typically adolescent image, "as cold as a witch's teat" becomes just "as cold as hell." In the typical Caulfieldian expression, "they got a bang out of things, though—in a *half-assed* way, of course," the italicized word becomes "whimsical." Dr. Ulherr explains that "translating 'half-assed' by "*schrullig*" in itself would not be so bad, since it seems next to impossible to find a German equivalent for the original word; but the whole passage in the translation doesn't make much sense when it goes on into the next sentence—'that sounds mean to say,' which is translated literally." The worst blunder in the opening pages, however, is the complete omission, in the description of the head master's daughter, of the phrase "she had on those damn falsies that point all over the place." When the translator comes at last, near the end of the book, to the famous vulgar word that has caused criticism of the original novel, it is indicated simply by the conventional "——."

While the translator, my correspondent continues, expresses Salinger's idea of adolescent tribulation, the German edition "completely fails to convey the hero's language to the German reader" and is, therefore, "not suited to inspire any enthusiasm among the younger generation." No translator, of course, can be blamed for failing to re-create as colloquial a style as Holden's in another language. Since they, unlike the author, are not in a strong enough position to insist upon the integrity of the text, translators must also make concessions to public taste. The point of this discussion is not to criticize the translation so much as to show the basis for Dr. Ulherr's final observation that, after comparing the two versions of *Catcher*, "I am more determined than ever not to read the translation of a book whose original language I can understand."[15]

Very probably the same comments could be made about other translations. The novel was a flop when Robert Laffont first published it in Paris in 1953,[16] and Claude Julien, writing in *Le Monde* on January 13, 1962, still found it necessary to explain to French readers that *Catcher* outclasses several other American novels with adolescent heroes that have attracted nothing like the same kind of response in the United States. Fortunately, the situation in Europe is not so bad as it might be if *Catcher in the Rye* could be known there only in translation, for far more literary-minded German, French, and Scandinavian students read English than American students read their languages. It is very likely, as Bungert implies, that adolescents abroad will become acquainted with Holden in the unadulterated, original form, and that his style of speaking may even flavor their own English.

NOTES

*Figures in parentheses. throughout this chapter refer to page numbers in the original edition of *The Catcher in the Rye* (Boston: Little, Brown, 1951). This same pagination is preserved in the undated Modern Library edition and also in the Grosset and Dunlap reprint.

1. Warren French with Marc Rosenberg, "The Beast that Devours Its Young," *CCC: The Journal of the Conference on Composition and Communication*, XIII, 7 (May, 1962).

2. Ernest Havemann, "The Search for the Mysterious J.D. Salinger," *Life* (November 3, 1961), p. 141.

3. Grunwald, *Salinger*, p. 255.

4. *Ibid.*, p. 151.

5. *Ibid.*, p. 252.

6. J.D. Salinger, *"Raise High the Roof Beam, Carpenters" and "Seymour: An Introduction"* (Boston, [1963]), p. 123.

7. R.G.G. Price, "Booking Office," *Punch*, CCXXI, 192 (August 15, 1951).

8. Grunwald, *Salinger*, pp. 125–26.

9. Hugh MacLean, "Conservatism in Modern American Fiction," *College English*, XV, 317 (March, 1954).

10. David Leitch, "The Salinger Myth," *Twentieth Century*, No. 168 (November, 1960), p. 431. Grunwald does not reproduce the footnote containing this figure.

11. Price, *loc. cit.*

12. This imaginative and allusive Norwegian title has led to a fascinating correspondence. The translation given has been graciously supplied by Rolf L. Bergendahl, Cultural Attaché of the Norwegian Embassy in Washington, who explains that the literal translation is "Each Takes His—And the Rest of Us Gets None," which would not convey the proverbial connotations of the Norwegian title. Gerard Vanneck of the United Nations Terminology Unit, New York, further explains that the title is derived from the words of a familiar Norwegian children's singing game and that the general idea of the title might best be conveyed by "Odd Man Out." Donald Fiene informs me that translator Åke Fen, shortly before his death, received an annual Norwegian Translators' Society award for his rendition of *The Catcher in the Rye*.

13. Quoted in W.S. Field, "Hermann Hesse as Critic of English and American Literature," *Monatshefte*, LIII, 156 (April–May, 1961).

14. The bibliography in *American Literature* for May, 1962, lists an article, "J.D. Salinger" in Japanese by Hisao Kanesaki in *Jimbun Kenkyu*, a publication of the University of Osaka, for June, 1961. Donald Fiene is preparing a bibliography of other foreign reactions to Salinger. One of the most interesting foreign criticisms of *The Catcher in the Rye* is Panova's "J.D. Salinger's Novel," *Inostrannaya Literatura* (Foreign Literature), November, 1960, pp. 138–41, prepared to accompany a translation of the novel which appeared in that issue of the magazine. Miss Panova denounces Holden as a *stilyaga* (Russian Beatnik) with many unacceptable traits, yet finds him ultimately sympathetic because he is a victim of a heartless capitalistic society symbolized by the sated funeral director Ossenburger, who "grows rich on the mortality of the poor."

15. Since this chapter was written, the German translation of *The Catcher in the Rye* has been "reworked" by the distinguished German novelist, Heinrich Böll, author of *Billiards at Half Past Nine*, and published with the title literally translated *Der Fänger im Roggen*. The employment of an artist of such stature to revise the translation suggests the increasing importance that is being attached to Salinger's novel in Europe.

16. *New York Times Book Review*, January 7, 1962, p. 8.

SANDRA WHIPPLE SPANIER

Hemingway's "The Last Good Country" and The Catcher in the Rye: More Than a Family Resemblance

"The Last Good Country" is one of Ernest Hemingway's works that has attracted little attention so far. Found among the papers he left behind, it was edited by Mary Hemingway and, along with several other previously unpublished pieces, made its debut in 1972 in the Scribner's collection called *The Nick Adams Stories*. Hemingway rarely dated his manuscripts, but three of the 110 loose pages of this one do bear dates of 1952, 1955, and 1958.[1] Thus, it is the last Nick Adams story Hemingway wrote. But "story" is a misnomer. Judging by its length and the pace and progression of events, it most likely is the beginning of a rather long novel, which Hemingway for some reason abandoned. It is an intriguing work, though, because its genre— it has been called "sky-blue pastoral"[2]—is unique in Hemingway's writings. The story of a disillusioned young man's escape from a corrupt society into the unspoiled wilderness, "The Last Good Country" is rooted solidly in the tradition of American Romanticism. It bears a striking resemblance to two of its predecessors in particular. The kinship of Hemingway's Nick Adams stories and Mark Twain's *Adventures of Huckleberry Finn* has already been definitely examined by Philip Young,[3] but *this* Nick Adams story also appears to be intimately related to a twentieth-century rendering of the same theme: J.D. Salinger's *The Catcher in the Rye*. This study will examine "The Last Good Country" and *The Catcher in the Rye* as contemporary American

From *Studies in Short Fiction* 19, no. 1 (Winter 1982): 35–43. © 1982 by Newberry College.

romances with some surprising similarities in detail. It will end with a suggestion as to why Hemingway may have decided to abandon at Camp Number One the idyllic journey of Nick and his sister through the Michigan woods.

A basic element in the Romantic tradition is the escape from civilization to the unspoiled "territory." Hemingway's and Salinger's heroes are both young outcasts of unusual sensitivity, pursued by agents of a corrupt society. Nick Adams, a reform school alumnus, accidentally has killed a deer out of season, and two unsavory game wardens are after him. With his sister, Littless, the only person in the world he cares for, Nick takes off for a remote section of the upper Michigan wilderness. In *The Catcher in the Rye*, Holden Caulfield, freshly flunked-out of Pencey Prep School, spends a few days in New York City amid an assortment of thugs, "perverts," and "phonies" so that he can be with *his* beloved sister, Phoebe, before he sets off for the West. Holden's story differs from Nick's in that Holden actually gets to his "good country," but only because he was committed to a California institution to "take it easy." Although Holden's basic sense of alienation, his relationship with his sister, and the preparations he makes for his escape correspond closely to Nick's, we actually follow Nick and Littless into the wilderness, while we never see Holden making his journey. But this structural difference in the stories is overshadowed by their similarities.

The characters in these two works are surprisingly alike, even in their idiosyncrasies, and their similarities extend beyond the family resemblances to be expected among characters of a type. Both avid readers and good writers, Nick and Holden share a contempt for arbitrary authority and conventions and hold a dark view of life that worries their loving little sisters. Nick's survival pack includes plenty of books, and the story ends just as he is about to read *Wuthering Heights* aloud to Littless. Nick wants to be a writer when he gets older, but his stories are already too "morbid" for publication in his favorite magazine. Littless gently inquires, "'Couldn't you maybe make it if you wrote cheerfuller things? That isn't my opinion. Our mother said everything you write is morbid'" (LGC 90).[4] In *The Catcher in the Rye*, Holden refers to a dozen or more books and explains, "I'm quite illiterate, but I read a lot" (CR 18).[5] He cares enough about good writing to be contemptuous of his brother, who wrote "this terrific book of short stories," but who now is in Hollywood writing movie scripts, "being a prostitute" (CR 1–2). Holden himself has a reputation for being a "hot-shot in English." To help out his roommate, he spends an evening absorbed in writing a paper about the baseball mitt that had belonged to his dead brother, Allie, who had scribbled poetry all over it to read in the outfield. The assignment, however, was to describe a room. Like Nick, who continues to write "morbid" stories that no one will publish, Holden is a serious enough writer to be true only to his material. *His* sister, also, accuses him of being too negative, although her approach is less delicate than Littless's: "'You don't like *anything* that's happening,'" Phoebe charges. "'You don't like any schools. You don't like a million things. You *don't*'" (CR 169). Angrily, she challenges Holden to name one thing he likes, which he has a hard time doing. Incidentally, even Nick's speech in the unedited manuscript is more like Holden's—notorious among the nation's high school librarians for its four-letter words—than the published version of the story would indicate.

Not only are Nick and Holden themselves alike in many ways, but they have similar friends. Each boy has one trustworthy adult to whom he can turn—a kind of father-figure, who, while successfully functioning in society himself, is cynical enough to be sympathetic to the boy's plight and to help him make provisions for his escape. Mr. Packard and Mr. Antolini provide the guidance and support that Nick and Holden cannot receive from their own ineffectual parents (in both stories the boys' fathers are invisible and their mothers prone to "sick headaches"). These men encourage the boys' writing ambitions, are interested in their families and girlfriends, know the boys' characters well, and offer them concerned advice based on that knowledge.

Before setting off on his journey through the woods, Nick stops at the Packards' store to trade some trout for food and supplies. John Packard is a witty, irreverent man. He teases his wife about the "change of lifers" who vacation at the hotel she runs, says he likes Nick Adams because he has original sin, and prefers camp meetings and revivals to Chautauquas and Self-Betterment Courses because "at least there was some sexual intercourse afterward by those who got really aroused although he never knew anyone to pay their bills after a camp meeting or a revival" (LGC 99). Although he claims not to understand "culture," he advises Nick, "'You going to be a writer you ought to get in on it early. Don't let them get too far ahead of you!'" (LGC 100). Mr. Packard is interested also in how Nick and his girlfriend, Trudy, have been getting along. When Nick reports that he heard she was working up at the Soo, Mr. Packard replies, "'She was a beautiful girl and I always liked her.'" They talk about more serious matters, too. Mr. Packard predicts that Nick will someday have "things to repent," which is perfectly all right because, he tells Nick, "'you're alive and you're going to do things.'" But, although everybody has to lie sometimes to survive, he advises Nick to pick out one person he will never lie to. They both agree it will be Mr. Packard.

Although his visit with Mr. Antolini ends uncomfortably with what Holden interprets as a homosexual advance, Holden and his former English teacher had had a similar relationship. To preserve his meager resources, Holden has gone to the Antolinis' apartment to sleep on their couch the night before he plans to start West. Mr. Antolini, Holden tells us, is "a very witty guy," who, like John Packard, teases his wife about the company she keeps. Asking Holden to excuse the messiness of the living room, he explains, "'We've been entertaining some Buffalo friends of Mrs. Antolini's ... Some buffaloes, as a matter of fact'" (CR 182). He is interested in Holden's writing and threatens to show him to the door in short order if he had flunked English. In a dialogue much like Nick and Mr. Packard's, Mr. Antolini expresses interest in Holden's social life, asking about Sally Hayes and remarking, "'Helluva pretty girl'" (CR 191). Their conversation, too, takes a philosophical turn and ends with a bit of advice. Mr. Antolini worries that Holden is heading for "'a special kind of fall, a horrible kind'" (CR 187). He is afraid that Holden some day will die nobly for a highly unworthy cause, and he writes out a quotation on the subject for Holden to keep and think about.

While this father substitute figures prominently in Hemingway's and Salinger's stories, a more important character in American Romanticism is the loving companion who accompanies the hero on his journey. In their quest to establish a separate peace, the hero and his companion are two against the world, and no one else matters. Hemingway writes that Nick and Littless "loved each other and they did not love the others. They always thought of everyone else in the family as the others" (LGC 71). Holden and Phoebe feel the same. To heighten the contrast between the pair's goodness and civilization's corruption, their love for each other must be innocent and selfless. Hints at physical attraction only serve to show how pure their actual relationship is. Philip Young cites the ancestors of Nick and Littless and Holden and Phoebe—Huck and Jim, Ishmael and Queequeg, Deerslayer and Chingachgook—and notes, "Without the overtones, we would never stop to think how immaculate is the conception."[6]

There are plenty of overtones in both stories. (Some were actually edited out of "The Last Good Country.") Both Nick and Holden sense that the love they share with their sisters must be carefully controlled. Littless wishes that she and her brother could live together always and even get married. She wants cards printed saying, "Mrs. Nick Adams, Cross Village, Michigan-common-law wife" (LGC 122). Although Nick responds playfully, he discourages even this jest, saying, "'I won't let you file'" and "'I don't think it would work.'" When Littless persists, the incestuous implications are obvious: "'I've got another scheme. We'll have a couple of children while I'm a minor. Then you'll have to marry me under the Unwritten Law.'" Nick continues to protest and finally steers the conversation in a safer direction.

American romances have included memorable scenes of the companions innocently sleeping together (for example, Ishmael and Queequeg), or at least of one tenderly watching over the other sleeping (as in Huck's and Jim's moonlit vigils on the raft). So do "The Last Good Country" and *The Catcher in the Rye*. Nick and Littless sleep together back to back in a bed Nick has prepared on the ground, and in the morning he watches her sleeping and admires the way her lashes lie on her cheeks: "He loved his sister very much and she loved him too much. But, he thought, I guess those things straighten out. At least I hope so" (LGC 119). When Holden sneaks home late at night to visit Phoebe, he, too, watches over his sister sleeping and, like Nick, admires the way she looks. Although his description is less than lyrical, it is loving: "Kids look all right. They can even have spit all over the pillow and they still look all right" (CR 159). When he awakens her, they sit on the bed talking, and then, as if they were lovers, they get up and dance to music on the radio. Like Nick, Holden senses that the love he shares with his sister must be limited. He says of Phoebe, "She's very affectionate. I mean she's quite affectionate, for a child. Sometimes she's even too affectionate" (CR 161).

Littless comes from a long line of Hemingway heroines. Like Catherine *in A Farewell to Arms*, she promises to go home "'If I'm a bother or a nuisance or an expense'"; like Maria in *For Whom the Bell Tolls*, "she looks like a small wild animal" to Nick; and like Renata in *Across the River Into the Trees*, she has a profile that could break your heart. But although she is as devoted to her "man" and serves him as selflessly as her older sisters did theirs, Littless Adams is unique among them for her youth and spunk—and she bears a remarkable resemblance to Phoebe Caulfield. Besides loving and being loved by their brothers, wanting to protect and help them, aiding them in gathering supplies for their escapes, and insisting on running away with them, Littless and Phoebe even look alike, with their short-cropped, no-nonsense haircuts exposing well-informed little ears.

Both girls are lovably tough, well-read, intelligent, and worldly for their ten or eleven years. Littless practices being a boy, trying out various ways of clasping her hands and crossing her legs. She loves to read and brings along three books, two of which are "too old" for her, according to Nick. She is also rather theatrical and well-versed in the ways of the world. As Littless sits on Nick's lap, they carry on a spirited dialogue in which she declares she wishes she had got him some knockout drops (to use on the game wardens pursuing them) from the Royal Ten Dollar Gold Piece Inn and Emporium in Sheboygan by working as an assistant to the Queen of the Whores. When Nick asks her how a whore's assistant talks, Littless demonstrates, saying, "Well, ma'am, it must be pretty tiring on a hot day like today to be just a bird in a gilded cage. Things like that" (LGC 113–4).

Phoebe is as spirited a little girl as Littless Adams. She is taking belching lessons from a friend, looks fine wearing tailored suits, writes books about a girl detective named Hazle Weatherfield, and is looking forward to being Benedict Arnold in the class play. Holden says of her, "I mean, if you tell old Phoebe something, she knows exactly what the hell you're talking about. I mean you can even take her anywhere with you" (CR 67). Like Littless, she likes things that are "too old" for her, and she is quite dramatic. She knows films by heart, and whenever Holden takes her to see *The 39 Steps*, Phoebe never fails to say aloud in the theater in unison with the film actor, "'Can you eat the herring?'"

Even the nature of the "good country" itself is as similar as it could be for two stories with settings as different as upper Michigan and midtown Manhattan. Each boy finds sanctuary in an unspoiled, unchanging tract of nature familiar especially to him. It is far removed from the dangers and irritants of society and is peopled only by simple Indians, America's "noble savages." The place inspires solemn, worshipful feelings in the travelers (which is as close as they ever come to being religious), the land abundantly provides, and it never rains there. Littless is awed by the solemn majesty of the forest, where the tree trunks rise sixty feet before branching out. The woods make her feel "awfully religious," and Nick replies, "'That's why they build cathedrals to be like this'" (LGC 90). The land is rich with trout, berries, and wild grouse, and the sky is blue and cloudless. Only Nick and the Indians know this country. Nick says, "'This is about the last good country there is left. Nobody gets in here ever'" (LGC 89).

Holden, too, has a favorite tract of nature, even in New York City—the Museum of Natural History. He is as familiar with it as Nick is with the forest: "I knew that whole museum routine like a book," he says (CR 119). The museum, too, is unspoiled and timeless. Holden says

> The best thing, though, in that museum was that everything always stayed right where it was. Nobody'd move. You could go there a hundred thousand times, and that Eskimo would still be just finished catching those two fish, the birds would still be on their way south, the deer would still be drinking out of that water hole, with their pretty antlers and their pretty, skinny legs, and that squaw with the naked bosom would still be weaving that same blanket. Nobody'd be different (CR 121).

Holden describes the Indian room in solemn tones, and, like Nick's forest, it resembles a cathedral: "It was a long, long room and you were only supposed to whisper," the floor is the kind that would make a "helluva racket" if marbles were dropped on it, and children file in two-by-two like choirboys. The land is rich here, too, and is peopled only by Indians. Like the woods, it is a safe place and the weather is always clear. Holden says, "It always smelled like it was raining outside, even if it wasn't, and you were in the only nice, dry, cosy place in the world. I loved that damn museum" (CR 120).

"The Last Good Country" is an American romance. It is Hemingway's *Huckleberry Finn*. But although the pattern is familiar—"an odyssey of a loving couple in escape of society"[7]—Nick and Littless Adams are twentieth-century young people who talk and act remarkably like Holden and Phoebe Caulfield. Nick Adams, is, of course, Hemingway's own character; he appears in a couple of dozen other stories, after all. But critics have noticed that he is somehow different here. One reviewer of *The Nick Adams* Stories is unhappy with the change, charging that Nick here is "too crafty and knowledgeable," that instead of a "shaken and confused Nick Adams" such as we see in "The Killers," Hemingway now presents us with "the embarrassing spectacle of a 'they'll-never-take-me-alive' Nick Adams."[8] Philip Young passes a different judgment while noting that he "is not quite the same taciturn, rather impersonal and understated Nick we have long known":

> Far more fleshed out as a character, if no more impressive still far more "alive," he is more like his creator than when he was more of a sketch. But I do not think Hemingway has spoiled him any, or hurt him much—just that in rounding him out he has changed him some, by filling in some blanks.[9]

Hemingway did draw on a childhood experience of his own for this last Nick Adams story. The plot is derived from a tale he used to tell as fact (and it is sometimes a delicate operation to separate fact from fiction when Hemingway talks about his own life) about how he as a boy illegally shot a big game bird, was warned by a sister that game wardens were after him, and then eluded his pursuers by taking off into the Michigan woods. Accounts of the incident vary,[10] but what is important is that Hemingway perceived it as a major event of his youth, one to be taken dead seriously. Carlos Baker comments:

> He had tangled with the law. He had been a bad boy. All the rest of his life he regarded game wardens with the utmost suspicion. The older he grew, the larger the episode bulked in his memory. In his fifties, he solemnly assured a professor of English that two game wardens had once chased him all over Michigan and that he was lucky not to have been sent to reform school.[11]

"He also set down a puerile story based on the incident," Baker adds.

The brother–sister relationship in the story may be rooted loosely in autobiography as well. A letter Hemingway wrote to Malcolm Cowley in 1945 casts an interesting light on the feelings Nick and Littless have for each other, as long as one is careful to take into account the playful tone of braggadocio. Hemingway wrote: "Have one very social sister and three damned nice sisters. One used to be in love with me and can tell you, if you ever had any doubts, that incest is fun."[12] Our hero *is* rounded out and somehow changed in this Nick Adams story, and, with caution, the developments in his character may be partially explained autobiographically. But perhaps knowing Holden Caulfield also helped Hemingway to fill in some of the blanks.

In his biography of Hemingway, Carlos Baker reports that Hemingway and Salinger had a cordial meeting at the Ritz in Paris in 1944 and that in 1948 Salinger wrote to Hemingway saying he had accomplished some writing, including part of a play about a boy named Holden Caulfield and his sister, Phoebe, and two more of what he called his "incestuous" short stories.[13] In December, 1945, *Collier's* published one of them (a story about Holden visiting his sister after leaving prep school, apparently a warmup for the bedroom scene he expanded in the novel); Hemingway had been writing dispatches for *Collier's* throughout World War II. It seems quite likely that he would have been familiar with Holden's story. *The Catcher in the Rye* was published in 1951; the first dated page of the manuscript which Mary Hemingway later titled "The Last Good Country" is marked July 23, '52. One can hardly help wondering if the similarities between this work and Salinger's are not too striking to be entirely coincidental.

A mystery remains. Why did Hemingway put away his story unfinished, the young people suspended forever in the peace of their good country? Young says, "There is nowhere to go from a dream."[14] The story is over; we cannot follow Huck into the territory or Holden through the Holland Tunnel, either. But I would venture another explanation as well. By the time he was working on "The Last Good Country," that childhood incident may have been just too far away and the facts of it too blurred by the legend of "bad boy" for Hemingway to have known what he really felt, rather than what he had grown accustomed to feeling about it over the years. He had once described his struggles to achieve "the real thing, the sequence of motion and fact which made the emotion and which would be as valid in a year or in ten years or, with luck and if you stated it purely enough, always."[15] Perhaps, in an effort to rescue this tale from becoming fairy tale and his characters from turning caricatures, Hemingway, in writing "The Last Good Country," dipped for life-giving "motion and fact" into a store of accumulated memories and impressions from his life, the legends of his life, and the works and lives of others, unable anymore to distinguish their sources. "The Last Good Country" is a vivid and charming rendering of an American myth, but Hemingway is not renowned for charming idylls. Perhaps he lost enthusiasm for his work in progress when he began to sense that it was not new or real or even truly his own. Perhaps Hemingway quit when he realized he was coming awfully close to a story that had already been written.

NOTES

1. Philip Young and Charles W. Mann, *The Hemingway Manuscripts: An Inventory* (University Park and London: The Pennsylvania State University Press, 1969), p. 47.

2. Philip Young, "'Big World Out There': *The Nick Adams Stories*," *Novel*, 6 (Fall 1972), 11.

3. Philip Young, *Ernest Hemingway: A Reconsideration* (University Park and London: The Pennsylvania State University Press, 1966).

4. Ernest Hemingway, "The Last Good Country," *The Nick Adams Stories* (New York: Charles Scribner's Sons, 1972). This and all other page numbers in the essay designated "LGC" refer to this edition.

5. J.D. Salinger, *The Catcher in the Rye* (Boston: Little, Brown and Company, Bantam edition, 1964). This and all other page numbers in the essay designated "CR" refer to this edition.

6. Young, "'Big World Out There,'" p. 12.

7. Young, "'Big World Out There,'" p. 11.

8. Douglas Wilson, "Ernest Hemingway, *The Nick Adams Stories*," *Western Humanities Review*, 27 (Fall 1973), 298.

9. Philip Young, "Posthumous Hemingway, and Nicholas Adams," in *Hemingway in Our Time*, ed. Richard Astro and Jackson J. Benson (Corvallis: Oregon State University Press, 1974), p. 16.

10. For discussions of the incident, see Carlos Baker, *Ernest Hemingway: A Life Story* (New York: Charles Scribner's Sons, 1969), pp. 20–1 and Philip Young, "'Big World Out There,'" pp. 10–11.

11. Baker, p. 21.

12. I quote from an auction catalog of Sotheby Parke Bernet, Inc., Sale #4035, Thursday, October 20, 1977 to October 22, 1977, item #425; letter of 15 July 1948 from Ernest Hemingway to Malcolm Cowley. This letter is not included in Carlos Baker's *Ernest Hemingway: Selected Letters 1917–1961* (New York: Charles Scribner's Sons, 1981).

13. Baker, pp. 420, 646.

14. Young, "'Big World Out There,'" p. 11.

15. Ernest Hemingway, *Death in the Afternoon* (New York: Charles Scribner's Sons, 1932), p. 2.

EDWIN HAVILAND MILLER

In Memoriam:
Allie Caulfield in
The Catcher in the Rye

Although J.D. Salinger's *Catcher in the Rye* deserves the affection and accolades it has received since its publication in 1951, whether it has been praised for the right reasons is debatable. Most critics have tended to accept Holden's evaluation of the world as phony, when in fact his attitudes are symptomatic of a serious psychological problem. Thus instead of treating the novel as a commentary by an innocent young man rebelling against an insensitive world or as a study of a youth's moral growth,[1] I propose to read *Catcher in the Rye* as the chronicle of a four-year period in the life of an adolescent whose rebelliousness is his only means of dealing with his inability to come to terms with the death of his brother. Holden Caulfield has to wrestle not only with the usual difficult adjustments of the adolescent years, in sexual, familial and peer relationships; he has also to bury Allie before he can make the transition into adulthood.[2]

Life stopped for Holden on July 18, 1946, the day his brother died of leukemia. Holden was then thirteen, and four years later—the time of the narrative—he is emotionally still at the same age, although he has matured into a gangly six-foot adolescent. "I was sixteen then," he observes concerning his expulsion from Pencey Prep at Christmas time in 1949, "and I'm seventeen now, and sometimes I act like I'm about thirteen."[3]

On several occasions Holden comments that his mother has never

---

From *Mosaic* 15, no. 1 (Winter 1982): 129–140. © 1982 by Mosaic.

gotten over Allie's death, which may or may not be an accurate appraisal of
Mrs. Caulfield, since the first-person narrative makes it difficult to judge.
What we can deduce, though, is that it is an accurate appraisal of Holden's
inability to accept loss, and that in his eyes his mother is so preoccupied with
Allie that she continues to neglect Holden, as presumably she did when Allie
was dying.

The night after Allie's death Holden slept in the garage and broke "all
the goddam windows with my fist, just for the hell of it. I even tried to break
all the windows on the station wagon we had that summer, but my hand was
already broken and everything by the time, and I couldn't do it. It was a very
stupid thing to do, I'll admit, but I hardly didn't even know I was doing it,
and you didn't know Allie" (p. 39). The act may have been "stupid"—which
is one of his pet words to denigrate himself as well as others—but it also
reflects his uncontrollable anger, at himself for wishing Allie dead and at his
brother for leaving him alone and burdened with feelings of guilt. Similarly,
the attack on the station wagon may be seen as his way of getting even with
a father who was powerless either to save Allie or to understand Holden.
Because he was hospitalized, he was unable to attend the funeral, to witness
the completion of the life process, but by injuring himself he received the
attention and sympathy which were denied him during Allies illness. His
actions here as elsewhere are inconsistent and ambivalent, but always
comprehensible in terms of his reaction to the loss of Allie.

So too is Holden's vocabulary an index to his disturbed emotional
state—for all that it might seem to reflect the influence of the movies or his
attempts to imitate the diction of his older brother, D.B. At least fifty times,
something or somebody *depresses* him—an emotion which he frequently
equates with a sense of isolation: "It makes you feel so lonesome and
depressed" (p. 81). Although the reiteration of the word reveals the true
nature of his state, no one in the novel recognizes the signal, perceiving the
boy as a kind of adolescent clown rather than as a seriously troubled youth.
As his depression deepens to the point of nervous breakdown, furthermore,
Holden—who at some level of awareness realizes that he is falling apart—
seeks to obscure the recognition by referring to everything as "crazy" and by
facetiously likening himself to a "madman."

"Crap," another word he uses repeatedly, is similarly self-reflexive.
Although it is his ultimate term of reductionism for describing the world, like
"crazy" it serves to identify another of his projections. He feels dirty and
worthless, and so makes the world a reflection of his self-image. Similarly, if
he continually asserts, almost screams, that the phony world makes him want
to "puke," it is because Holden's world itself has turned to vomit. In his
troubled, almost suicidal state he can incorporate nothing, and, worse, he

believes there is nothing for him to incorporate. In turn, the significance of his repeated use of variations on the phrase "that killed me" becomes almost self-evident: reflecting his obsession with death, it tells the unsuspecting world that he wishes himself dead, punished and then reunited with Allie.

Although his consistently negative and hostile language thus reflects Holden's despair and is his way of informing the world of his plight, if no one listens it is primarily his own fault. For with the usual fumbling of the hurt he has chosen a means which serves his purposes poorly. While his language may serve to satisfy his need to act out his anger, at the same time it serves to isolate and to punish him further. If in his hostile phrases he is calling for help, he makes certain that he does not receive it. Ashamed of his need—a sixteen-year old crying for emotional support—and unable to accept kindness since in his guilt he feels he does not deserve it, Holden is locked into his grief and locked out of family and society.

In this respect, the first paragraph of *Catcher in the Rye* is one of the most deceptively revealing possible. Although Holden, the would-be sophisticate, relegates his familial background to "David Copperfield kind of crap," he talks about little else except his "lousy childhood." Arguing that he will not divulge family secrets so as not to cause pain, and pretending to respect the feelings of his parents, he verbally mutilates them, and in an ugly way; but if he is to suffer, so must they. He retaliates in kind, not in kindness. Yet the aggressive, assertive tone masks a pitiful, agonized call for emotional support and love.

Equally revealing of Holden's problem is his observation, as he stands alone on a hill that cold December, his last day at Pencey Prep, looking down at the football field where his classmates are participating collectively in one of the rites of adolescence: "it was cold as a witch's teat, especially on top of that stupid hill" (p. 4). What he wants is the good mother's breast. And why he needs this maternal comfort so much is implicitly suggested when he descends the hill to say good-by to his history teacher, who cannot understand why in answering a question about Egyptian history on an examination Holden should have begun and ended with a description of the preservation of mummies. The teacher cannot know that Holden has no interest in the Egyptians, only in what happened to Allie, and that he cannot focus on ancient history until he has come to terms with his own past. Nor can he know that Holden has misinterpreted as rejection his father's concern for his future, that the boy wants to be at home, and that to accomplish his goal he has failed in four different schools.

But lest one think that this insensitivity is a fault of the older generation, Salinger next portrays the response of one of Holden's peers to the first of a number of roles he will play in his desperate attempt to disguise his obsession with Allie's death, on the one hand, and his need for parental comfort, on the other. Thus when Holden pulls his red hunting cap over his eyes and says histrionically, "I think I'm going blind.... Mother darling, everything's getting so *dark* in here.... Mother darling, give me your hand," the response of his classmate is: "You're nuts.... For Chrisake, grow up" (pp. 21–22). Ackley cannot know that Holden assumes Allie's red hair when he puts on the red cap, that the simulated blindness is descriptive of Holden's state, or that he uses the script as a (futile) means of asking for the maternal hand that he believes has been denied to him.

If Ackley does not appreciate the extent to which the death of Holden's red-haired brother informs his posturing, even less is his roommate Stradlater aware of the chain of associations that he sets off when he asks Holden to write a composition for him. Unable to write about a "room or a house" Holden writes about Allie's baseball mitt—an object which is a complex version of a child's security blanket, a sacred relic of the living dead, at the same time that it reminds Holden of betrayal. And thus as he writes about the mitt, we learn directly for the first time of Allie's death and of Holden's self-punishing rage.

By coincidence, Stradlater has a date that evening with Jane Gallagher, the girl to whom Holden had shown the glove in a combined attempt to sympathize with her for her unhappy childhood and to solicit her sympathy for himself. Worried that Stradlater will make "time" with an attractive girl with whom Holden plays checkers—the only kind of play of which the self-styled sex maniac is capable—Holden presses to know what has happened on the date. And when Stradlater implies that he got what he wanted, Holden lashes out with the hand he injured on the day of Allie's death. Subsequently pinned to the floor until he promises to stop his ridiculing insults, as soon as he is released, Holden shouts, "You're a dirty stupid sonuvabitch of a moron," and then he receives the blow that subconsciously he wants. "You asked for it, God damn it," Stradlater says, and he is right for reasons he does not understand (pp. 44–45).

And so on his last day at Pencey Prep Holden makes a clean sweep of it: he writes off the school, his chums, and even Jane. There is no Tom Sawyer to rescue him when he eventually quotes Huck Finn: "I felt so lonesome, all of a sudden. I almost wished I was dead" (p. 48). Suddenly Holden decides to leave late that evening even though his family is not expecting him until the following Wednesday. His Mark Cross luggage packed, he is "sort of crying. I don't know why. I put my red hunting hat on, and turned the peak around to the back, the way I liked it, and then I yelled at the top of my goddam voice, '*Sleep tight, ya morons!*'" Thus, in his usual hostile fashion, Holden makes sure that he will be rejected. Protected only by the red hat, which he now wears like a baseball catcher as he evokes Allie's favorite sport, he stumbles down the stairs and "damn near broke my crazy neck" (p. 52).

On the train to New York he strikes up a conversation with a Mrs. Morrow, who turns out to be the mother of one of his former classmates. He lies through his teeth praising her son who is "about as sensitive as a goddam toilet seat" (p. 55). But "Mothers are all slightly insane. The thing is, though, I liked old Morrow's mother," who happens to be proud of her moronic son. When she wonders whether Holden is leaving school before the beginning of vacation "because of illness in the family," he casually informs her, "I have this tiny little tumor on the brain" (p. 58). The fib achieves the expected result, Mrs. Morrow's genuine sympathy for an ill "son."

Though Holden plans to spend the next few days in a hotel, he is "so damn absent-minded" that he gives the cab driver his home address. After he realizes his "mistake," they drive through Central Park, and Holden asks the driver whether he knows what happens to the ducks in the pond during the winter. The "madman" replies angrily, "What're ya tryna do, bud? ... Kid me?" (p. 60). Worried that he has antagonized the man, Holden invites him for a drink. When the driver refuses, Holden, "depressed," retaliates against "father": "He was one of those bald guys that comb all their hair over from the side to cover up the baldness" (p. 61).

In the hotel he is bored but "feeling pretty horny" (p. 63), as a sixteen-year-old is supposed to feel, and he calls up a whore but lets her put him off. ("I *really* fouled that up.") Then he thinks of telephoning his sister Phoebe, who "has this sort of red hair, a little bit like Allie's was" (p. 67), but he is afraid his mother will answer. He goes to the bar in the hotel and dances with some older women from Seattle who are in New York to see the celebrities, not to provide Holden with entertainment or solace. He punishes them for neglecting him when he fibs that Gary Cooper has just left the room. On the way to a bar frequented by his older brother D.B., who is now, according to Holden, prostituting himself in Hollywood, he asks a cabby named Horwitz about the ducks in the lagoon in Central Park. Horwitz gets "sore" and counters in a typical New York taxi discussion that "The *fish* don't go no place" (p. 82). Desperate for companionship, Holden invites Horwitz for a drink. The driver refuses and has the last word: "If you was a fish, Mother Nature'd take care of you, wouldn't she? Right? You don't think them fish just *die*, when it gets to be winter, do ya?" (p. 83). Holden does not comment, but Horwitz unwittingly summarizes the boy's dilemma.

Later, in D.B.'s nightclub Holden glosses over his loneliness by observing the behavior of the phonies in the club, and then rejects the invitation of one of D.B.'s girlfriends as others have rejected him. When

Holden returns to his hotel, an elevator operator named Maurice sets him up with a call girl, but when "Sunny" arrives, he is "more depressed than sexy" (p. 95), and asks her to stay and talk. He pays her $5.00 and then "depressed" begins "talking, sort of out loud, to Allie" (p. 98).

Maurice returns with Sunny and demands another $5.00 for services not rendered. Holden tries to defend his rights but begins to cry. Sunny wants to leave quietly after she takes money from Holden's wallet, but Maurice "snapped his finger very hard on my pajamas. I won't tell you *where* he snapped it, but it hurt like hell." (The sudden self-protective chastity is an amusing and effective detail.) When Holden calls Maurice "a stupid chiseling moron," for the second time that evening he is smacked, with a "terrific punch" in his stomach (p. 103). Hardly able to breathe, fearing he is drowning, he stumbles toward the bathroom. "Crazy," he acts out a scenario: with a bullet in his gut, he goes down the stairs and puts six shots into Maurice's "fat hairy belly," and then throws the gun down the elevator shaft. He calls up Jane, who comes over and bandages his wound: "I pictured her holding a cigarette for me to smoke while I was bleeding and all." Finally he goes to sleep: "What I really felt like, though, was committing suicide. I felt like jumping out the window. I probably would've done it too"—except for the "stupid rubbernecks" (p. 104).

Holden's protestations to the contrary, the associations in this scene are only superficially from the "goddam movies." Maurice threatens Holden with castration, even though he has not had sex with Sunny, and then pummels him in the stomach. In retaliation Holden commits parricide. In his fantasy he summons Jane, who is associated with Allie through her knowledge of the baseball mitt, and has her play the role of mother.

When Holden thinks of jumping out the window, he is recalling an event which the reader does not learn about until later. A few years earlier Jimmy Castle, a classmate, was so tortured and brutalized, presumably genitally, by a bunch of students that he leaped from a window, wearing Holden's turtleneck sweater. As though Holden is not sufficiently burdened with his unresolved grief for Allie, he has had to cope with this tie to an unfortunate classmate. Sunny, the prostitute, anticipates the appearance of Phoebe, who is both the kid sister and by mythic association the sun goddess. Sunny offers Holden sex, Phoebe will offer him love. Unable to handle sex, Holden wants Sunny to be a confidante, a role which she is unable to handle. Yet she tries unsuccessfully to protect him from Maurice's aggression, which may be Holden's construction of his mother's ineffectual role in the Caulfield household.

At breakfast on the following morning he meets two nun school teachers, and begins a conversation which shortly turns to *Romeo and Juliet*.

If the scene with Sunny reveals that Holden is not ready for sexual relationships—he is a "sex maniac" only in his head—his comments on the tragedy solely in terms of Romeo's culpability in Mercutio's death confirm the arrestment. He is attracted to the nuns, or mothers, who remind him of "old Ernest Morrow's mother" (p. 112), but they also remind him that his father was a Catholic until he "married my mother." This leads him to recall some unpleasant associations with Catholics, and when he says good-by to the nuns, "by mistake I blew some smoke in their faces. I didn't mean to, but I did it" (p. 113). In atonement for his unkindness Holden makes a symbolic apology to the nuns when he imagines them standing in front of a department store raising money for charity. He tries "to picture my mother or somebody, or my aunt, or Sally Hayes's crazy mother, standing outside some department store and collecting dough for poor people in a beat-up old straw hat. It was hard to picture." Since his "picture" of his mother is too harsh, and anxiety-producing, he guiltily corrects it: "Not so much my mother, but those other two" (p. 114).

Walking along the street, he sees a family coming from church—"a father, a mother, and a little kid about six years old." Holden "sees" the family, but only in terms of his own situation. Without evidence he initially assumes that the parents are neglecting the boy who walks along the curb singing to himself, "If a body catch a body coming through the rye"—or so Holden imagines. For it is doubtful that the six-year old, if he knows the poem in the first place, duplicates Holden's misreading of the famous lines. What Holden "hears" anticipates the grandiose fantasy he will later relate to Phoebe in which he catches and saves children. For a moment he is charmed with his fantasy of a self-contained kid whose parents are at hand to protect him: "It made me feel not so depressed any more" (p. 115).

In the afternoon Holden escorts Sally Hayes to a Broadway show and goes ice skating at Rockefeller Center. Then they sit down for a chat—about Holden. He pours out his anger at the phony world, and when Sally tries to be sensible, he almost screams at her, "I don't get hardly anything out of anything. I'm in bad shape. I'm in *lousy* shape" (p. 131). Sally can hardly be expected to understand how empty he feels, or know how to respond to his cry for sympathy. Then he proposes what he knows she cannot agree to, that they run off together to New England. When she objects to the scheme, he verbally assaults her but not without self-pity: "she was depressing the hell out of me" (p. 133).

After this rejection, which in his usual fashion he makes inevitable, he tries to lift the depression by evoking earlier, happier days when the Caulfield family was intact. He goes to Radio City Music Hall, where, with the parents in another part of the theater, Allie and he had sat by themselves watching a favorite drummer. But pleasant memories of Allie cannot rescue him, and he goes to a bar to meet a former classmate named Luce. Although Holden wants Luce's companionship and assistance, he subjects him to an offensive, crude interrogation about his sex life. Twice Luce asks, repeating the question put earlier by Ackley, "When are you going to grow up?" (p. 144). After Holden confesses that his sex life "stinks," Luce reminds him that once before he had advised him to see an analyst. At once Holden asks for more information and comes as close as his pride permits to begging for the kind of aid which Luce of course cannot provide. When Luce gets ready to leave for his date, Holden implores, "Have just one more drink. Please. I'm lonesome as hell" (p. 149).

Now "*really* drunk" and wounded, because Luce like the others betrays him, he replays the scenario of "that stupid business with the bullet in my guts again. I was the only guy at the bar with a bullet in their guts. I kept putting my hand under my jacket, on my stomach and all, to keep the blood from dripping all over the place. I didn't want anybody to know I was even wounded. I was *concea*ling the fact that I was a wounded sonuvabitch" (p. 150). Even in fantasy his self-pity turns into self-disparagement: he hates himself as he screams for attention.

He decides to call up Jane Gallagher, but by "mistake"—it is almost a comedy of errors—he dials Sally Hayes and makes up for his insults. Then he goes to the men's room, dunks his head in a washbowl, and sits on a radiator to dry himself. When the pianist, a "flitty-looking guy," enters, Holden asks him to arrange a date with the singer at the club. The pianist tells him to go home.

> "You oughta go on the radio," I said. "Handsome chap like you. All those goddam golden locks. Ya need a manager?"
> "Go home, Mac, like a good guy. Go home and hit the sack."
> "No home to go to. No kidding—you need a manager?"
> (p. 152)

Holden, who needs "a manager," is crying as he goes for his coat. When the middle-aged attendant gives him his coat even though he has lost his check, he returns the kindness by asking her for a date. She laughs, but not derisively, and, intuiting the role he wants her to play, makes him put on his red hunting hat. His teeth chattering, Holden goes to Central Park to "see what the hell the ducks were doing" (p. 153). On the way, one "accident" following another, he drops the phonograph record he has bought for Phoebe. If, as he believes, nothing has been given to him, he cannot give even to his favorite sister and must punish her as he has been punished.

When he finds the pond he nearly falls in. "Still shivering like a bastard," he imagines that he has pneumonia and dies.

In this fantasy he acts out his anger against his parents and inflicts upon them the ultimate punishment, his death. His funeral is mobbed and everybody cries: "They all came when Allie died, the whole goddam stupid bunch of them." He feels "sorry as hell for my mother and father. Especially my mother, because she still isn't over my brother Allie yet" (p. 155). In this reenactment of Allie's funeral he displaces his brother and enjoys exclusively the love of his mother. But not for long, since his "picture" cannot lift his guilt, dissolve his rage, or make over reality. People will not mourn him long, no longer than they mourned Allie, and life in the phony world will go on without him. Like Allie he will lie in the cemetery exposed to the elements.

To take his "mind off getting pneumonia and all," he skips "the quartets and the nickel" across the lagoon. "I don't know why I did it, but I did it." Perhaps he imitates a game Allie and he played together, but when he throws away his money, there is only one place he can go—home. Which he does, although he disguises the desire by preserving his fantasy: he goes there to see Phoebe "in case I died and all" (p. 156). In the foyer of the Caulfield apartment he recognizes "a funny smell that doesn't smell like any place else" (p.158), and he finds Phoebe asleep in D.B.'s bed: "I felt swell for a change" (p. 159). Safe and protected, he begins to relax and no longer worries "whether they'd catch me home or not" (p. 163). What he does not say is that he would like to be caught. At first Phoebe is "very affectionate" until she guesses that he has been kicked out of Pencey Prep. Then, hurt and angry, a reaction which he cannot understand, she beats him with her fists and says over and over, "Daddy'll *kill* you!" At last Holden tellingly replies, "No, he won't. The worst he'll do, he'll give me hell again, and then he'll send me to that goddam military school. That's all he'll do" (p. 166).

In this climactic scene Phoebe plays a double role. About Allie's age when he died, she is the sister disappointed in the failures of her idealized brother, but she is also an underaged, undersized mother figure. Firmly but affectionately Phoebe presses Holden to explain why he has been expelled. He pours forth all his phony rationalizations, most of which begin and end with something or somebody "depressing" him. When Phoebe suggests that the fault may be his—"You don't like anything that's happening"—he is "even more depressed" (p. 169). She insists, now perhaps not unlike the lawyer father, that he name some things he likes. Unable to "concentrate" on her disturbing questions, Holden thinks of the two nuns and of Jimmy Castle's suicide—kind mothers and a dead son. Relentlessly but not without a concession, Phoebe asks him to tell her "one thing'" he likes.

"I like Allie," I said. "And I like doing what I'm doing right now. Sitting here with you, and talking, and thinking about stuff, and—"

"Allie's *dead*—You always say that! If somebody's dead and everything, and in *Heaven*, then it isn't really—"

"I know he's dead! Don't you think I know that? I can still like him, though, can't I? Just because somebody's dead, you don't just stop liking them, for God's sake—especially if they were about a thousand times nicer than the people you know that're *alive* and all." (p. 171)

Phoebe is silent. Holden believes that "she can't think of anything to say." More perceptive than her older brother, she gives him time to recognize the significance of what he has said: that Allie is dead. Then, like the parents and the teachers, but with an affection that dilutes his anger, she tries to direct Holden to a consideration of a future which—as she tactfully does not say—must be lived without Allie. When she suggests that he may want to be a lawyer, Holden is unable to reply precisely, not merely because he is trapped in his negations, but also because, in spite of his anger, he can only attack the father by indirection. "Lawyers are all right, I guess," he replies, with wayward antecedents, "but it does not appeal to me." He draws a picture of lawyers "saving innocent guys' lives"—which is another rescue fantasy and a disguised self-reference. When he discusses, from his hurt viewpoint, the role of the corporation lawyer, he deflects the indictment of his father through use of the second-person pronoun: "All you do is make a lot of dough and play golf and play bridge and buy cars and drink Martinis and look like a hot-shot" (p. 172). Ironically, Holden emulates his father's behavior, from his Mark Cross luggage to his drinking and "hot-shot" attacks on phonies.

Soon Holden confides his most heroic fantasy, undeterred when Phoebe corrects the misquotation of Burns's poem on which it is based.

"I thought it was 'If a body catch a body,'" I said. "Anyway, I keep picturing all these little kids playing some game in this big field of rye and all. Thousands of little kids, and nobody's around—nobody big, I mean—except me. And I'm standing on the edge of some crazy cliff. What I have to do, I have to catch everybody if they start to go over the cliff—I mean if they're running and they don't look where they're going I have to come out from somewhere and *catch* them. That's all I'd do all day. I'd just be the catcher in the rye and all. I know it's crazy, but that's the only thing I'd really like to be. I know it's crazy." (p. 173)

This is the most complex of all the rescue fantasies. Holden has the "crazy" idea that he should have saved Allie, and that in the future he will save children abused by adults. If he is savior, he is also victim. For he himself is at "the edge of some crazy cliff" and feels himself, as he puts it later, going "down, down, down" (p. 197). He acts out the role he wants the adult world, particularly his father, to play: that of rescuer.

When a moment later Phoebe and Holden horse around and dance about the bedroom, the youth's delight illuminates his desire for a childhood where there are no fears, only joy and protection. The idyll ends abruptly when the parents come home, and Holden, fearing rejection, hides in a closet. Before he leaves, he borrows Phoebe's Christmas money. For the fourth time he begins to cry: "I couldn't help it. I did it so nobody could hear me, but I did it." For the first time he achieves what he has cried for from the beginning: Phoebe, now the mother, not the little sister, "put her old arm around my neck, and I put my arm around her, too, but I still couldn't stop for a long time" (p. 179). Before he goes, he almost tells the truth about himself as well as about the catcher-in-the-rye fantasy. "I didn't give much of a damn any more if they caught me. I really didn't. I figured if they caught me, they caught me. I almost wished they did, in a way" (p. 180).

Holden leaves to spend the night with a former teacher at a preparatory school, now an English professor at New York University. Antolini has been a role model, a good father, for Holden: he carried the body of Jimmy Castle to the infirmary after his suicide, and he banters in the witty style of D.B. Holden is disappointed when Antolini informs him that he has had lunch with Mr. Caulfield and shares the father's concern that "you're riding for some kind of a terrible, terrible fall" (p. 186). The professor tries intellectually to check the boy's self-destructive tendencies, as Phoebe does in her quite different way. Antolini puts the boy to bed on a couch in the living room, and says "Good night, handsome." Later Holden wakens to find "something on my head, some guy's hand" (p. 191). "Shaking like a madman," he concocts an excuse to leave and spends the rest of the night sleeping on a bench in Grand Central Station. "I think," he writes, "I was more depressed than I ever was in my whole life" (p. 194).

Although initially Holden interprets Antolini's caress as a sexual advance, in the morning he has doubts, "I mean I wondered if just maybe I was wrong about thinking he was making a flitty pass at me" (pp. 194–95). Whatever his intentions, sexual or paternal, Antolini sets off the not unusual homosexual panic of adolescents. But Holden's problem is not primarily sexual. He cannot connect with anyone in any way until the burden of Allie's death is lifted.

Alone, depressed, he walks up Fifth Avenue in the morning looking for the two nuns—looking for mother—when something "very spooky" happens. "Every time I came to the end of a block and stepped off the goddam curb, I had this feeling that I'd never get to the other side of the street. I thought I'd just go down, down, down, and nobody'd ever see me again." Once more he is at the cliff, and there is no one to catch him, to keep him from going "down, down, down"—except Allie. He cries out, "Allie, don't let me disappear" (pp. 197–98).

Holden has at last touched bottom, although he is not to be spared further indignities, some of his own making. Never again will he summon Allie, which means that he begins to turn from the past and death and to move into the present and toward the living. The inevitable fantasy that he creates in moments of crisis subtly changes. He plans to go "out West, where it was very pretty and sunny and where nobody'd know me" (p. 198). When Holden proposes to Sally that they run off to Vermont or Massachusetts, the flight is in the direction of Maine, where Allie died. In going west he moves toward the living, for D.B. is in Hollywood. Still damaged and still hungering for security, he pictures himself as a deaf mute working at a filling station and—most important—married to another deaf mute. "If we had any children," he declares, with obvious reference to his own lot, "we'd hide them somewhere. We could buy them a lot of books and teach them how to read and write by ourselves" (p. 199). At last Holden's locked world is opening up.

He goes to Phoebe's school to say good-by and to return her Christmas money. He is upset to find "Fuck you" scrawled on a wall, no doubt more upset than the kids who share neither his naive ideas of purity, despite his verbal profanities, nor his fears of sexuality. While he waits for Phoebe at the museum, two boys ask the way to the mummies. As Holden leads them to the Egyptian room, he begins to repeat the information given in his history examination at Pencey Prep about the process of preservation, and frightens the lads who do not share his obsession with death. Instead of a savior or a catcher, Holden turns out to be a bogey man—as unfeeling as the unfeeling adults who have never understood him. Alone in the tomb, he is mocked again by the ugly epithet of sexual assault which he finds on the walls. Typically he overreacts and at the same time punishes himself as he pictures his tombstone: Holden Caulfield—"Fuck you" (p. 204).

If this debasement is not enough, he suddenly has diarrhea, and passes out on the floor of a toilet. It is as though he must experience an elemental purging—get all the "crap" out of his distorted picture of life and of himself. Compulsively he creates still another fantasy of flight. This time he is a thirty-five-year-old man living by himself: "I even started picturing how it would be when I came back. I knew my mother'd get nervous as hell and start to cry and beg me to stay home and not go back to my cabin, but I'd go anyway" (p. 205). If he is still punishing his mother—and himself—at least he pictures himself alive and at the middle of the journey.

When Phoebe comes to the museum with her luggage because she plans to go west too, once again she reaches out to her brother. The act of love is almost too much for Holden. "I got sort of dizzy and I thought I was going to pass out or something again" (p. 206). But he does not fall nor pass out. Instead like the loved-hated parents or like a protective older brother— in short like all the other adults—he automatically advances all the sensible reasons why Phoebe's plans are "crazy." When he begins genuinely to think of someone else's lot, he assumes responsibility. He is no longer the kid who needs and demands everybody's attention.

When Phoebe proves stubborn, he returns her gift of love with another gift. He escorts her to Central Park, not to the duck pond—with its associations with death—but to the carrousel. "When she was a tiny little kid, and Allie and D.B. and I used to go to the park with her, she was mad about the carrousel" (p. 210). In the bedroom Holden and Phoebe had danced together like two kids, but at the carrousel Holden refuses to ride with her and watches her reach for the gold ring. In turn, when he promises to go home with Phoebe, he delights her and at the same time achieves the goal hinted at on the first page of his narrative: "I felt so damn happy all of a sudden, the way old Phoebe kept going around and around. I was damn near bawling. I felt so damn happy" (p. 213).

In the epilogue, Chapter 26, Holden writes of himself at age seventeen in an institution near Hollywood, not far from D.B. After a period of rest and therapy there has been no fabulous transformation, although there has been change. His language is no longer negative, nor is his attitude. He is not sure that he is going to apply himself when he returns to school in September: "I *think* I am, but how do I know? I swear it's a stupid question" (p. 213). Although he has to put up token resistance—after all, he is Holden Caulfield—he is ready to go "around and around" in the game of life and no longer needs Allie's mitt or hat to protect him. Nor must he picture himself as the victim of insensitive adults; the psychoanalyst's advice is not "bull."

When D.B. asks him about "all the stuff I just finished telling you about," he replies truthfully, without a defensive wisecrack. "About all I know is, I sort of *miss* everybody I told about." At last he cuts through his "crap," his evasions and hostile defenses. He wants, as he has always wanted, to establish connections, and he is well on his way to doing just that, for in his narrative he has at least established connections with readers.

"Don't ever tell anybody anything," he writes at the conclusion; "if you do, you start missing everybody" (p. 214). But telling is precisely what he has been doing and in the process Holden has finished mourning. Allie now rests in peace.

NOTES

1. Holden Caulfield has been called "a lout," a saint, a "sad little screwed-up" neurotic, and a "beatnik Peter Pan," but he deserves none of these epithets, positive or negative. The novel has been read as a critique of "the academic and social conformity of its period" (Maxwell Geismar), as a modern version of the Orestes-Iphigeneia story (Leslie Fiedler), as a commentary on the modern world in which ideals "are denied access to our lives" (Ihab Hassan), or as a celebration of life (Martin Green). These essays appear in *Salinger—A Critical and Personal Portrait*, ed. Henry Anatole Grunwald (New York, 1962).

2. James Bryan recognizes that "the trauma" behind Holden's problems is the death of his brother Allie, but he proceeds to examine the work in terms of Holden's psychosexual growth when clearly the youth's development is emotionally arrested. See "The Psychological Structure of *The Catcher in the Rye*," *PMLA*, 89 (1974), 1065–74.

3. J.D. Salinger, *The Catcher in the Rye* (New York, 1964), p. 9.

MARY SUZANNE SCHRIBER

Holden Caulfield, C'est Moi

If Holden Caulfield set out to study the criticism of *The Catcher in the Rye*, he would find himself the hero of an "awesome" (in today's Pencey Prep idiom) novel that sold a million and a half copies in the ten years following its publication and millions more since 1961.[1] A major figure in what George Steiner referred to, as early as 1959, as "the Salinger industry,"[2] Holden would find himself the subject, by 1981, of 344 essays and reviews, 21 books, 142 references and articles and chapters, and 14 dissertations and theses in the United States alone.[3] Perhaps most phenomenal of all, he would discover that critics have imposed on him and his story an enormous freight of sign value, of significance, in the sense both of meaning and of importance. Holden Caulfield has been construed as a classic American hero, the American adolescent, and the whole of American youth. The novel in which he appears has been associated with the classics of American literature, with the Quest, with the American dream, and with the myth of America. How have critics managed to magnify to such proportions a protagonist who is, after all, but a sixteen-year-old urban, male, WASP preppy? How has it happened that critics have persuaded themselves that this carefully delimited young male is the whole of youth, male and female, and the whole of America as well?

The popularity and magnification of Holden Caulfield and his story are

From *Critical Essays on Salinger's The Catcher in the Rye*. Edited by Joel Salzberg. Boston: G.K. Hall & Co. (1990): 226–37. © 1990 by Joel Salzberg.

101

rendered yet more peculiar by the propensity of critics to doubt the importance of the elusive J.D. Salinger, fallen silent since 1965, and of his one novel, *Catcher*. Critics apologize for their industriousness while in the act of producing the criticism that canonizes Salinger. Thus the 1963 Pocket Books collection of critical essays on Salinger begins with this observation by Henry Grunwald: "There is a feeling in many quarters that altogether too much fuss is being made about J.D. Salinger"; sympathetic critics classify him as a "good minor writer" while insisting that he holds the imagination as other good minor writers do not; unsympathetic critics who otherwise relegate those deemed minor to the oblivion of critical silence feel called upon to put this particular "minor writer" in his place at length.[4]

A cynic might note that the wedding of academic tenure and publication accompanied the Salinger industry, and that the flap over the decency of its language conveniently provided axes to grind and arguments to be made in print. Harvey Swados offers as reasons for the massive critical attention that has in turn designated *Catcher* an American epic Salinger's "supposed profundity," his "tantalizing physical inaccessibility," and the "legend of mysterious private suffering cohabiting with a singularly Christian literary morality ... conducive to excited appraisals of a writer's importance."[5] Or perhaps *Catcher* has been the high school and college novel of choice because of the age of its protagonist and because of its genre: the novel of adolescence. Yet neither sheer pedagogical appropriateness to the interests of the young (if the term includes both males and females) nor literary interest in novels of adolescence (if the term designates a period in the lives of the young of both genders) accounts for *Catcher* being required as classroom reading; there are other contemporary novels of female adolescence, such as Carson McCullers's *A Member of the Wedding* and Ella Leffland's *Rumors of Peace*, that have fared considerably less well both in the marketplace and in academic journals.

The essential ingredient in the phenomenal success and the critical reception of *The Catcher in the Rye* is the propensity of critics to identify with Salinger's protagonist. Holden Caulfield, c'est moi. Falling in love with him as with their very selves, they fall in love with the novel as well. The criticism indicates that they see in Holden, and in themselves through his agency, an incarnation of their youth. Having identified with Holden, critics then engage in a procedure that magnifies him. Undeterred by and apparently oblivious to Holden's gender (and his social and economic class as well), they first assume maleness as the norm. Next, they are reinforced in this assumption by male-identified and gender-inflected theories of American literature, regnant for thirty years, within which more than a generation of readers has been taught to situate American novels. Developed by scholars who have themselves conflated the human and the male, these theories guide critics as they construe and construct the meaning of *Catcher* and its place in American literary history. They enable critics to find in Salinger's novel that which has been defined as archetypally American and thus classic, a literary work of timeless and universal significance.

Describing unabashedly the degree of identification of the male reader with Holden Caulfield, Robert Gutwillig writes: "What was it about the novel that struck Americans so squarely ten years ago and continues to hit the mark still? ... the shock and thrill of recognition. Many of my friends and this writer himself identified completely with Holden.... After reading the novel, several of us went out and bought ourselves red caps and earflaps, and we all took to calling each other 'Ace' and 'Prince.'" What is more surprising is that even as an adult Gutwillig apparently continues to identify with Holden: "I believe that, despite its flaws, it will continue to be read.... Holden takes Phoebe to the carrousel. He stands in the rain, watching her 'going around and around in her blue, coat and all.' 'God,' he says, 'I wish you could have been there.' We *are* there" (emphasis added), writes Gutwillig in 1961, just as "we" were there in 1951.[6]

Fifteen years later, *c'est la même chanson* is sung by Sanford Pinsker. Pinsker declares that, having early fallen in love with *Catcher*, he has been "trying to figure out what that has meant ever since.... Like Holden, I yearned for a world more attractive, and less mutable, than the one in which we live and are forced to compete.... Holden was my 'secret sharer,' the part of me that knew, deep down, that whatever Life was, it was decidedly *not* a game.... Holden said in bald print [what] I dared only whisper *sotto voce*." Like Gutwillig, Pinsker carries his love for Holden with him into manhood: "Holden Caulfield still has an honored place in the minds of what might well be the last generation to have formed its imagination, its sense of who we were, from the pages of a formative book."[7]

While identifying with Holden in their manhood as well as in their youth, critics have failed "to consider gender a relevant factor in either the configuration of identity or the institution of literature itself."[8] This occurs even when the critic is less than fond of the novel but perceives it nonetheless, like Ernest Jones, as "a case history of all of us," apparently defining "us" as male.[9] Presuming that the male is synonymous with the human, critics absorb the female into the male, particularly in their treatment of Holden and sexuality. Brian Way, for example, writes that in New York Holden embarks "on a dream" that is "universally adolescent": "the offer of unbelievable possibilities of sexual adventure and satisfaction." Way does not perceive this as a male's sense of adventure but, rather, he takes it to be normative; he praises Salinger for going "straight to the fundamental biological situation. [Salinger] sees that all the contradictions, agonies, and exaltations of adolescence stem from the central fact: that the adolescent has newly gained the physical potentialities for sexual experience but has not learnt to integrate them either within himself or in any consistent relation to the demands of society."[10] The notion of a "fundamental biological situation" overlooks the differential development, place, and manifestations of sexuality for males and females in the adolescent years.

On those occasions when critics are forced, by choice of texts, to consider female and male protagonists simultaneously, gender differences are sometimes recognized, but not necessarily sustained. Writing about "The Adolescent Hero" of both genders, James W. Johnson notes that sexual confusion "is nearly always more pronounced when the protagonist is a girl." Using Carson McCullers's Frankie Addams as "a conspicuous example of this bisexuality with her boyish haircut and her silver wedding frock," her calling cards that trace her "uncertainty about her sexual nature" and mark "the stages of her sexual as well as psychological maturation," Johnson insightfully observes that "such overt sexual ambiguity does not appear in their [the young women's] male counterparts, who are aware of their biological nature though they may be unsure as to what that nature involves." Nonetheless, having articulated a significant gender difference in the presentation of experience in novels of adolescence, Johnson backs away from his insight, as if unable to assimilate what he has himself detected. He makes no attempt to account for the difference, to convert it into critical capital. Moreover, and seemingly forgetful by the end of his essay of the heroines he earlier distinguished from heroes, he reinstates the male as adolescence itself, reducing the "new school of adolescence" to "the boy-hero" who "may some day achieve the relatively positive vantage-point of intellectualism."[11]

In the insatiable rhetoric of critics, the male is next made synonymous with the nation itself. Listen to Edgar Branch as he claims that *Catcher* and *The Adventures of Huckleberry Finn* are "brothers under the skin because they reflect a slowly developing but always recognizable pattern of moral and social meaning that is part of the active experience of young Americans let loose in the world, in this century and the last.... each author has probed beneath surface facts ... to the experiential continuity of American life."[12] Branch provides here an unmistakable instance of what Sidonie Smith calls "the naive conflation of male subjectivity and human identity" by assimilating the female into the male, and in tropological terms, he casts Holden Caulfield as a synecdoche of America when he is in fact a metonymy: a part is made to represent a whole as if it included all of the other parts that, like it, are merely parts; male *contains* female rather than existing as just another equal part within a larger unit, such as humanity.[13] Branch's rhetoric here immasculates, or renders male, "young Americans" as well as American life itself.

There are of course those who recognize the boundaries within which Salinger sets Holden Caulfield. Harold L. Roth, for one, describes the novel as an attempt to picture "a boy's analysis of himself," and "a young man's thoughts and actions."[14] Rather than subsuming under Holden all adolescents, from the urban slum to the Kansas farm, Maxwell Geismar recognizes that Holden's "is surely the differential revolt of the lonesome rich child, the conspicuous display of leisure-class emotions, the wounded affections never quite faced, of the upper-class orphan."[15] Yet certain observations that appear to take into account the embedding of Holden in a fictive reality, including that of gender, are insidiously phallic. Carl F. Strauch, for example, seemingly confident that he knows how women talk among themselves, describes Holden's much-heralded language as "the idiom of the American male."[16] While this statement appears to take gender differences appropriately into account, it may in fact stand on a stereotype of women, a throwback to notions of the "lady" and a ladylike idiom that eschews four-letter words. Typically the criticism of *Catcher* begins in the symbiosis of male critics and the boy-hero Holden and takes possession of everything in its path, immasculating the whole of adolescence and the nation itself. Holden now magnified, critics claim for *Catcher* the status of a classic on the traditional grounds of universality.

Female critics have been less inclined, proportionately, to identify with Holden Caulfield and then inflate him to cosmic proportions. Of the 344 essays and reviews of *Catcher* listed in the Sublette bibliography, some twenty-three are the work of women. While this figure may simply reflect the lesser number of women publishing literary criticism, it may also indicate that women readers do not identify as readily as male readers with male protagonists. Several female essayists show a sharp awareness of gender and its bearing on literature. Marjorie G. Perloff, for example, contrasts Sylvia Plath's *The Bell Jar* with *Catcher* and observes that while Holden Caulfield is in flight from his world, Plath's Esther Greenwood is the perfect "'good girl' who has always played the roles others have wanted her to play.... Her dilemma seems to have a great deal to do with being a woman in a society whose guidelines for women she can neither accept nor reject."[17] Sally Bostwick and Carol Murphy take Holden's sexual attitudes toward female characters into account; Murphy notes that "there is no real sex in Salinger stories."[18] Nona Balakian includes Salinger in her study of the anti-heroine and observes that in Salinger's work "there is not a single woman of maturity or stature;" in Salinger "the good angel" invariably "bears the face of a little girl (or sometimes a nun)."[19] Most recently, describing Holden Caulfield as a character in "revolt against the life of an adult male," Josephine Hendin avoids the conflation of the adolescent experience of young men and young women.[20]

Other female essayists, however, identify with Holden and immasculate adolescence as fully as male critics. Nancy C. Ralston sees Holden as the forerunner of "the disenchanted young person of today," and she is joined by Leonora Woodman and Molly Workman in the normalizing of Salinger's protagonist.[21] A prize-winning essay on *Catcher* written by a high school student, Amy Fogel, reveals not simply that female readers learn early to identify with male protagonists, as Judith Fetterley establishes in *The Resisting Reader*,[22] but also that they understand this to be required if a story is to win a reader's assent. Testifying unwittingly to the pedagogical importance of fiction that presents female protagonists with whom women can readily identify, Fogel writes: "To understand the positive values of *Catcher*, it is necessary for the reader to identify with Holden, because Salinger's affirmation of humanity comes through Holden's very existence; in his character is the essence of man's nobility."[23]

The gender of a critic, then, is not the sole determinant of a reader's perspective and the meaning that he or she ascribes to Salinger's novel. In the face of the work of women who have identified with Holden, the success and acclaim of *Catcher* cannot accurately be attributed to the single factor of the anatomy of most of those who make up the critical establishment. Rather, critics have been assisted and even directed in their reading by theories of American literature that privilege the male, assume that he is normative, and make intellectual males of us all. Androcentric criticism, that is, is the child of androcentric literary theories. The deconstruction of the critical frameworks that have governed the reading of American literature, together with the understandings enabled by feminist, structuralist, and reader-response theory, explain the powerful impulse among readers, male and female alike, to identify with Holden Caulfield, expand him to cosmic proportions, and then, completing the hermeneutic circle, claim for him a universality that makes *Catcher* a classic.

There are several explanations of the process whereby the male becomes all of us, male and female. According to Dorothy Dinnerstein it begins in human nurturing arrangements in which babies of both sexes, dependent on their mothers, come to resent them and all females. As a result, even a female child identifies with the male and attempts "to preserve her 'I'ness by thinking of men, not women, as her real fellow creatures."[24] According to this theory, girls as well as boys are, from a very early age, in the process of becoming male-identified and would happily merge with male protagonists.

Whether or not we find this persuasive, we know that girls and boys go off to school and learn to be readers. Until recently, becoming a reader meant becoming mentally a male. Carolyn Heilbrun points out that it was only seventeen years ago, in 1971, that readers were asked for the first time to be other than male-identified, to "look at literature as women; we, men, women and Ph.D.'s, have always read it as men."[25] Examining in that same year the evidence of the literary curriculum to which the female student is introduced, Elaine Showalter established that by the end of her freshman year a woman student, supposedly learning "something about intellectual neutrality ... would be learning, in fact, how to think like a man."[26] Pursuing shortly thereafter the thesis that what represents itself in education and in literary interpretation as neutral and objective and whole is in fact masculine and subjective and partial, Judith Fetterley analyzed the impact on women of reading like men and concluded: "As readers and teachers and scholars, women are taught to think as men, to identify with a male point of view, and to accept as normal and legitimate a male system of values."[27] All readers become male readers in the process of learning to read, enabling female critics to identify with Holden Caulfield, to immasculate themselves as young Amy Fogel did.

Having identified with Holden, female critics then approach the novel in much the same way as their male counterparts. And what is this way? Structuralism, reader-response theory, and experiments in cognitive psychology, linguistics, and communication theory have drawn attention to the extent to which reading and the construction of meaning are enabled by theories that, far from being transparent, are in fact mediators between readers and texts. Structuralists find the chief mediators in the text itself a work "has structure and meaning because it is read in a particular way" and is "actualized by the theory of discourse applied in the act of reading"; the readers' understanding of the operations of literary discourse tells them what to look for in a text.[28] Reader-response theorists, on the other hand, contend that the mediators are outside of the text in the reader; "even the simplest understanding and recollection depend on knowledge that the reader brings to the task."[29] While leaving unresolved the vexing question of whether readers control texts or texts control readers, cognition research shows that "comprehension is mediated by generalized knowledge structures, or schemata, that exist in the mind of the reader. The schemata that are activated in the process of understanding a text provide a framework for the construction of meaning."[30]

It is at this juncture that the presumed tendency of human beings of both genders to identify with the male, whether because of nurturing arrangements or schooling, joins theories of American literature that have dominated the American academic marketplace for some thirty years and have become staples in the educational process: the Quest, the Dream, the Rebel, the American Adam, the Romance as quintessentially American. Whether these theories are initially in or out of the text in the mind of the reader, whether they enable the critic to abstract patterns embedded in the fiction or to create and impose patterns from the outside, they nevertheless are now outside American fiction. They have taken on lives of their own, apart from any specific literary work. They are enlisted to situate individual novels in relation to tradition; they are sockets into which novels are routinely plugged in order to be charged with meaning. They are major agents in the construing and constructing of sign value and thus significance. These same theories are unmistakably present in *Catcher* criticism and are unmistakably masculinist, ratifying the identification of readers with that which is male and leading critics to normalize, universalize, and canonize Holden Caulfield.[31]

The regnant theories of American literature and of American literary history; those of such major critics as Lionel Trilling, Joel Porte, F.O. Matthiessen, Daniel G. Hoffman, Marius Bewley, R.W.B. Lewis, and Richard Chase,[32] have located the essence of American culture, and hence of American literature, in the sort of experience that, thanks to gender roles, has been accessible primarily to the male, is fictionalized primarily by male writers, and appeals to the androcentric bias of our culture. Nina Baym has explained how the quest of critics for "Americanness" and for the "American character," foregrounding fiction "that ignores details of an actual social milieu" and casting female characters as antagonists, has served to deny women's fiction and women writers a canonical position in American literary history.[33] Because these theories of American literature that privilege male fictions have been in the ascendancy in the academic study of American literature, the majority of American fiction to which students are exposed is the work of male writers whose protagonists incorporate that elusive, essential "Americanness" defined by theorists.

Yet there is perhaps a more insidious consequence of the imperialism of these formulations of our literary history. They perpetuate the masculinist status quo. Readers who have been taught to situate fiction within the regnant schemata of American literature are enabled by these schemata to make the most meaning from, and find to be most significant and therefore most important, those fictions that the schemata favor. Consequently, a process of self-selection is set in motion; other and perhaps equally meritorious fictions are rendered invisible in the glare of these masculinized dream and quest patterns. Moreover, features of canonical texts themselves that stand in the foreground of other frameworks are obscured if not rendered invisible because theory directs readers to fasten repeatedly on the matter that theory inescapably privileges; as cognition research demonstrates, "the schema activated determines the particular details that will be recalled, and, in the case of ambiguous passages, the nature of what is understood and remembered."[34]

The criticism of *The Catcher in the Rye* shows the degree to which literary theory is responsible for the attribution of global significance to the tale of a WASP preppy male youth. Critics clearly impose on or find in (as the case may be) Holden Caulfield and his adventures the definitions of essential "Americanness" that characterize the work of Trilling and Bewley and others. The trend began as early as 1956, in Charles Kaplan's essay entitled "Holden and Huck: The Odysseys of Youth." As the title forewarns us, Huck and Holden are about to become "youth" itself, apparently entirely male, as it sets off, in Kaplan"s words, on "an adventure story in the age-old pattern of a young lad making his way in a not particularly friendly adult world." Having immasculated "youth," it is easy to immasculate "adolescence" as well, as Kaplan proceeds to do: "In addition to being comic masterpieces and superb portrayals of perplexed, sensitive adolescence, these two novels thus deal obliquely and poetically with a major theme in American life, past and present—the right of the nonconformist to assert his nonconformity, even to the point of being 'handled with a chain.' In them, 1884 and 1951 speak to us in the idiom and accent of two youthful travelers who have earned their passports to literary immortality."[35] Notice how that which is associated with the male, in Kaplan's rhetoric, has progressively absorbed everything in its path. "Youth" and "adolescence" are first implicitly masculinized. Next, that which has been masculinized is expanded into a theme in the whole of "American life," and even immortalized by being projected into both "past and present." Then this all-consuming male, encompassing "youth" and "adolescence" and "America ... past and present" draws the "nonconformist" into its system. The coup de grâce, however, the most chilling manifestation of the insidious power of this androcentric habit over the perceiving mind—insidious because it remains invisible while selecting that which will become visible—occurs in the quote: "handled with a chain."

Kaplan's relentlessly immasculating rhetoric first does its work on "nonconformist" and then, ironically, on Emily Dickinson's "Much Madness Is Divinest Sense." Having assimilated everything into the male, Kaplan's rhetoric then either contradicts the equation of "nonconformist" with the male or manages to immasculate none other than Emily Dickinson. Theories of American literature that implicitly govern Kaplan's reading can be credited with this, theories that conflate American and male experience and proceed to blind the critic even to so strong a female presence as that of Emily Dickinson and to the implicit contradictions in his own critical text.

Perhaps the most anthologized essay on *Catcher*, Heiserman and Miller's "J.D. Salinger: Some Crazy Cliff," manages like Kaplan's essay to place *Catcher* within a frame of reference that, allowing the male to stand for the whole of humankind, turns the whole of America into a company of men. Heiserman and Miller's treatment articulates up front, however, the process whereby a novel like *Catcher* is canonized at the expense of that which is female. These critics place *Catcher* in the "ancient and honorable narrative tradition, perhaps the most profound in western fiction ... the tradition of the Quest. We use the medieval term because it signifies a seeking after what is tremendous, greater than the love of a woman ... somewhere on the arc of the Quest, the love of woman must be eschewed or absorbed: the hero must bind himself to the mast, or must seek his Ducalinda because she is Virtue, not because she is Female." Heiserman and Miller could not be more clear: Quest fiction is perhaps the most profound fiction; Quest fiction is male; Quest fiction is about heroes made tremendous by seeking the tremendous, and that which is tremendous is that which is dissociated from woman and her love. Along with Judith Fetterley and others, one wonders how a female reader can possibly identify with such heroes without identifying against herself. In this tradition, questers are the outcast and, according to Heiserman and Miller, "American literature seems fascinated with the outcast, the person who defies traditions in order to arrive at some pristine knowledge, some personal integrity." In the brief compass of two pages, woman has first been excluded from the quest and then from that with which American literature is fascinated. Holden Caulfield, of course, "is one of these American heroes.... Salinger translates the old tradition into contemporary terms." In the course of the essay, Holden is ranged with Eugene Gant, Natty Bumppo, Huck Finn, Hans Castorp, Huxley's heroes, Dostoyevski's Idiot, Quentin Compson, Ishmael, Nick Adams, "Stephen Dedalus and Leopold Bloom rolled into one crazy kid."[36] Assisted by genre theories and theories of American literature that encourage the construction of impressive meanings and spectacular family credentials for *Catcher*, small wonder that critics have attributed to Salinger's novel such imposing sign value and significance.

Other favorites of American literary theory, in addition to "Americanness" as nonconformity and as inherent questing, come into play in *Catcher* criticism, most of them inaccessible to a female reader short of the partial lobotomy performed in the educational process. Ihab Hassan, for example, finds in Salinger's novel "the tough western hero" delivering an "embarrassed testament of love" and "the American rebel-victim," as well as "the new look of the American dream."[37] Leslie Fiedler associates Holden with the "good bad boy" tradition, the very epithet ensuring, according to Fiedler, a best-seller: "How much longer it took for a book to be called *Bad Girl* and how different the connotations of the title!" Fiedler claims that the "good bad boy" is America's vision of itself—crude and unruly in his beginnings "but endowed by his creator with a sense of what is right.... Sexually as pure as any milky maiden, he is a roughneck all the same, at once potent and submissive, made to be reformed by the right woman."[38] The critical faculties readied and alert for the tradition of the "good bad boy," Fiedler goes on to classify *Catcher* with *Huckleberry Finn*, *Tom Sawyer*, and *On the Road*. Salinger's novel is rendered particularly meaningful and important, that is, by its conformity to unifying theories of the American literary tradition in which critics are steeped. Critics are prepared to tease these patterns out of texts and to acclaim those presumably significant books that fit that old favorite notion of American literature as a "literature of boys. Many of our classics have survived as classics for boys ... for adolescents."[39] The terms in which critics have created a reputation for *Catcher* testify to the continued viability of that tradition in the academic mind.

Thus the popularity and the ascription of broad significance and exceptional literary importance to *The Catcher in the Rye* can be traced to nurturing arrangements, to assumptions that the male is the normative, and to androcentric theories of American literature in which American fiction is routinely framed and taught. Yet a qualification is in order here. The reading experience of many of us, female as well as male (and rural as well as urban, Catholic and Jewish as well as WASP), is articulated in many of the claims made for Salinger's novel. Reader response, and not just the rhetoric of critics, suggests that *Catcher* is a fiction that *does* capture and express recognizable parts of adolescence. Does Salinger's novel more than "seemingly" escape, somehow, the confines of gender to touch broad if not universal human sensibilities? Perhaps the response to this novel should warn us that "concentrating on gender difference can lead us to slight the affinity of women and men ... the common ground shared by all humans."[40] Moreover, if the criticism of *Catcher* manages by and large to articulate the intuitions of many readers of both genders, how can that criticism fairly be labeled androcentric and accused of a masculinist imperialism that mistakes part of human experience for the whole? Or on the other hand, have we been duped into finding ourselves in Salinger's novel by the androcentric logic in which we are schooled? Is the reading of *Catcher* an instance in which "androcentricity *may* be a sufficient condition for the process of immasculation"?[41]

Catcher criticism is guilty of androcentricity as charged because it fails to be self-reflexive. It remains oblivious to the possibility of a female perspective; it fails to problematize the male (and the urban and the WASP); it remains shackled to "false and damaging 'universals' that saddle the major intellectual discourses."[42] It does not declare its assumptions and explain where *Catcher* gets "its power to draw us into its designs," whether from an appeal to authentic desires for liberation and maturity or sheer complicity in our androcentric conditioning.[43] *Catcher* criticism arrogantly assumes that the male includes, unproblematically and unquestionably, the female, the adolescent, and the nation itself, as if this were a given in the natural order of things, requiring no comment and no explanation. Having spoken to and for an exceptionally large audience for four decades, *The Catcher in the Rye* perhaps legitimately deserves its popularity and its designation as a "classic." The critical case for *Catcher*, however, remains to be made. Contrary to the silences and assertions of Salinger criticism to date, an adolescent male WASP is not automatically nature's designated spokesperson for us all.

NOTES

1. Robert Gutwillig, "Everybody's Caught *The Catcher in the Rye*," *New York Times Book Review*, 15 January 1961, 38; reprinted in *Studies in J.D. Salinger*, ed. Marvin Laser and Norman Fruman 1963), 1; hereafter cited as *Studies*.

2. George Steiner, "The Salinger Industry," *Nation*, 94 (14 November 1959); reprinted in *Studies*, 113.

3. Jack R. Sublette, *J.D. Salinger: An Annotated Bibliography, 1938–1981* (New York: Garland, 1984).

4. Henry Anatole Grunwald, introduction to *Salinger: A Personal and Critical Portrait* (New York: Pocket Books, 1963), ix.

5. Harvey Swados, "Must Writers Be Characters?" *Saturday Review* 43 (1 October 1960); reprinted in *Studies*, 121.

6. Gutwillig, *Studies*, 5.

7. Sanford Pinsker, "*The Catcher in the Rye* and All: Is the Age of Formative Books Over?" *Georgia Review* 40 (1986):953–56, 961.

8. Sidonie Smith, *A Poetics of Women's Autobiography* (Bloomington: Indiana University Press; 1987), 15.

9. Ernest Jones, "Case History of All of Us," *Nation*, 1 September 1951, 176.

10. Brian Way, "'Franny and Zooey' and J.D. Salinger," *New Left Review*, May–June 1962; reprinted as "A Tight Three-Movement Structure" in *Studies*, 194, 196.

11. James W. Johnson, "The Adolescent Hero." *Twentieth Century Literature* 5 (1959):6–7,10.

12. Edgar Branch, "Mark Twain and J.D. Salinger: A Study in Literary Continuity," *American Quarterly* 9 (Summer 1957); reprinted in *Studies*, 49.

13. Smith, *Poetics*, 17. I am indebted to my colleague, James M. Mellard, for this tropological observation.

14. Harold L. Roth, "Salinger, J.D., *The Catcher in the Rye*," *Library Journal* 86 (1951):7.

15. Maxwell Geismar, "J.D. Salinger: The Wise Child and the *New Yorker* School of

Fiction," in *American Moderns: From Rebellion to Conformity*, ed. Maxwell Geismar (New York: Hill and Wang, 1958); reprinted in *Studies*, 76.

16. Carl F. Strauch, "Kings in the Back Row: Meaning through Structure, A Reading of Salinger's *The Catcher in the Rye*," *Wisconsin Studies in Contemporary Literature* 2 (Winter 1961); reprinted in *Studies*, 146.

17. Marjorie G. Perloff, "'A Ritual for Being Born Twice': Sylvia Plath's *The Bell Jar*," *Contemporary Literature* 13 (1972):509–11.

18. Sally Bostwick, "Reality, Compassion, and Mysticism in the World of J.D. Salinger," *Midwest Review* 5 (1963):30–43; Carol Murphy, "Some Last Puritans," *Approach: A Literary Quarterly* 53 (1964):24.

19. Nona Balakian, "The Prophetic Vogue of the Anti-Heroine," *Southwest Review* 47 (1962):137.

20. Josephine Hendin, *Vulnerable People: A View of American Fiction since 1945* (New York: Oxford University Press, 1978), 114. While it is tempting to attribute this gender awareness to the resurgence of the women's movement and the development of feminist criticism, the facts of publication show otherwise, note the dates of these essays by women: Perloff, 1972; Bostwick, 1963; Murphy, 1964; Balakian, 1962; Hendin, 1978.

21. Nancy C. Ralston, "Holden Caulfield: Super-Adolescent," *Adolescence* 6 (1971):431; Leonora Woodman, "Teaching Literature Thematically," *English Journal* 55 (1966):564–68; Molly F. Workman, "*The Catcher* in the Classroom," *Virginia English Bulletin* 10 (1960):1–6.

22. Judith Fetterley, *The Resisting Reader* (Bloomington: Indiana University Press, 1978).

23. Amy Fogel, "Where the Ducks Go: *The Catcher in the Rye*," *Ball State Teachers' College Forum* 3 (1962):76.

24. Dorothy Dinnerstein, *The Mermaid and the Minotaur* (New York: Harper, 1976), 107.

25. Carolyn Heilbrun, Millett's *Sexual Politics*: A Year Later," *Aphra* 2 (1971):39.

26. Elaine Showalter, "Women and the Literary Curriculum," *College English* 32 (1971):855.

27. Fetterley, *Resisting Reader*, xx.

28. Jonathan Culler, *Structuralist Poetics* (Ithaca, N.Y.: Cornell University Press, 1975), 113–14.

29. Mary Crawford and Roger Chaffin, "The Reader's Construction of Meaning: Cognitive Research on Gender and Comprehension," in *Gender and Reading; Essays on Readers, Texts, and Contexts*, ed. Elizabeth A. Flynn and Patrocinio P. Schweickart (Baltimore: Johns Hopkins University Press, 1986), 4; hereafter cited as *Gender and Reading*.

30. Patrocinio Schweickart and Elizabeth Flynn, introduction to *Gender and Reading*, xii. E.D. Hirsch, Jr., as well, sets out the importance of schemata in his *Validity in Interpretation* (New Haven, Conn.: Yale University Press, 1967).

31. In Salinger criticism there is an amusing instance of the role of theory in the reader's assessment of a text. Harold Orel, in "What They Think About Teen-Agers in Books" (*College English* 23 [1961]:147–49), reports that students in his high school honors English class accused Holden of lacking good sense. We can assume that some of these same students, once in college and introduced to theory and following in the footsteps of their professors, will learn to see Holden as a hero and his story as a classic.

32. These important studies include studies such as Marius Bewley, *The Eccentric Design* (New York: Columbia University Press, 1963); Richard Chase, *The American Novel*

and Its Tradition (Garden City: Anchor Books, 1957); R.W.B Lewis, *The American Adam* (Chicago: University of Chicago Press, 1955); Joel Porte, *The Romance in America* (Middletown, Conn.: Wesleyan University Press, 1969); Lionel Trilling, "Manners, Morals, and the Novel" and "Reality in America" in *The Liberal Imagination* (New York: Viking, 1950); Daniel Hoffman, *Form and Fable in American Fiction* (New York: Oxford University Press, 1961); Leslie Fiedler, *Love and Death in the American Novel* (New York: Criterion Books, 1960); F.O. Matthiessen, *American Renaissance* (New York: Oxford University Press, 1941).

33. Nina Byam, "Melodrama of Beast Manhood: How Theories of American Fiction Exclude Women Authors," *American Quarterly* 33 (1981): 131.

34. Crawford and Chaffi, *Gender and Reading*, 8.

35. Charles Kaplan, "Holden and Huck: The Odysseys of Youth," *College English* 18 (November 1956); reprinted in *Studies*, 31, 37–38.

36. Arthur Heiserman and James E. Miller, Jr., "J.D. Salinger: Some Crazy Cliff," *Western Humanities Review* 10 (Spring 1956) reprinted in *Studies*, 23–25

37. Ihab Hassan, "J.D. Salinger: Rare Quixotic Gesture," in *Radical Innocence: Studies in the Contemporary American Novel* (Princeton: Princeton University Press, 1961) and in a slightly different form in *western Review* 21 (Summer 1957); reprinted in *Studies* 58, 66, 67.

38. Leslies Fiedler, *Love and Death in the American Novel* (New York: Criterion Books, 1960), 267–68.

39. Van Wyck Brooks, *the Writer in America* (New York: E.P. Dutton, 1953), 64.

40. Schweickart and Flynn, *Gender and Reading*, xxix.

41. Patrocinio Schweickart, "Reading Ourselves: Toward a Feminist Theory of Reading," in *Gender and Reading*, 42.

42. Schweickart and Flynn, *Gender and Reading*, xxix.

43. Schweickart, "Reading Ourselves," in *Gender and Reading*, 42–43.

A. ROBERT LEE

"Flunking Everything Else Except English Anyway": Holden Caulfield, Author

I

Few self-accounts, whether autobiography or novel, display quite so take-it-or-leave-it a bravura as *The Catcher in the Rye*. From Holden's opening disparagement of his early childhood as "all that David Copperfield kind of crap"[1] through to his last, peremptory "That's all I'm going to tell about" (213), J.D. Salinger has his narrator sound the very model of skepticism about whether indeed we do "really want to hear about it" (1). Yet given the book's spectacular popularity. since its publication in 1951, clearly only the most obdurate of readers have proved resistant to "hearing about it" and to Holden's different virtuoso flights of scorn or dismay or selective approval. For however we have come to think of Holden Caulfield—as one of the classic isolates of modern times, as the savvy but endlessly vulnerable witness to crassness and bad faith, as postwar American adolescence itself even—still another figure presses out deep from within. At virtually every turn Holden gives notice of his endemic and unremitting will to a style of his own, to writerliness, to showing himself, knowingly or not, as nothing less than the very author in waiting of *The Catcher in the Rye*.[2]

In part, this identity inevitably has something to do with Salinger's originality in conceiving as his narrator the seventeen-year-old who hovers dauntingly at "six foot two and a half," whose hair has turned its celebrated

From *Critical Essays on Salinger's The Catcher in the Rye*. Edited by Joel Salzberg. Boston: G.K. Hall & Co. (1990): 226–37. © 1990 by Joel Salzberg.

and premature gray on the right side of his head, and who writes of Pencey Prep and his all but Lost Weekend in New York from a West Coast psychiatric ward in the wake of his nervous breakdown. But, to use a key term from the novel, the "composition" Holden puts before us offers anything but the merely offbeat recollections of a put-upon and precocious teenager. This "composition" is the latest in a career that time upon time has seen Holden "composing" other themes, other selves, and other identities. Each, however, has hitherto been of the moment, a spontaneous if never other than highly particular creation conjured into being to meet a required part, or to win or deflect attention, or to fill up the spaces of his loneliness, or, often enough, simply to make good on his sheer creative overdrive. Whatever the occasion, these made-up identities are for the most part extraordinarily affecting and often wickedly funny, a kind of inspired ventriloquy on Holden's part, and at the same time a set of rehearsals, a repertoire, to be called back into play by the eventual author-autobiographer.

In this connection, too, it does not surprise that nearly all the values and people Holden most prizes possess a humanity marked out by style, by an authenticity not only of the heart and senses, but also of art. Indeed, these people are like Holden himself—the Holden who can be wilful, contrary, often impossible, yet in a manner insistently of his own making and at odds with whatever he deems dull or conformist. Each "phony," "and all," and "crumby" is reiterated as often as needed to install his own special signature as writer or monologist, a signature that would be impossible to think anybody's but his alone.

The Catcher in the Rye, as often enough noted, does indeed thereby yield a portrait of the artist, but one that, more than other comparable narratives, operates within its own rules. For a start it makes Holden's every authorial tic and habit as much an equal part of the narration as all the supposedly actual events being unfolded. One thinks not only of his use of "phony" and the like but also of the jibes at his own expense: "I'm the most terrific liar you ever saw. It's awful" (16). He automatically assumes that he has the reader's ear: "She's all right. You'd like her" (67), he says, notably, of Phoebe, and in almost the same phrase, of Allie. And in his off-hand way he makes frequent and meanly well-targeted judgments: "Pencey was full of crooks" (4) or "That guy Morrow was about as sensitive as a goddam toilet seat" (55). Holden seems, ostensibly to tell the one story that bears on "this madman stuff" only to reveal himself, fugitively, in the margins as it were, also telling another, that in which he writes himself imaginatively into being. Both stories are told by the ultimately larger self of Holden as author, the Holden who can editorialize gloriously, fire off opinions, imitate screen celebrities or his fellow preppies, and even, as it appears, brazenly flaunt his resentment at all the unlooked-to burdens of writing autobiography. But if any one overwhelming clue can be said to indicate his essential vocation, it has to do with his strongest and most symptomatic fear, that of disappearing, be it in crossing Route 202 to see "old Spencer" or Manhattan's Fifth Avenue as he talks to the dead Allie. At the very moment of making that fear articulate, transposing it from life into narrative, it is actually being dissolved and conquered.

Analogies have been much proposed for *Catcher*, particularly Dickens's *David Copperfield*, Twain's *Huckleberry Finn* and Joyce's *Portrait*.[3] Each novel, as life, rite of passage, or journey, offers clear similarities in terms of type and situation. But Salinger's novel belongs still more precisely to the company of those fictional autobiographies which show their protagonists discovering their truest being in the call to authorship and in the "self" they see themselves shaping as the words precariously, yet inevitably, take sequence upon the page. Memorable as each is, Copperfield, Huck, and Dedalus tell their stories from positions of retrospect (even Copperfield with his teasing "Whether I shall turn out to be the hero of my own life ... these pages must show"). Holden is altogether more extemporaneous, his account more volatile and rapid, or so Salinger persuades us to feel. Holden's essential styling of things—his every transition, dissolve, off-the-cuff commentary, and wisecrack—could hardly fail to implicate us from first to last in the heady business whereby as for the first time and in the mirror of his own "composition" he sees himself whole and clear. In no way can he ever disappear again, even if he does "sort of *miss* everybody I told about" (214).

To some extent an experiment like Gertrude Stein's *The Autobiography of Alice B. Toklas*, Stein's invention of herself through the persona of her Paris companion and memoirist, bears a resemblance to *The Catcher in the Rye*.[4] Yet Stein's modus operandi never wholly frees itself of the suspicion of staginess or formula. Two other American first-person classics, Ralph Ellison's *Invisible Man* and *The Autobiography of Malcolm X*, however, unlikely as they might at first perhaps be thought, come closer.[5] Both, in an overall sense, obviously tell a more consequential story than Holden's, that of the black American odyssey as against the turnings of white bourgeois New York and its satellite outposts in New Jersey and Pennsylvania. But they do so in a manner and with an improvisational daring greatly of a kind. Each depicts a self, in the face of historic denial, discovering itself as it goes along, a self that, as it moves from blank to identity, marginality to center, does so as though exhilarated and even astonished at its own formulation in writing.

No one would suggest Holden to be some exact fellow traveller of Ellison's black underground "spook" or the oratorical whirlwind who becomes Malcolm X. But the story he offers in *The Catcher in the Rye* delineates a figure who equally, and equally powerfully, draws the energies of self-discovery into his own narrative. This drama of self-inscription, if we can call it so, in and of itself thereby becomes the parallel of all Holden's other doings at Pencey and in Manhattan. Not the least part of it, furthermore, is that whatever Holden's protestations to the contrary, his is a finished autobiography, a story posing as a fragment as may be but wholly complete in its beginning, middle, and end. It would do less than justice to who he is, or at least to who and what he has become, and to Salinger behind him, to think otherwise.

Holden, then, takes to the writer's life out of several kinds of necessity. Despite the contrariness of his signing-off—"I'm sorry I told so many people about it" (214)—his "composition" represents nothing less than a path to psychological health. He has, so to speak, remade himself. Moreover, the privileges of authorship, in addition, have given him his occasion as for the first time to elicit pattern, order, from what throughout his troubled young life has overwhelmingly been flux and loss. Writing, too, has ended his isolation by giving him access to a community that will read and respond to him. Above all, he has achieved his apotheosis, that of an artist writing from the fullest wellsprings of his being and so "unprostituted"—the jokily risqué term he uses about his Hollywood screenwriter brother, D.B.[6] He has made one world into another, one prior self or circle of selves into another. Acknowledging the "author" in Holden thus becomes a critical necessity if we are to get anything like the full measure both of the tale he tells and of himself as teller.

II

From start to finish Holden qualifies as a "performing self," in Richard Poirier's phrase, "authorly" to a degree in how he sets up terms and conditions for his story.[7] Nowhere does he do so more cannily than in the opening of *Catcher*, where his mock brusqueness in saying what he *won't* do "I'm not going to tell you my whole goddam autobiography or anything" (1)—and his equally mock doubts about any readerly good faith we might be assumed to possess—"If you really want to hear about it" (1)—combine not so much to put us off as positively to commandeer our attention. "Where I was born," "my lousy childhood," and "anything pretty personal" about his absentee parents are to be withheld, though not, apparently, the happenings behind this "madman stuff" and his being "pretty run down." How better, it could be asked, to stir curiosity or lay down guidelines as to what is to follow? His every denial and insistence betrays the "authorly" Holden, a narrator about his duties with all the animus of one who can do nothing to stop the storytelling impulses within him.

D.B., the brother who "used to be just a regular writer" but who on Holden's estimate is "being a prostitute" in Hollywood, similarly helps to position Holden as author. D.B. has forfeited this "regularity" for the movies, for the Jaguar, and, we learn at the end, for "this English babe" who comes with him to visit Holden. But he once wrote "this terrific book of short stories" (1) whose title piece, "The Secret Goldfish," Holden has taken to because it delineates a body of private feeling strongly held—that of "this little kid that wouldn't let anybody look at his goldfish because he'd bought it with his own money" (2). As narcissistic as the "kid" may be, he has made of the goldfish a thing of his own, an icon or even artwork. D.B. also points ahead to remind us that Holden comes from a family of writers, not only himself as the Hollywood "prostitute" but Allie who wrote poems on his baseball mitt and Phoebe who composes her "Old Hazle Weatherfield" detective stories. All the Caulfield siblings, in fact, are compulsive fabulists, imaginers.

A number of selective highlightings, first from the Pencey scenes and then those in New York, will help unravel the rest of the pattern. The interview with "old Spencer" has rightly been admired as a comic tour de force, from the "ratty old bathrobe" worn by Spencer and the Vicks Nose Drops through to "the terrific lecture" about "Life is a game" and the dazzlingly awful nose-picking. As a parody of dead rhetoric and set-piece counseling, the episode works to perfection. But in addition to the comedy, it also serves to open up another round of perspectives on Holden as author. Whatever else Holden has failed, he has "passed English," or, as he says in his note added to the exam answer written for Spencer on the Egyptians, "It is all right if you flunk me though as I am flunking everything else except English anyway" (12). A boy who can wonder where the ducks in Central Park go in the winter or see through received cliché—"Game, my ass. Some game"—might well "pass English." In the first instance he is about the search for some kind of benign spiritual principle and in the second about the quest for a language untrammeled by inertness or mere hand-me-down phrasing. He seeks an "English" that expresses him, his situation, not that of "phony" institutionalism.

Little wonder, then, that Holden also shows himself as a virtually insatiable reader. If he can "act out" his contrition for Spencer, assuage the history teacher's need to play the stentorian, he has books in plenty to draw upon. Not only has he been exposed to "all that Beowulf and Lord Randal My Son stuff," but to a literary syllabus as extensive as it is various. *David Copperfield* he brings into play in his first sentence. Clad in his red hunting hat while rooming with Stradlater he reads Isak Dinesen's *Out of Africa*—"I wouldn't mind calling this Isak Dinesen up" (18). Within a trice he adds to the roster Ring Lardner, Somerset Maugham, and Thomas Hardy—"I like that Eustacia Vye" (19). On the train to New York he delivers himself of his thoughts on "those dumb stories in a magazine," obviously no fan of tabloid popular culture. The sex book he has read at Whooton, "lousy" as he thinks it with its view "that a woman's body is like a violin and all" (93), comes pressingly to mind as he waits for his prostitute at the Edmont Hotel. He delivers himself about his views of the Bible—"I like Jesus and all ..." but the Disciples "... were about as much use to Him as a hole in the head" (99). With the nuns Thomas Hardy again comes into his mind: "you can't help wondering what a nun thinks about when she reads about old Eustacia" (110), and *Romeo and Juliet* and *Julius Caesar*. He remembers a discussion of *Oliver Twist* in a film seen with Allie, a novel obviously familiar to him. His meeting with Carl Luce has him invoking Rupert Brooke and Emily Dickinson as, incongruously, a pair of "war" poets, and in turn Hemingway's *A Farewell to Arms* ("a phony book") and Fitzgerald's *The Great Gatsby* ("Old Gatsby, Old sport. That killed me," as his eye for style causes him to remark). For good measure, given the novel's title, he throws in Robert Burns, the writer from whose ditty he has conjured up his fantasy of himself being a catcher in the rye. All of these allusions he contrives to wear lightly, passing stopovers as might be in the passage of his own gathering imagination. In fact, they speak to him from within the community he will shortly join, that of authors and artists who have also and at every risk made over the world on their own creative terms.

A key moment in the process manifests itself in "the big favor" solicited of him by Stradlater, namely a "composition" that can be about anything "just as long as it's descriptive as hell." More than a little revealingly, Stradlater instructs him not "to stick all the commas and stuff in the right place." In part, this advice is to cover up Holden's authorship, but as Holden himself realizes only too well, it typifies how neither Stradlater nor much of the rest of Pencey has the faintest appreciation of what "English" means. The date with Jane Gallagher, who for Holden is the girl individualized by keeping her kings at the back at checkers but for Stradlater is no more than another sexual scalp, stirs in him the memory of Allie, live or dead his one dependable imaginative ally alongside Phoebe. Unsurprisingly he chooses to write about the mitt, the poems in green ink "written all over the fingers and the pocket and everywhere" (38). Holden writes, too, in his "pajamas and bathrobe and my old hunting hat" (37), as if he were kitted out for the job like some updated Victorian man of letters. Everything he pours into his "description," predictably, is wasted on Stradlater, flush as the athlete is with sexual conquest and with concerns a universe away from whatever Holden may have encoded about Allie's death—his traumatized night in the garage and the near self-mutilation of putting his writing hand through "all the goddam windows." "I sort of like writing" (39), he confides, almost shyly, as though dimly aware that we have caught him about his most intimate and essential business. Authorship, whether he likes it or not, pursues him.

Literal authorship, however, is one thing. Holden also revels in "authoring" himself in other ways—as the student penitent for Spencer, as the scholar-prince and then canasta player for an uncomprehending Ackley, as the "goddam Governor's son" who prefers tap-dancing to government and then the no-holds-barred pugilist for Stradlater, and as "Rudolf Schmidt," the name he borrows from the dorm janitor to discuss Ernest Morrow with Mrs. Morrow when they part share a compartment on the train journey between Trenton and Newark.

This latter impersonation again helps establish Holden's drive to invention, his relentless and high-speed fabulation. His version of Morrow as "adaptable," "one of the most popular boys at Pencey," "original," and "shy and modest," not only plays to a fond mother's heart, but also shows Holden on a great improvisational jag, one invention barely put forward before another follows suit. His lie, too, about leaving Pencey early on account of needing an operation for a "tumor on the brain" smacks of a matching versatility of invention, alibiing as an art as in turn does his excuse for not visiting the Morrows in Gloucester, Massachusetts, on account of a promise to see his grandmother in South America. He even starts reading the timetable to stop inventing or lying—"Once I get started, I can go on for hours if I feel like it. No kidding. Hours" (58). He cannot resist, too, trying on the role of "club car" roué, a man who knows his cocktails and has the chutzpah to ask Mrs. Morrow to join him. This is wit, style, ventriloquy, all to symptomatic good purpose. More "authoring," literary and otherwise, however, lies directly ahead as Holden alights at Penn Station and embarks upon his weekend tryst with New York.

III

"I'm traveling incognito" (60) Holden tells the cab driver who takes him to the Edmont Hotel and who has to field the questions about where the ducks go when the Central Park lagoon freezes over in winter.[8] Much as Holden gamely affects to apologize for the B-movie implications of the phrase—"When I'm with somebody that's corny, I always act corny too" (60)—it again emphasizes his uninhibited and ever-burgeoning passion for invention. Doubtless the "loneliness" that tears at him always, together with his fear of disappearance and sheer nervous fidget, propel him more and more into these impersonations. Yet whatever their cause, they mark him as a peerless and habitual fantasist. And are they not, also, instance for instance, the contrivances, of a self that as yet is truly "incognito," that of Holden as yet again the author? Each con-man routine and verbal sleight-of-hand virtually bespeaks authorship, an inventing self as well as invented selves. Is there not, even a hint of the embryonic author in Holden's subsequent query to the cabbie about which band might be playing at the Taft or New Yorker and about joining him for a cocktail—"On me. I'm loaded"? For this is Holden as returnee Manhattanite, back for a good time, a glad-hander, knowing in the city's ways and willing to say the hell with expense. That he is also under-age to be drinking merely points up the masquerade. But who Holden truly is, here as elsewhere, indeed does lie "incognito."

Yet even *his* role-playing risks eclipse when he witnesses the routines being acted out at the Edmont. One window reveals the transvestite recomposing himself as a woman and then "looking at himself in the mirror." Holden does not fail to note that he is "all alone too." A second window exposes him to the "hysterics" of the couple squirting water in each other's mouth, with a possible third party just out of view. "Lousy with perverts" is Holden's reaction, much as he concedes that this "kind of junk is sort of fascinating to watch" (62). But mere voyeur Holden is not. He wants, indeed needs, to be in the action, the absolute participant observer. To watch this urban cabaret relegates him to consumer not maker. Within a trice he is back to his own efforts, the would-be suitor to Faith Cavendish, burlesque stripper and Eddie Birdsell's "ex." Much as he fails to talk her round—"I should've at least made it for cocktails or something" (66)—it leads him on to the person he knows to have a truly creative center, none other than his fellow writer and infant sister, Phoebe.

"Old Phoebe," Holden muses, "You never saw a little kid so pretty and smart in your whole life" (67). But no sooner has he made an inventory of all that makes Phoebe an object of passionate fondness for him—the straight A's, the short red hair stuck behind her ears, her "roller-skate skinny" body, her ability to speak Robert Donat's lines in *The 39 Steps* and stick up a finger with part of the middle joint missing—than he also adds a detail as close as could be to his own impulses. Alongside D.B. and Allie, "a wizard," Phoebe is a writer. Holden gives the information as follows:

> Something else she does, she writes books all the time. Only, she doesn't finish them. They're all about this kid named Hazel Weatherfield—only old Phoebe spells it "Hazle." Old Hazle Weatherfield is a girl detective. She's supposed to be an orphan, but her old man keeps showing up. Her old man's always a "tall attractive gentleman about 20 years of age." That kills me. Old

Phoebe. I swear to God you'd like her.... She's ten now, and not such a tiny kid any more, but she still kills everybody—everybody with any sense, anyway. (68)

Holden recognizes in Phoebe not just a sister but a figure whose creative quirks amount to perfection. She cannot finish her stories. She gets her proportion all out of joint (the twenty-year-old father). The name "Hazle" is either an inspired abbreviation or a misspelling, not to say an ironic echo of Faith Cavendish's "Cawffle" for Caulfield. And she makes her detective an orphan with a parent: The logic here, of course, is that of a child's imagination, the logic of splendid fantasy more than hard fact or chronology. Holden recognizes in it the same authenticity as in D.B.'s "The Secret Goldfish" or Allie's poems in green ink, a Caulfield energy of imagination by which he, too, is wholly possessed. Nonetheless, his own "compositions" have still supposedly to take written shape, even though they are in fact being realized even as he describes Phoebe and everybody else.

His other "authoring" goes on, however, as unstoppable and fertile as ever. He tells "the three witches," Laverne, Old Marty, and Bernice, with whom he drinks and dances in the Lavender Room, that his name is "Jim Steele," that if not Peter Lorre then he has seen Gary Cooper "on the other side of the floor," and that "sometime" he will look them up in Seattle. But when, once more rebuffed, he again calls to mind Jane Gallagher, it is as another literary ally, another fellow traveler in the ways of the imagination. She may well lose eight golf balls, be "muckle-mouthed," keep her kings at the back, be "terrific to hold hands with," and get hold of his neck at the movies, but she also has a redeeming affinity with "composition" and the written word. Once again Holden alights on aspects of someone else that mirror his own writerly alter ego: "She was always reading, and she read very good books. She read a lot of poetry and all. She was the only one, outside my family, that I ever showed Allie's baseball mitt to, with all the poems written on it. She'd never met Allie or anything, because that was her first summer in Maine—but I told her quite a lot about him. She was interested in that kind of stuff" (77).

Jane belongs in a companionship of style, and Holden responds accordingly. Like D.B. before the "prostitution," Allie, and Phoebe, she recognizes and opens to the things of the imagination. Others, too, will embody this for Holden: the black piano-player at Ernie's—"He's so good he's almost corny" (80); the two nuns (one of whom teaches English); "this colored girl singer" Estelle Fletcher whose record of "Little Shirley Beans" he buys for Phoebe; Miss Aigletinger who took them to the Museum of Natural History; "Old James Castle" who was bold enough to tell Phil

Stabile he was conceited, would not take it back, and was driven to jumping to his death at Elkton Hills school (a boy, significantly, with "wrists about as big as pencils"); and Richard Kinsella, who during "Oral Comp" always gets derided for his "digressions" (of which Holden observes, "I mean it's dirty to keep yelling 'Digression!' at him when he's all nice and excited" [184]). Like all of these, Jane appeals to his need for alliances against the dead hand of uncreativity and "phoniness."

His trip to Ernie's, and the Catch-22 conversation en route in which the cab driver Horwitz tries to find the logic of his question about the Central Park ducks—he unwittingly comes close with "If you was a fish, Mother Nature'd take care of you, wouldn't she?" (83)—again call into play Holden's skills as literary impresario. "Old Ernie" he quickly marks down as a "phony," a mere exhibitionist rather than legitimate piano-player who is given to "putting all these dumb, show-offy ripples in the high notes, and a lot of other very tricky stuff that gives me a pain in the ass" (84). He hates the clapping, the instant "mad" applause. He even; teasingly, thinks of himself as "a piano player or actor or something" to the effect that "I wouldn't want them to *clap* for me.... I'd play in the goddam closet" (84). As if from instinct, Holden knows that good music—good writing or good art in general—needs a right, intimate, true response and not mere noise. But such surrounds him, especially when he runs into Lillian Simmons who asks him about D.B. who "went with" her for a while ("In *Holly*wood!," she gushes, "How marvelous! What's he *do*ing?") Lillian he can just about tolerate, but not the "Navy guy" with her. In a last stab of invention he designates Lillian's date "Commander Blop or something."

His experiences with "the elevator guy" Maurice and Sunny might be thought a case of art outrunning life. Holden's virginity, his sex-book good manners as he thinks them when the girl gets to the room—"'How do you do,' I said. Suave as hell, boy" (93)—his parlor-game attempt at conversation in the guise once again of "Jim Steele," and his excuse of having had an operation on his "clavichord" hovers between pathos and French farce. When Maurice returns for the rest of the money, he knows just whom he is dealing with, however—"Want your parents to know you spent the night with a whore?" (102). "A dirty moron" Holden can call him, but he can't "act" his way out of getting slugged. What he can, and does, do, typically, is reinvent himself as a movie hero, a bleeding, tough-guy private eye. He acts out in life what he will go on to act out in his writing:

> About half way to the bathroom, I sort of started pretending I had
> a bullet in my guts. Old Maurice had plugged me. Now I was on
> the way to the bathroom to get a good shot of bourbon or

something to steady my nerves and help me *really* get into action. I pictured myself coming out of the goddam bathroom, dressed and all, with my automatic in my pocket, and staggering around a little bit. Then I'd walk downstairs, instead of using the elevator. I'd hold on to the bannister and all, with this blood trickling out at the side of my mouth a little at a time. What I'd do, I'd walk down a few floors—holding on to my guts, blood leaking out all over the place—and then I'd ring the elevator bell. As soon as old Maurice opened the doors, he'd see me with the automatic in my hand and he'd start screaming at me, in this very high-pitched, yellow-belly voice, to leave him alone. But I'd plug him anyway. Six shots right through his fat hairy belly. Then I'd throw my automatic down the elevator, shaft after I'd wiped off all the finger prints and all. Then I'd crawl back to my room and call up Jane and have her come over and bandage up my guts. I pictured her holding a cigarette for me to smoke while I was bleeding and all.

The goddam movies. They can ruin you. I'm not kidding. (103–4)

As pastiche Chandler or Hammett or Erle Stanley Gardner this would take some beating—film noir from an expert. But Holden is also "scripting" his own part, an author-director writing himself into his own text. The way ahead has once more been richly indicated.

It is so, again, in Holden's meeting with the two nuns as he awaits his link-up with "old Sally Hayes." His mind drifts effortlessly across his life present and past, Sally with her flurry of words like "grand" and "swell" and the recollection of Dick Slagle who pretended Holden's suitcases were his own at Elkton Hills (despite Holden's gesture of putting them out of sight under his bed). Slagle has taken refuge in the word "bourgeois," an intended put-down of Holden, but as tired a form of language as Sally's schoolgirlisms. In encountering the nuns, however, Holden again finds himself recharged by their evident genuineness, the one next to him especially with her "pretty nice smile," her warm thank-you for his contribution, her being an English teacher, and perhaps most of all her enthusiasm on hearing "English was my best subject." As much as he cannot resist two "digressions" of his own—on what a nun thinks about the "sexy stuff" in *The Return of the Native* or *Romeo and Juliet* and on his father's one-time Catholicism—he sees in his listeners a decency that all but humbles him. He also upbraids himself for having even to think of money in connection with them and for blowing smoke in their faces. "They were very polite and nice about it" (113), he reports; as unfeignedly charitable about his rudeness as about not bringing "Catholicism" into the conversation. Holden writes of them as of Jane or Phoebe or the hat-check girl, women for whom one of his wilder "performances" would be wholly wrong.

Holden's next foray into a literary arena, or at least something close, arises out of his date with Sally Hayes ("the queen of the phonies") to see Alfred Lunt and Lynn Fontanne in the Broadway benefit show *I Know My Love*. No sooner does he buy the tickets than his mind takes off on "acting," the whole nature of "performance" itself. He thinks as a veteran of bad or unauthentic "performances"—those of Spencer, Stradlater, Ackley, Buddy Singer from The Lavender Room, Old Ernie, and "white girl" singers of "Little Shirley Beans," among others. The latter, who lack Estelle Fletcher's "very Dixieland and whorehouse" feel, can also be compared with the "terrific whistler" Harris Macklin and the "swell" kid he hears "singing and humming" Burns's lines "If a body catch a body coming through the rye." The child's obvious unphoniness "made me feel better." Such are his touchstones for his dislike of "acting" ("I hate actors") and his irreverent slaps at Laurence Olivier's Hamlet ("too much like a goddam general, instead of a sad, screwed-up type guy"). Holden's own touch of Hamletism also, no doubt, plays into these judgments, his own need to find out how exactly to "act" for himself. The other touchstone he turns to lies in the exhibits in the museum, "unactorly" "glass case" art that does not "move," is "warm," and is free of all the "dog crap and globs of spit and cigar butts from old men" that deface Central Park. "Performance" as seen in the museum—whether the Indians rubbing sticks or the squaw with the bosom weaving a blanket or the Eskimo fishing or the deer and birds—all strike Holden as things that "should stay the way they are," natural and "forever" as indeed exhibits in a natural history museum might be expected to be.

His verdict on the Lunts has exactly to do with their unnaturalness. They overact, or rather "didn't act like people and they didn't act like actors"; theirs are performances whose off-centeredness he rightly thinks "hard to explain." Matchingly hard for him to explain to Sally is his own "performance": his hatred of the "dopey movie actor" type he sees at the intermission and of Sally's Ivy League "buddyroo," of conversation about the Lunts as "angels," and even of Sally herself. On he persists, however, through a risingly frenetic inventory of New York, taxicabs, Madison Avenue buses, "phony guys that call the Lunts angels," and his own experience of boys' prep schools. But when he tries to "author" an alternative, Sally and himself as pastoral homesteaders in Massachusetts and Vermont, he finds himself speaking—writing—in the air, cut down by the unimaginativeness of Sally's response. Their exchange ends in disaster ("I swear to God I'm a madman"), but as he takes stock he also thinks that at the time of "writing" his script for Sally and himself "I *meant* it." Holden, once again, has become most alive and most himself in making an imagined world.

Nor does Holden find his direction from the two would-be mentors he seeks out, Carl Luce and Mr. Antolini. Both betray him, or at least fail to grasp the essential human and creative purposes behind Holden's turning to them. Luce he has been drawn to because he knows or pretends to know the mysteries of sexual life. He also has "the largest vocabulary of any boy at Whooton" and "intelligence." But Holden suspects him from the outset of being a "flit" himself, a mere "hot shot" parader of his own ego and vanity. As to Antolini, his betrayal cuts even deeper. Yet another English teacher, he has won Holden's admiration for trying to talk D.B. out of going to Hollywood and for being his "best" teacher. But he also has his not-so-hidden purposes in calling Holden "you little ace composition writer," in welcoming him to the Antolini apartment for the night, and for playing the sage with his citations from William Stekel on "brilliant and *creative* men." The game is revealed in his homosexual pass, that "something perverty" which for Holden is not only sexual but also a sell-out of all the "literary" advice he has had served up to him by Antolini. Only in Holden's *own* will to make good on the artist in himself, Salinger invites us to recognize, can lie his salvation.

The pointers in that direction are given in abundance. Holden tellingly casts his mind back to D.B.'s conversation with Allie about war writing and about Rupert Brooke, Emily Dickinson, Ring Lardner, and *The Great Gatsby*. Out in the park again looking for ducks he starts "picturing millions of jerks coming to my funeral and all" (154). At his parents' apartment he goes into his "bad leg" routine for the new elevator boy. In Phoebe's room he experiences a near shock of recognition on reading the entries in her notebooks, one stylist's salute to another. She, in her turn, understands the broken record pieces he is carrying for her; the significance of his "I passed English"; the parable of James Castle and Holden's related "catcher" fantasy; and what they are about in dancing the "four numbers" to her radio. The "something very spooky"—his fear of disappearing on Fifth Avenue—serves to indicate the ebb before the storm, his lowest point. Not only must he erase all the "fuck you"s from the walls in order to make a world worthy of each Allie and Phoebe, he also must write himself back into being and into a health to the other side of the "dizziness" and "crazy stuff" that threatens his very existence. "Mad," euphoric, certainly, though he appears in company with Phoebe on the carrousel (that modern incarnation of a medieval art pageant) as it plays "Smoke Gets in Your Eyes" in the rain, Holden can in fact combat his fear of disappearance only through art, authorship. What greater apprenticeship, after all, could anyone have served?

"That's all I'm going to tell about" (213) may indeed be his parting shot, but it is an "all" of whose variety, drama, or fascination, we have been left in no doubt. Only an author of his vintage, too, could offer the advice "Don't ever tell anybody anything. If you do, you start missing everybody" (214). For in making text of life, "goddam autobiography" of experience, he has separated the observer in himself from the participant. He has become, willingly or not, the person he himself has most sought out from the beginning and who in return has most sought him out, none other than Holden Caulfield, author.

NOTES

1. J.D. Salinger, *The Catcher in the Rye* (New York: Bantam Books, 1964), 1. Subsequent page references in the text are to this edition.

2. Oddly, this aspect of Holden has not been much covered in the criticism. But I do want to acknowledge, however, the following: Eugene McNamara, "Holden as Novelist," *English Journal* 54 (March 1965): 166–70, and Warren French, "The Artist as a Very Nervous Young Man" (chapter 8), in *J.D. Salinger* (New York: Twayne, 1963), 102–29. Other criticism with a bearing includes Maxwell Geismar, "The Wise Child and the *New Yorker* School of Fiction," in *American Moderns: From Rebellion to Conformity* (New York: Hill and Wang, 1958), 195–205; Donald P. Costello, "The Language of *The Catcher in the Rye*," *American Speech* 34 (October 1959): 173–81; and Carl F. Strauch, "Kings in the Back Row: Meaning Through Structure—A Reading of Salinger's *The Catcher in the Rye*," *Wisconsin Studies in Contemporary Literature* 2 (Winter 1961): 5–30.

3. See, notably, Charles Kaplan, "Holden and Huck: The Odysseys of Youth," *College English* 18 (November 1956): 76–80; Edgar Branch, "Mark Twain and J.D. Salinger," *English Journal* 44 (September 1957): 313–19; and Malcolm M. Marsden, ed., *If You Really Want to Know: A "Catcher" Casebook* (Chicago; Scott-Foresman, 1963).

4. Fiction that poses as autobiography has, to be sure, a long ancestry, but other American examples would include James Weldon Johnson, *The Autobiography of an Ex-Colored Man* (1912), John A. Williams, *The Man Who Cried I Am* (1967), and Ernest Gaines, *The Autobiography of Miss Jane Pittman* (1971). Given the arguments I make about an analogy between Afro-American fiction and *The Catcher in the Rye*, it will be no surprise that all these were written in fact by black authors.

5. This is not to propose that *Catcher, Invisible Man*, or *The Autobiography of Malcolm X* fall into a single shared category of "fictions of fact." But they do have in common the "dual" aspects of a story being told and the storyteller's recognition of how that "story" helps establish his or her identity.

6. Holden and the movies offers a complementary perspective to Holden as author. Time and again he cites film, film actors, different scenes. In this respect, see Bernard S. Oldsey, "The Movies in the Rye," *College English* 23, no. 3 (1961): 209–15.

7. Richard Poirier, *The Performing Self: Compositions and Decompositions in the Languages of Contemporary Life* (New York: Oxford University Press, 1971).

8. Compare, once again, Ralph Ellison's narrator in *Invisible Man*, typically the following: "I'm shaking off the old skin and I'll leave it here in the hole. I'm coming out, no less invisible without it, but coming out nevertheless...." Both the prologue and epilogue underscore the narrator's "incognito" status.

JOYCE ROWE

Holden Caulfield and American Protest

O n a gray winter afternoon Holden Caulfield, frozen to the quick by more than icy weather, crosses a country road and feels he is disappearing. This image of a bleak moral climate which destroys the soul is not only the keynote of J.D. Salinger's *The Catcher in the Rye* but of much that now seems representative of the general tone of American cultural commentary in the aftermath of World War Two, when the novel was conceived. By 1951 (the year of *Catcher*'s publication) the ambiguities of the cold war, of American global power and influence, were stimulating a large popular audience to find new relevance in well-worn images of disaffection from the modern world. These, which historically had been identified with an aesthetic or intellectual elite, were increasingly being adapted to popular taste as they bore on current social and political concerns. The impact of David Riesman's classic sociological study, *The Lonely Crowd*, published one year before *Catcher*, may have paved the way for a new public concern with the disturbing subject of American character; but the immediate interest Riesman's book aroused and its relatively large sale suggest a readership already sensitized to the kind of anomie which Riesman described and from which Holden Caulfield suffers.[1]

In a sense, Salinger's novel functions at a crossroads, a point on an aesthetic and spiritual journey that he was soon to leave behind.[2] Not unlike the author of *David Copperfield* and *Oliver Twist*, whom he is all too anxious

From *New Essays on The Catcher in the Rye*. Edited by Jack Salzman. New York: Cambridge University Press (1991): 77–95. © 1991 by Cambridge University Press.

to mock, Salinger created a work that is rich enough in language, reference, and scene to captivate innocent and sophisticated readers alike. Indeed, it is only through the democratic nature of his audience that Salinger achieves any version of that ideal community of sensibility and response whose essential absence determines Holden's resistance to the world as it is.[3]

Putting aside the many pleasures of authorial wit, narrative skill, and aesthetic energy that are the first fruits of a reading of *Catcher*, I want to concentrate on a perspective which, thus far, has not received any real critical scrutiny. This is Salinger's ability to infuse a rather formulaic disaffection not merely with the tormented urgency of an individual adolescent voice, but with a resonance that suggests much about the contemporary state of traditional American ideals and aspirations. Holden's brand of alienation gains in significance when viewed not only laterally, in relation to contemporary styles of resistance (as many critics have already done), but historically, in its relation to and displacement of cultural themes which had preoccupied many earlier American writers.[4] To trace such a pattern is, I hope, to deepen our sensitivity to the role that literature plays in shaping the social and moral options that define identity in an historical culture.

Like earlier social resisters in American literature, Holden holds to his own vision of authenticity in the teeth of a morally degraded society. Unlike his forebears, however, he has little faith in either nature or the power of his dreams to compensate for what his "own environment [cannot] supply."[5] The "perfect exhilaration" that Emerson once felt, crossing the snow puddles of Concord Common at twilight, has been transmuted in Holden's urban, modern consciousness to a puzzled speculation: periodically he "wonders" where the ducks in Central Park go in winter when the lagoon in which they live freezes over.[6] The contrast of freezing and freedom, a keynote of Salinger's style, reminds us that the spiritual freedom traditionally symbolized by migratory birds is the remotest of possibilities for Holden. From beginning to end of his journey, from school to sanitarium, Holden's voice, alternating between obscenity and delicacy, conveys his rage at the inability of his contemporaries to transcend the corrosive materialism of modern American life. Many critics have berated him for being a rebel without a cause, asking, in Maxwell Geismar's words, "But what does he argue *for*?"[7] But this inability to move forward and assert a positive goal would seem to be precisely the point of his character.

As a precocious but socially impotent upper-middle-class adolescent who is entirely dependent upon institutions that have failed him, Holden has none of the resources—spiritual, economic, or vocational—that might enable him to become Thoreau's "majority of one." In Thoreau's claim that each of us can become a sovereign unit if we act according to the dictates of conscience, we have a classic American "Antinomian" statement, in which the highest form of individualism, of true self-reliance, is to become, paradoxically, an image of the community's best self. *Walden* opens with "Economy," an account of Thoreau's expenditures for building his house, and ends with a vision of spiritual regeneration spreading through the land. In this conception, to rebuild the self is to regenerate the community. Thoreau's Antinomianism is thus not merely a private or eccentric choice but one that manages to fuse all elements of experience—aesthetic, spiritual, social, national—into a unified endeavor. All need not go to the woods, but all must live as if they had discovered Walden Pond within themselves. Although Holden, lacking faith in the power of self-regeneration, is no Thoreau, neither is his dilatory rebellion merely the measure of his own eccentricity. It too symbolizes a pervasive social failure. Like Pencey Prep, an elite boarding school full of crooks, materialist America desecrates and debases whatever falls to its care. A society that had once expressed its redemptive hopes in symbols of great moral or millennial power— Winthrop's City on the Hill, Melville's *Pequod* going down with a "living part of heaven" nailed to its mast—now finds its goals in the platitudes of "adjustment" psychology and the regenerative therapeutic of the sanitarium. What, indeed, is it *for?*

In Holden's postwar lexicon, America and the world are interchangeable terms. And American global hegemony is given its due in the "Fuck you" expletives which Holden sees as an ineluctable blight spreading through space and time—from the walls of his sister's school, to the tomb of the Egyptian mummies at the Metropolitan Museum, to his own future gravestone. ("If you had a million years ... you couldn't rub out even *half* the "Fuck you" signs in the world" [202].) Like Scott Fitzgerald, Salinger envisions American society as a kind of gigantic Midas, frozen at the heart and thus unable to mature. For all its wealth, its members cannot generate enough respect for their own humanity to care either for their past or their future.

But while Holden lacks the moral energy to make resistance signify as an individual action, he shares with his classic forebears (Hester Prynne, Ishmael, Jay Gatsby) an unwillingness to recognize the ambiguous truths of his own nature and his own needs.[8] This lack of self-awareness characteristic of American heroes, this refusal to probe the tangled underbrush where psychological and social claims intertwine, leads to a familiar pattern: a sense of self-versus-world, an awareness so preoccupied with a lost ideal that any real social engagement is evaded. Thus, paradoxically, rebellion only reinforces the status quo.

Holden's evasion is embodied in a strategy familiar to those who recognize that when Huck Finn lights out for "the Territory" he is making a bid for a hopeless hope—freedom from human contingency; and that when Nick Carraway returns to the West he is following the same path to an unrepeatable past that he has consciously rejected in the pattern of Gatsby's life. Like these dreamers, Holden too is committed to a hopeless vision that makes all the more acute his disgust with the actual. But, in comparison to his forebears, Holden's ideal is a far more diminished thing. It lies in a sunlit childhood Eden, dominated by the image of his dead brother, Allie, who stands for whatever is most authentic in Holden's inner life. Unlike Gatsby, who sacrifices himself to his passion for the past, Holden cannot deceive himself: there is no resurrecting the past, because Allie is dead. This hard fact reduces what was in Gatsby a buoyant, if misguided, hope, to a barren and ineffectual nostalgia. As a mordant comment on American dreamers, it is the last twist of the knife.

Allie's death occurred when Holden was thirteen, the age when puberty begins. On Allie's side of the border it is still childhood; a time when self and world seem, at least in memory, to exist in an enchanted unity. The painful rupture of this sense of self-completion by adolescent self-consciousness and self-doubt is figured in Holden's ritual smashing of the garage window panes at the news of Allie's death. The fact that Holden breaks his own hand in the act—a kind of punitive self-sacrifice—only underscores its symbolic relation to the greater self-mutilation which the loss of childhood signifies for him. The psychic wilderness into which he falls leaves him in a state of continuous nervous anxiety—of being and belonging nowhere, of acute vulnerability to the aggressions and depredations of others against his now-diminished sense of self. But this anxiety never catalyzes any recognition of the enormity of his needs, or of the inevitable limitations of his character. By the end of the story Holden does realize that his vision of himself as catcher was only a daydream. He cannot save either himself or those he loves. ("The thing with kids is.... If they fall off, they fall off, but it's bad if you say anything to them" [211].) But this hard-won insight—sustained through his feeling for his little sister Phoebe—is as close as Holden ever comes to establishing any reciprocity with others, or any awareness of the imperatives that operate in their lives.

The notion of the fall into experience as spiritual castration or social betrayal—the dark legacy of romanticism—has had particular importance for those American artists who have viewed American experience from the vantage point of the country's historic ideals. Of course, among those writers we term "classic" there are distinctions to be made. In "The May-Pole of Merry Mount" Hawthorne allegorized adulthood in terms of the marriage ritual, whereby a man and a woman, brought to moral consciousness through their feeling for one another, sublimate the primitive passions of childhood in the social responsibilities of communal life.[9] But Hawthorne's view of the potential for human happiness in adult life (which becomes his own form of idealism) is something of an exception to the more common, albeit complex, ambivalence of nineteenth-century American writers toward the value of what Wordsworth called "the still sad music of humanity"—a melody which can be heard only by those who relinquished their longing for the intuitive glories of childhood.

Indeed, as the century wears on and industrial society assumes its characteristic modern shape, the American sense of despair at and revulsion from the norms of adult life seems to increase. Writers as diverse in sensibility, experience, and social orientation as Dreiser, Wharton, and Hemingway have created, in *Sister Carrie*, *The House of Mirth*, and *The Sun Also Rises*, works that are remarkably congruent in their protagonists' ultimate response to their world. Hurstwood, disintegrating under the pressure of his confused longings, can find solace only in the rhythmic motion of his rocking chair pulled close to the warmth of the radiator. Similarly, Lily Bart, overcome by her tortuous social battles, seeks a lost primal warmth by imagining herself cradling a baby in her arms as she relapses into a final narcoticized sleep; and Jake Barnes, made impotent by the war, is unable to imagine a way out of that no-man's-land of lost souls whose wayward pleasures postpone forever the psychosexual dilemmas of adult life. In one form or another, the regression to childhood serves as an "over-determined" response to the limitations of social and individual reality confronting these protagonists. So Holden, praying to the image of his dead brother, fights to hold onto what he fears most to have lost, struggling through a barren present peopled by Stradlaters and Ackleys—"slobs" secret or pathetically overt; moral ciphers who exploit by arrogance or by whining manipulation. The bathos of American society turns out to be the real illness from which Holden suffers. In the degree to which we respond to his voice, to the bid his apostrophes make for our allegiance, his condition of loneliness and longing becomes a mirror of our own predicament.

What Holden shares with, indeed inherits from, such classic American prototypes as the new man of Emerson's essays, the narrator of *Walden*, or of "Song of Myself," or of *Adventures of Huckleberry Finn*, is both a way of perceiving reality—a "horizon of expectations," in the words of E.H. Gombrich—and a way of speaking that enforces this view on the reader/auditor by discrediting or delimiting all potentially competing voices.[10] Both his overt aggression and his more subtle hostility toward others are regularly redeemed by the vitality of his compassion, intelligence and wit. The reader, like one of Holden's loyal though exasperated teachers, is continually persuaded to acknowledge Holden's innate superiority to those around him. All his conflicts seem designed to reinforce this persuasion, to bind the reader closer to him. The startling intimacy of his address, beginning with "if you really want to hear about it," but quickly becoming "You should have been there," "You would have liked it," flatters the reader by implying that he or she shares in Holden's delicacies of feeling and taste. In effect, the reader fills the space that Allie's death leaves vacant, his silent allegiance the token of an ideal communion in which Holden might find his authenticity confirmed. Indeed, Holden's idiosyncratic friendship with the reader compensates proleptically for the final loss he suffers in freeing his sister from her sacrificial loyalty to him. But such an "ideal communion," demanding nothing less than the absolute acceptance and mutual joy of his lost relations with Phoebe and Allie, leads to a profound distortion of the reciprocal norm implied in the term. By trying to convert us to his way of seeing and feeling—incorporating us, as it were, into his consciousness while distancing himself from others—Holden unconsciously makes clear that such a bond could never be the basis for the dialogic tensions, sympathies, and re-visions upon which real community depends.

Although Holden's consciousness, like that of all first-person narrators, is the lens through which we view his world, it does not follow that the perspective which the reader shares with the narrator must be as restricted as it is here. Not that Holden is so thoroughly reliable that we cannot see his own confusions and pretensions; there are obvious discrepancies between what he says about himself and the truth of his situation and feelings. His boarding school precocity masks a vulnerability to social humiliation; his pride in his looks and intelligence does little to assuage his guilty fascination with and fear of female sexuality; and his displaced aggression only underscores his doubts about his own sexual potency. But these effects are all too obvious. They exist not for the sake of challenging or complicating our empathy with Holden, but of reinforcing it by humanizing him with the same falsities and fears, the same ambiguous mix of "crumby" and decent impulses, that we can accept in ourselves. They make us like him better, believe in his innate decency as we wish to believe in our own, and so encourage us to accept his view of experience as an adequate response to the world. Indeed Holden, "confused, frightened and … sickened" by the behavior of others, flatters the reader's sense of his own moral acumen; it is all too easy to accept Holden as an exemplar of decency in an indecent age.

Although Holden claims that in telling his tale he has come to "miss" Ackley, Maurice, and the others, his presentation of these figures hardly suggests a deep engagement with the substance of their lives. Like Thoreau's Walden neighbors, whose prodigal habits are introduced only to reinforce the superiority of the narrator's "economy," the characters that Holden meets have little depth apart from their function as specimens of a depressingly antithetical world. If one cares about the three female tourists from Seattle with whom Holden tries to dance, it must be for the sake of one's own humanity, not theirs. They are like flies on the wall of Holden's consciousness—their own histories or motivations need not trouble us. Thus Holden's plunge into the urban muddle, while it seems to provide images of the social complexity of modern America, turns out to be a curiously homogeneous affair: each class or type merely serves as another reflection of a predetermined mental scheme. In this hall of mirrors the apparent multiplicity of experience turns out to be largely a replication of the same experience, in which those who act out of purpose, conviction, or faith are heartbreakingly rare.

In place of authenticity Holden finds an endless appetite for the glamour of appearance, for the vanity of effect and approval. The story that he writes for Stradlater about the poems on Allie's baseball mitt is rejected by his "unscrupulous" roommate because it doesn't follow the rules of the English composition assignment: "'You don't do *one damn thing* the way you're supposed to,'" says the infuriated Stradlater. "'Not one damn thing'" (1). Holden, of course, resists the rules in order to explore his own nascent artistic integrity, while around him those with more claim to our respect than the obtuse Stradlater betray talent and spirit alike by modeling themselves on one another and conforming their behavior to the regulations of a standardized "performance."

Ernie, the talented "colored" piano player who runs his own New York nightclub, is a case in point. He has learned to capture the attention of his customers by performing, before a spotlighted mirror. His face, not his *fingers*, as Holden points out, is the focus of his style. Once very good, he now parodies himself and packs in the customers who, themselves anxiously performing for one another, applaud Ernie wildly. "I don't even think he *knows* any more when he's playing right or not," Holden says (84). Holden's sense of artistry thus serves as a measure of all false values. To the degree that we endorse his authenticity we, who would "puke" along with him, are enabled to share it.

Because there is no other character in the book to provide serious commentary on, or resistance to, Holden's point of view, his experience lacks the kind of dialectical opposition, or reciprocal sympathy, through which he, and we, might develop a more complex sense of the imperatives of American social reality. As he says about the abortive attempt of Mr. Spencer to focus his attention on his failed history exam: "I felt sorry as hell for him.... But I just couldn't hang around there any longer, the way we were on opposite sides of the pole ..." (15). It is this need to polarize and abstract all personal relations that defeats any possibility of normative social connection and engagement. Though Holden complains that people "never give your message to anybody," that "people never notice anything," it is his dominating consciousness, setting himself and the reader in a world apart, that insures his isolation.

Holden's continuous need to defend himself from the encroachments of others generates the verbal disguise he uses to fictionalize all his encounters with adults. The games he plays with Mr. Spencer and Mrs. Morrow, "shooting the bull," telling each what he thinks will most interest and please, enable him to distance himself from the false self his false phrases create as he attempts to protect the true core of his being. As the psychoanalyst D.W. Winnicott has described it, "the true self" is a core of identity which is always invulnerable to external reality and never communicates with it. In adolescence, "That which is truly personal and which feels real must be defended at all cost." Winnicott's description of what violation of its integrity means to the true self—"Rape and being eaten by cannibals ... are mere bagatelles" by comparison—brings to mind the emotional horror that Hawthorne displays toward the violation of another's deepest self, which he calls the Unpardonable Sin.[11] This sense of an integrity to be defended at all cost shapes the Antinomianism, as it does the duality, of Hester Prynne, Huck Finn, and Melville's most notable protagonists. But unlike these forebears, whose need for self-protection is clearly denoted by their double lives, Holden has very little inner or secret freedom in which to function. If society is a prison, then, as in a nightmare tale of Poe, the walls have moved inward, grazing the captive's skin.

Seen in this light, Holden's constant resort to obscenity serves as a shield, a perverse rite of purification that protects him from the meretricious speech of others, which threatens his very existence. Language, for Holden, is a moral matter. In the tradition of Puritan plain-speech, which has had such a marked influence on American prose style, the authenticity of the word derives from, as it points toward, the authenticity of the mind and heart of the speaker. But unlike the narrators of *Walden* and "Song of Myself," who give voice to a language fully commensurate with their visionary longings, Holden's imprecations and expletives ultimately serve to define his impotence; they reveal the degree to which he is already contaminated by the manners, institutions, and authorities of his society. The inadequacy of his vocabulary, upon which he himself remarks ("I have a lousy vocabulary" [9]) is a reflection not merely of his adolescent immaturity, but of the more abiding impoverishment from which he as a representative hero suffers—the inability to conceptualize any form of social reciprocity, of a reasonably humane community, in which the "true self" might feel respected and therefore safe. Lacking such faith there is finally nothing that Holden can win the reader to but complicity in disaffection.[12]

It is a literary commonplace that the English novel—from Austen, Dickens, and Conrad to writers of our own day, like Iris Murdoch—has regularly focused its critical energies on the interrelation of social institutions and individual character. In the work of English and European writers generally, society is the ground of human experience. Although many English protagonists enter their stories as orphans, their narratives lead toward a kind of self-recognition or social accommodation to others that represents the evolving meaning of their experience. One grows, develops, changes through interactions with others in a web of social and personal forces which is simply life itself.

But classic American heroes never make such accommodations. Their identities are shaped, not by interaction with others but in resistance to whatever *is*, in the name of a higher social, ethical, or aesthetic ideal. This, as I have noted, is the ground of their Antinomianism—a public or exemplary heroism, designed to be the only morally respectable position in the narrative. Orphanhood has functioned quite differently for American heroes than for European. More than a starting point from which the hero must evolve a social and moral identity, it represents a liberation from the past that is a totalizing condition of existence—spiritual, psychological, political, and metaphysical. American heroes, seemingly alone, free, and without family or history, test the proposition that a new world might bring a new self and society into being. Although in each case the hero's or heroine's effort issues in failure, there is no conventional recognition of this experiential truth on the part of the protagonist, no willingness to recalculate his or her relations to society or history. American individualism thus reshapes the archetypal pattern of the orphaned young man (or woman) seeking an adult identity by coming to terms with him or herself in the matrix of family life.

Indeed, the family, as the basis for individual as well as social identity, hardly exists in classic nineteenth-century American literature. Almost invariably American heroes lack the memory of past roots. Hawthorne's *The Scarlet Letter* is perhaps the proof text for this statement. Hester Prynne, having shed her European past, stands before the Puritan community, her infant in her arms, unwilling to identify the father—a revelation that would establish a new family (in Hester's ideal terms) on these shores. The fact that Pearl returns to Europe at the story's end, that Dimmesdale tortures himself to death rather than acknowledge his paternity, and that Hester herself remains alone, dreaming of the New World community yet to be, suggests how thoroughly discouraged this most "social" of our classic novelists was about the prospects for authentic family relations in American society.

American heroes like Ishmael and Gatsby are fatherless by choice as well as circumstance. Ishmael will continue to wander as he searches for his lost homeland; Gatsby reaches toward an impossible transcendence whose measure lies precisely in its ineffable difference from the world he knows. Thus Holden's initial dismissal of family history as "all that David Copperfield kind of crap" suggests his affinity with the traditional American rejection of the kind of bildungsroman which *David Copperfield*, among other Dickens novels, exemplifies. But while Holden fully shares, on the deepest spiritual level, in the isolation of the traditional American hero, nothing enforces our sense of his impotence more than his ineffectual play at orphanhood in an urban wilderness. Enmeshed as he is in a labyrinth of social roles and family expectations, escape—to a sunny cabin near, but not in the woods—is envisaged in terms of a cliché whose eerie precision illuminates the core of desperation that sustains the image. Salinger's hero is wedded to a pattern of thought and aspiration in which he can no longer seriously believe. He invokes it because it is the only form of self-affirmation his culture affords.

If the old dream of regeneration through separation has become both terrifying and foolish, society remains for Holden what it has always been for American heroes—an anti-community which continues to betray its own high birthright for a mess of commercial pottage. Holden's fear of disappearing—an image which joins the beginning and end of the story—as he crosses from one side of the road or street to the other, aptly expresses his sense of the diminishing ground for authenticity in America. The peculiar sense of a materialism so blanketing that it produces a pervasive, deadening of affect becomes the mark of the age. One thinks of Sylvia Plath's *The Bell Jar*, whose heroine finds a correlative to the terror of inner emptiness in the social sterility of Madison Avenue glamour—just that world which Holden imagines himself as headed for. Books such as *The Man in the Grey Flannel Suit* and *Sincerely, Willis Wayde*, written to attract a large popular audience, turn these perceptions into the simplified, world-weary clichés of growing up and selling out.[13] But whether cynical or sincere, the protagonists of these novels share with Holden an inability to conceptualize the future as anything but a dead end. "It didn't seem like anything was coming" (118), says Holden, conveying the sense of a world that seems to annihilate the possibility of growth.

Trying to imagine himself a lawyer like his father, Holden wonders if his father knows why he does what he does. Holden knows that lawyers who rake in the cash don't go around saving the innocent. But even if you were such an idealistic fellow, "how would you know if you did it because you really *wanted* to save guys' lives, or because what you really *wanted* to do was be a terrific lawyer, with everybody slapping you on the back and congratulating you in court ..." (172). In a society as replete with verbal falsities as this one, how do you trust your own words, your own thoughts? How do you know when you are telling yourself the truth?

Dickens's tales also show adolescence in an urban commercial society to be a dislocating and frightening process. But from *Nicholas Nickleby* through *Great Expectations* there is regularly a kindly, decent figure who provides aid, comfort, and tutelage in time of need. However bad the adult world seems, enough sources of social strength remain to make the protagonist's struggle toward maturity worthwhile. But Holden never finds such an adult. Mr. Spencer, the history teacher who *seems* to take a fatherly interest in him, is actually most interested in shaming and humiliating him. D.B., the older brother he admires, is as emotionally remote from him as is his father, and Holden takes revenge by reviling him for "selling out" to Hollywood. His mother, as he repeatedly notes, is too nervous and anxious herself to do more than pay perfunctory attention to her children's needs. His father is a shadowy abstraction—a corporate lawyer, defined by his preoccupations and vexations. We hear from Phoebe that "Daddy's going to kill you," rather than experience the father directly through any memory of Holden's.

Holden's anxiety, then, is of a specifically contemporary kind. Those adults who should serve as moral tutors and nurturers are neither wholly absent nor fully present. Perhaps, as David Riesman puts it in speaking of middle-class American parents, "they are passing on to him their own contagious, highly diffuse anxiety," as they look to others to define values and goals increasingly based upon socially approved ephemera.[14] Yet, however shadowy these adult figures may be, they are as controlling of Holden as is the impersonal, elusive corporate authority which, he knows, ultimately determines the values of his home. Like the corporate structure itself, these adults are profoundly ambiguous figures whose seeming beneficence it is dangerous to trust. All are effectively epitomized in the teacher Mr. Antolini, whose paternal decency may be entwined with a predator's taste for young boys, and whose advice to Holden turns out to be as puzzling, if not as specious, as his midnight hospitality.

Remarking that Holden is a natural student, Mr. Antolini urges education on him for its efficiency: "After a while, you'll have an idea what kind of thoughts your particular size mind should be wearing. For one thing, it may save you an extraordinary amount of time trying on ideas that ... aren't becoming to you. You'll begin to know your true measurements and dress your mind accordingly." Mr. Antolini's words, like his manners, are glibly seductive, and a trifle coarse. Ideas as garments that one slips on for the fit—

a ready-made identity—is a concept not far removed from the kind of stylized performance that Holden detects in the Lunts ("they were *too* good") and Ernie. It is suited to a society that increasingly emphasizes image and appearance as intrinsically valuable; a society in which the mess and pain of a real struggle with ideas and feelings is considered an unwelcome deviation from the approved norm of "personality."

Because Holden's final return to his family, his "going home," is never dramatized, we are deprived of the experience of a reckoning in which some genuine moral insight, in distinction to Mr. Antolini's sartorial version in the quest for knowledge, might occur. Instead, we are left with the sense of a society that Holden can neither accept nor escape. His encounter has only served to increase his sense of himself as a creature at bay. His anxiety is never allayed.

Because Holden is never allowed to imagine or experience himself in any significant struggle with others (his bloody fistfight with Stradlater emphasizes the futility of any gesture that *is* open to him), neither he (nor his creator) can conceive of society as a source of growth, or self-knowledge. In place of a dialectical engagement with others, Holden clings to the kind of inner resistance that keeps exiles and isolates alive. In response to the pressures for "adjustment" which his sanitarium psychiatrists impose, he insists upon the principle that spontaneity and life depend upon "not knowing what you're going to *do* until you do it" (213). If the cost of this shard of freedom is the continuing anxiety which alienation and disaffection bring—of life in a permanent wilderness, so to speak—so be it. Impoverished it maybe, but in Holden's sense of "freedom" one can already see foreshadowed the celebrated road imagery of the Beats.

Holden's struggle for a moral purity that the actual corruptions and compromises of American society, or indeed any society, belie is a familiar one to readers of classic American works. But as I have already suggested, for Holden the terms of that struggle are reversed. Unlike nineteenth-century characters, Holden is not an obvious social outsider or outcast to those he lives among. Well-born and well-favored, his appearance, abilities, and manners make him an insider—he belongs. And yet, as the heir of all the ages, blessed with the material splendors of the Promised Land, Holden feels more victim or prisoner than favored son. Like the country at large, he expresses his discomfort, his sense of disease, by squandering his resources—physical, emotional, intellectual—without attempting to utilize them for action and change. But the willful futility of his acts should of blind us to the psychic truth which they reveal. Ultimately Holden is performing a kind of self-mutilation against that part of himself which is hostage to the society that has shaped him. Moreover, while previous American heroes like Hester

Prynne and Huck Finn evaded social reality at the cost of denying their human need for others and their likeness to them, Holden's resistance concludes on a wistful note of longing for everybody outside the prison of his sanitarium—an ambivalence that aptly fixes the contemporary terms of his predicament.

Holden's self-division is thus reduced to the only form in which his society can bear to consider it—a psychological problem of acceptance and adjustment; yet Salinger's irony results in a curious double focus. The increasing prestige of American psychoanalysis in the 1950s may be attributed to its tendency (at least in the hands of some practitioners) to sever individual issues and conflicts from their connections to more obdurate realities in the social world. There is familiar comfort in the belief that *all* problems are ultimately individual ones which can, at least potentially, be resolved by force of the individual mind and will. This irony surely lies within the compass of Salinger's story.[15] But its effect is undercut by the polarized perspective that Salinger has imposed on his hero. As we have seen, the stoic isolation through which Holden continues to protect his authenticity is itself an ethic that devalues confrontation or action and so fixes human possibility in the mold of a hopeless hope. Indeed, it becomes a strategy for containment, as much an evasion of social reality as is the psychiatric imperative to adjust.

There is nothing finally in Holden's diffuse sympathies to offend or dismay the reader, nothing to keep him permanently on edge. By the end of the story the reader has seen his familiar social world questioned, shaken, only to be reconstituted as an inevitable fate.[16] Having been drawn to Holden's side we are finally drawn to his mode of perception and defense. To keep the citadel of the self intact by keeping others at a distance is the kind of social agreement that guarantees that the longed-for community which American experience forever promises will surely forever be withheld.

In discussing the romantic novelist in nineteenth-century European literature, René Girard remarks that the romantic establishes a Manichean division of self and other, refusing to see how "Self is implicated in Other." But since Gerard's concern is as much with the author as with the characters, he goes on to note that this situation is finally attributable to the novelist who stands behind the character and refuses to free either himself or his character from these limitations. In distinction, a "classic" novelist, such as Cervantes, transcends this opposition by distancing himself from his character and so frees himself from the character's perspective. Some form of reconciliation is then possible between protagonist and world.[17]

In Girard's terms, Salinger never frees himself, or therefore the reader, from the grip of Holden's perspective. What happens is just the reverse. We are initiated into a process of seeing in which we are either on the side of integrity and autonomy (Holden) or on the side of the predators and exploiters—from Maurice the pimp to the anonymous psychoanalyst who wants Holden to promise to "apply" himself. A Manichean choice indeed. For the reader, this duality preempts all other modes of perception. The corrosive materialism that blasts Holden as it does his world finally becomes irrelevant to any particular historical moment or reality. Instead, isolation, anxiety, the modern sickness of soul turns out to be the given, irremediable condition of our lives.

NOTES

1. David Riesman, with Reuel Denny and Nathan Glazer, *The Lonely Crowd: A Study of the Changing American Character* (New Haven: Yale University Press, 1950). By 1967 the book was in its thirteenth printing. An abridged version (New York: Doubleday, Anchor Press, 1955) has been widely available ever since, though I have not been able to obtain exact sales figures. Riesman derives the term *anomie* from the French sociologist Emile Durkheim's *anomique*, "meaning ruleless, ungoverned." But Riesman uses it in a broader sense than did Durkheim. For Riesman, anomic individuals are out in the cold, caught between the more desirable state of "autonomy" and the blind conformity of the "adjusted" (abridged ed., p. 278). For another perspective on the mass cultural anxieties which can be figured in Riesman's term, see Michael Wood's comments on the imagery of film noir in *America at the Movies* (New York: Basic Books, 1975).

2. For a consideration of the sacramental vision of experience, tentatively broached here, but confidently asserted in the later stories, especially "Raise High the Roof Beam, Carpenters" and "Zooey," see Ihab Hassan, "Almost the Voice of Silence: The Later Novellettes of J.D. Salinger," *Wisconsin Studies in Contemporary Literature* 4, no. 1 (Winter 1963).

3. In 1965 *Catcher* was listed as one of ten leading mass-market paperback bestsellers. In 1967 it was one of "the leading twenty-five best sellers since 1895" (*Facts on File*, quoted in Jack R. Sublette, *J.D. Salinger: An Annotated Bibliography, 1938–1981* [New York: Garland Publishing Co., 1984], p. 132). It has not been possible to obtain current sales figures, but the book still seems to be a perennial favorite among high school students. In a personal survey, every one of the college freshmen in my required English course (two sections, seventy students) was familiar with it.

4.   Two well-known views that place Holden in his own time suggest the range of many others. Maxwell Geismar ("J.D. Salinger: The Wise Child and *The New Yorker* School of Fiction," in *American Moderns: From Rebellion to Conformity* [New York: Hill and Wang, 1958]) exclaims that "*The Catcher in the Rye* protests, to be sure, against both the academic and social conformity of its period. But what does it argue *for*?" Contemptuous of what he detects as a faked Anglicized patina, glossing a deracinated Jewish world, Geismar dismisses the novel's perspective as "well-to-do and neurotic anarchism" (p. 198). David Galloway (*The Absurd Hero in American Fiction* [Austin: University of Texas Press, 1966]), far more sympathetic to Holden's plight, finds it readily assimilable to his own existentialist concerns. "Holden doesn't refuse to grow up so much as he agonizes over the state of being grown up." He stands for modern man (frustrated, disillusioned, anxious)— a "biting image of the absurd contemporary milieu" (p. 145). While Holden may indeed

stand for modern man, I find Galloway's argument, from absurdity to frustration, to be a circular one. The question remains: why should this time be more absurd than any other time; why must frustration be predicated upon absurdity? Holden has often been compared (unfavorably) to Huck Finn. But these comparisons are essentially; limited to differences in character and social scene. The deeper structural and thematic affinities between *Catcher* and earlier "classic" American works have either been ignored or dissipated in the generalities characteristic of the transcultural myth criticism so popular in the 1950s and 1960s. For an example of the latter, see Arthur Heiserman and James E. Miller, Jr., "J.D. Salinger: Some Crazy Cliff," *Western Humanities Review* 10 (Spring 1456): 129–37.

5. *The Catcher in the Rye* (New York: Bantam, 1964.), p. 187. All quotations will be from this edition and hereinafter will be cited in parentheses.

6. Ralph Waldo Emerson, *The Collected Works*, Alfred R. Ferguson, general editor (Cambridge, Mass.: Belknap Press of Harvard University, 1971), vol. 1, p. 10.

7. Geismar, *American Moderns*, p. 198. See also Mary McCarthy, "J.D. Salinger's Closed Circuit," *Harper's Magazine* 225 (October 1962): 46–7.

8. See the introduction to my *Equivocal Endings in Classic American Novels* (Cambridge University Press, 1988) for an outline of the pattern this resistance takes in classic American novels.

9. Nathaniel Hawthorne, *Centenary Edition* of *Collected Works*, ed. William Charvat and others (Columbus: Ohio State University Press, 1963–1985), vol. 9, pp. 54–67.

10. E.H. Gombrich, *Art and Illusion: A Study in the Psychology of Pictorial Representation* (Princeton: Princeton University Press, 1960), p. 60.

11. D.W. Winnicott, *The Maturational Process and the Facilitating Environment* (New York: The International Universities Press, 1965), pp. 190; 187. Winnicott stresses the value of isolation to the adolescent: "Preservation of personal isolation is part of the search for identity and for the establishment of a personal technique for communicating which does not lead to violation of the central self" (p. 190). The difficulty for Holden is that his culture offers no support for his struggle; it is as if the subject of identity has become such a chronic and pervasive cultural dilemma, generating so much anxiety, that the adolescent adults who surround him treat the problem (as his mother does) like a headache they have learned to live with and ignore.

12. Unusual among early critical responses to *Catcher* is Hansford Martin's "The American Problem of Direct Address," *Western Review* 16 (Winter 1952): 101–14. Martin notes that American writers almost invariably are concerned with the problem of voice, of "man-talking-to-you." He calls this "a literature of direct address," but attributes the phenomenon wholly to the artist's democratic concern with the interaction between art and society (p. 101).

13. Sloan Wilson, *The Man in the Grey Flannel Suit* (New York: Simon and Schuster, 1955); John P. Marquand, *Sincerely, Willis Wayde* (Boston: Little, Brown, 1955); Sylvia Plath, *The Bell Jar* (1963; rpt. New York: Bantam, 1971).

14. Riesman, *The Lonely Crowd*, p. 49.

15. Compare John Cheever's 1958 story, "The Country Husband," in *The Housebreaker of Shady Hill and Other Stories* (New York: Harper and Brothers, 1958), pp. 49–84. Similarly, the husband ends in the basement, devoted to his psychiatrically prescribed woodworking therapy as a cure for his unnameable angst.

16. Cf. Carol and Richard Ohmann, "Reviewers, Critics, and *The Catcher in the Rye*," *Critical Inquiry* 3, no. 1 (Autumn 1976): 15–38. The Ohmanns' review previous critics to point out how Salinger's precise social criticism has been generalized to deny its topical

force. They object to the general critical response that Holden's predicament has been left to him to solve, as a problem of more love, the search for identity, and so forth. Instead, the Ohmanns stress specific bourgeois capitalist relations, hypocrisies of class and exploitation to which they find Holden responding. While the Ohmanns rightly, I believe, assert that "the novel draws readers into a powerful longing for what-could-be, and at the same time interposes what is as an unchanging and immovable reality," they readily attribute to Salinger a political aim ("these values cannot be realized within extant social forms" [p. 351]) that is really their own. The critics who have read Holden's problem as his alone may indeed have missed a good deal of Salinger's social criticism, but, as I have tried to show, Salinger creates the ambiguity. In the end, the book offers ample warrant for just this kind of individualistic interpretation.

17. René Girard, *Deceit, Desire, and the Novel* (Baltimore: Johns Hopkins University Press, 1966), pp. 271, 308.

PAUL ALEXANDER

Inventing Holden Caulfield

1

Coming off an eventful spring, which saw him enjoy the dual accomplishments of having his first story published and of signing on with a literary agent, Salinger wanted to get out of New York for the summer. In the quiet surroundings of the countryside, he could better concentrate on his writing and produce even more stories for Dorothy Olding to submit to magazines.

In the early days of the summer of 1940, Salinger headed out of Manhattan. For some weeks, he stayed on Cape Cod, a calming and beautiful vacation spot. Then, by early August, he had moved on to Canada. On August 8, he mailed a postcard to Whit Burnett from Murry Bay, a charming resort in Quebec. On one side of the postcard was an elegant rendering of the Manor Richelieu—the hotel, Salinger pointed out on the other side of the card in a brief note he jotted to Burnett, where he was *not* staying. While Salinger was summering outside of New York, he was doing so on the sort of shoestring budget that was appropriate for a struggling young author. Salinger had not dropped Burnett a note to comment on Canadian hotels, however. He had written to tell him he was working on a long short story, a departure for Salinger since his stories tended to be relatively short. Finally, after revealing that he was playing bingo on

From *Salinger: A Biography*. Los Angeles: Renaissance Books (1999): 63–77. © 1999 by Paul Alexander.

Tuesday nights, Salinger signed off, offering good wishes to Burnett and his colleague at *Story*, Martha Foley.

On the surface Salinger's note appeared innocuous enough, but even at his young age, Salinger knew that to make it in the publishing business he needed to form and foster professional relationships that could further his career. To date, by publishing "The Young Folks," Burnett had helped Salinger more than anyone, something for which Salinger was obviously grateful. Salinger still got along with editors and publishers. He had not yet formed the opinions, as he would in years to come, that the author–editor relationship is adversarial and that most editors and publishers are uncaring and duplicitous. Of course, this general opinion—that he could not trust the very people whose job it was to publish his work—would later inform his decision to stop publishing his fiction. But that was later. At the moment, he had larger concerns, since he had not yet found that one invention—a character, a genre, a voice—that would inspire him to produce work that was special and original. By September, Salinger was back in Manhattan. On the fourth, he wrote to Burnett to say he had decided to try an autobiographical novel; naturally he would show it to Burnett first. As for why he had gotten away for the summer, he had done so, he said, because he was starting to have second thoughts about being a writer. When he began thinking about becoming an actor again, which he had started to do just before the summer, he realized he needed to get away. Back in New York, he planned on attacking the writing business with new zeal. Then, in a letter dated September 6, Salinger told Burnett he had decided to use the initials "J.D." instead of "Jerome," because he was afraid readers would confuse him with Jerome Faith Baldwin.

Finally, on September 19, Salinger revealed to Burnett, in yet another letter, that he had recently pulled out an old story called "The Survivors" and started looking at its ambiguous ending. Already Salinger was experimenting with a technique he would come to rely on in his writing. When he reached the end of a story, instead of closing it off with some kind of definitive piece of action, he would leave the ending unresolved, open to interpretation. In this way Salinger hoped the endings of his stories would force his readers to ask additional questions concerning the characters and events about which they had just read. With "The Survivors," Salinger had not yet developed enough confidence in what he was doing to leave the ending unclear. Ultimately, he rewrote the story and opted to finish off the story's action with a sure ending. In mid-September, when Salinger submitted "The Survivors" to *Story*, Burnett turned it down.

*   *   *

There was a presidential election in 1940. Franklin Roosevelt had first been elected in 1932, and he was now running for an unprecedented third term in office. This time, the Republicans had nominated as his challenger Wendell Wilkie, who could not have felt confident about running against Roosevelt, since in the 1936 election Roosevelt had defeated Kansas governor Alfred Landon in the electoral college by the staggering margin of 523 to 8. Since 1937, Roosevelt had been trying to focus attention in America on the cultural and political developments taking place in Europe and Asia. Roosevelt had repeatedly warned Americans about the threat to world peace posed by Fascism, which was taking hold in both Europe and Asia. Many Americans dismissed Roosevelt as a warmonger trying to scare people just to get reelected. Still, throughout the fall campaign, Roosevelt cautioned voters about the nationalism that was taking over important segments of the population in Japan, the moves Hitler was making in Europe, and the cooperation Mussolini was offering him in Italy. Regardless of whether the majority of Americans believed Roosevelt to be a warmonger, they still credited him with lifting the national economy out of the Great Depression, so, in early November 1940, they reelected him for the third time, a feat no other president had accomplished. Although Wilkie fared better than Landon before him—it would have been hard for him to get fewer electoral votes than 8—Roosevelt still won in the electoral college by a margin of 449 to 82. In November, Salinger voted for the first time in his life. He voted for Roosevelt.

*   *   *

Salinger ended 1940 on a positive note. Earlier in the year, he had submitted a story called "Go See Eddie" to *Esquire*, but the magazine had rejected it. Then, in the fall, he sent the story to a literary journal named the *University of Kansas City Review*. The editors accepted the story and ran it in the issue that appeared in December. It was Salinger's second published story, and it gave him, if he still needed it, the sort of reassurance young writers often require to keep on trying to make it in a business filled with criticism and rejection.

2

In the spring of 1941, Salinger was still living in his parents' apartment. He was strapped for cash because, while he had seen two of his stories in print, both had been published in small literary journals that did not pay well. In fact, for all of the effort he had put into starting a writing career, so far he had made only twenty-five dollars. One of his first efforts to make some money with his writing was a story called "The Hang of It." Remarkably, that spring, when Olding submitted the story to the editors at *Collier's*, they bought it. One of the most prosperous magazines in the publishing business, *Collier's* paid writers well—extremely well. For a story of normal length, the magazine paid as much as two to three thousand dollars. Salinger would not receive that much money for "The Hang of It" since it was a *short* short story. Still, he looked forward to seeing the story in print—the first time his work would appear in a national magazine. More to the point, he could hardly wait to get paid.

Collier's ran the story on July 12, 1941. In the story, which in a slogan below the story's title the magazine advertised as "A Short Story Complete On This Page," Salinger examined a subject that would play a vital role in his fiction—the lives of people in the military. Obviously this was also a timely topic, since serious political problems continued to plague Europe, raising the possibility that the American military might become involved at some point. In "The Hang of It," Salinger was writing about a father whose son, Harry, a foul-up in the Army, reminds him of another foul-up from years ago, Bobby Pettit, who was famous for telling his fellow soldiers that one day he would get "the hang of it." It's not until the very end of the story that the reader learns the father, now a colonel, is Bobby Pettit, which provides undeniable proof that he did get "the hang of it" and implies that his son will, too.

In many ways "The Hang of It" is an insignificant story—not at all in the same league as the important stories Salinger would go on to write. But the story represented something else for Salinger: his ability to craft stories that he could sell in the marketplace. At the time, *Collier's*, along with *Esquire* and the *Saturday Evening Post*, was among a small number of magazines that controlled the commercial fiction market. During the 1930s and 1940s, before television, magazines that published popular fiction attracted enormous audiences and generated substantial sums of money in advertising revenues. To ensure their competitiveness, magazines paid those writers who could produce material so much money that some authors were able to make a living writing nothing but short stories.

As he wrote his early stories, Salinger soon saw that to improve his chances of selling a particular story to the commercial magazines, he had to tailor that story for a certain publication. Take "The Hang of It," for instance. In 1941, with the prospect of another world war looming, the American public was interested in reading about Army life. So, Salinger chose the Army as the story's backdrop. What's more, Salinger wrote the story so that its success relied on an O. Henry-style twist at the end; he did this because readers judged a story successful if it pulled off just such a gimmick. *Collier's* was much more apt to accept "The Hang of It," which dealt with the United States Army in an entertaining way, than "The Young Folks," which dealt with the empty, aimless lives of spoiled rich kids from Manhattan—not the kind of subject a mainstream magazine editor could easily sell to America's middle-class reading public.

Of all the magazines Salinger dreamed about publishing in, however, the *New Yorker* stood out above all others as his ideal. Its audience was sizable and sophisticated. Its pay scale was among the highest in publishing. Its editorial staff was widely known for treating writers with respect and consideration. More than anything, to appear in the *New Yorker* meant that one had reached the upper echelon of the publishing business.

Through his agent, Salinger had been submitting stories to the *New Yorker* for some time, all to no avail. Just this year, 1941, on March 17, he had submitted "The Fishermen" to John Mosher at the magazine. Salinger had mailed in the story himself because Olding was in the hospital. On Salinger's letter, someone at the magazine had written in large block letters the word NO, then circled it, although Salinger would never know this. Instead, to Salinger, Mosher simply wrote a brief note turning the story down. Undeterred, Salinger already knew the next story he would submit to the *New Yorker*. As he had with "The Young Folks," he wanted to write about rich, jaded teenagers from Manhattan. This time, Salinger had come up with a new character around which to focus the story—an animated yet neurotic teenage boy from the Upper East Side with the unusual name of Holden Caulfield.

*   *   *

In the summer of 1941, while he was living and working at home, Salinger and William Faison, his friend from Valley Forge, went to visit Faison's sister, Elizabeth Murray, at her home in Brielle, New Jersey. Salinger was still grateful to Elizabeth for the informal editorial sessions the two had had over dinners in Greenwich Village some time back; at a point when he was unsure about how to proceed with his writing career, she had been encouraging to him. On this trip, they did not dwell on Salinger's work; mostly they just socialized. As a part of their socializing, one night Elizabeth took Salinger over to the home of a friend of her mother's to meet that woman's daughter—Oona O'Neill.

For some years, Elizabeth's mother had known Agnes Boulton, who lived in Manhattan but kept a summer home on the Jersey shore near Point Pleasant. Boulton had been the second wife of playwright Eugene O'Neill, who had written *Anna Christie, The Hairy Ape, Desire Under the Elms, The*

Emperor Jones, *Strange Interlude*, and *Mourning Becomes Electra*. In 1941, he was already one of America's most successful and respected playwrights. During their brief marriage, O'Neill and Boulton had one daughter, Oona, who was fifteen. Raised by her mother in Manhattan, Oona attended the exclusive all-girls Brearly School, where she was close friends with the daughters of other wealthy families, among them Carol Marcus and Gloria Vanderbilt. At an early age, she was a fixture of the New York social scene. In the spring of 1942, she would be nominated as Debutante Number One. This would happen in large part because Oona possessed an almost mythical beauty and a hauntingly distant personality. When another extraordinary debutante, Jacqueline Bouvier, appeared on the scene more than a decade later, she would be compared with Oona. With her classic features, her delicate looks, her dark hair, Oona routinely stopped conversation when she made an entrance into a crowded room, a simple act she found to be profoundly difficult since she suffered from a paralyzing shyness. "Oona had a mysterious quality to her," says Gloria Murray, Elizabeth's daughter. "She was quiet but she was stunning in her beauty. One night I remember going over to her house and she was getting ready to go out with some boy. So my grandmother asked her, 'Do you like this boy?' And she said, 'No, I can't stand him.' But she was going out with him anyway. She was a blank, but she was stunning in her beauty. You just couldn't take your eyes off her."

When Elizabeth took Salinger to meet Oona on that night in the summer of 1941, he had a typical reaction. "He fell for her on the spot," Murray says. "He was taken with her beauty and impressed that she was the daughter of Eugene O'Neill. For her part, she seemed to be impressed that he was a writer, too." Some connection must have taken place instantly between them, for by the end of the evening they had agreed to see each other after both of them returned to Manhattan.

Back in the city, they went to movies and plays. They met for dinner at cafes and restaurants. They took long walks through Central Park. It was an odd union, really—the classically beautiful young woman dating this wisecracking, intellectual young man (who was so "above it all" he had not even bothered to take college seriously. Oona obviously was attracted to Salinger's sharp wit and brilliant mind and Salinger was attracted to Oona's breathtakingly good looks. As they dated that summer, Salinger fell in love with Oona. Around this time, he got to see in print a story he had written, which dealt with the subject of love, although he probably had gotten the idea for the story well before he met Oona.

*   *   *

In September, *Esquire* published Salinger's "The Heart of the Broken Story." In "Backstage with *Esquire*," Salinger's photograph appeared. His dark, soulful eyes, his full lips, his black hair slicked back and combed to one side, all combined to create a studious and youthful look for Salinger, who was pictured in his sports jacket and tie. In a biographical note, Salinger was described as having been "born in Manhattan twenty-two years ago, educated in city schools, a military academy, and three colleges, never advancing beyond the freshman year." Then the note went on:

> He visited pre-Anschluss Vienna when he was eighteen, winning high honors in beer hoisting. In Poland he worked in a ham factory and slaughterhouse, and on returning to America he went to a small college in Pennsylvania where, he says, he wrote a smug little column for the weekly paper. Then he attended Columbia, and studied with Whit Burnett's short-story group. His satire on formula fiction, "The Heart of a Broken Story," appears on page 32.

Upon reading the story, the reader learned that it was actually about writing a story. The story-within-the-story concerns Justin Horgenschlag and Shirley Lester, would-be lovers who are supposed to meet in order for the boy-meets-girl story-within-the-story to take place, but who don't because the author in the story "couldn't do it with this one." Instead, in Salinger's version of the boy-meets-girl story, Justin and Shirley never meet. Shirley goes off to become involved with a man "with whom she [is] in love" but who is not—and never will be— in love with her, while Justin starts dating a woman "who [is] beginning to be afraid she [isn't] going to get a husband." In short, the boy and the girl do not fall in love with each other, but with people who do not love them and never will.

In his fourth published story, Salinger may have exhibited his considerable skill at handling irony and satire, but he also offered his first take on the idea of love, a subject on which he had little experience, except for his relationships with Oona and—perhaps—with the young girl in Vienna. Still, Salinger's impression of love was clear enough: He rejected it, or, more to the point, he rejected the possibility that a true and reciprocal love could exist. In Salinger's world, apparently, one did not end up with one's true love but with someone who had his or her own agenda—and more than a few ulterior motives.

3

But early in 1941, Salinger had found the subject matter about which he was supposed to write. For some time he had been searching for that special character or milieu; as it is with most writers, much of this process of discovery had been unspoken, even accidental, as if he were going about it by instinct. Then, even though he was only in his early twenties, he came to understand that the vehicle through which he was destined to examine the world in such a way as to make his fiction distinctly his own was Holden Caulfield.

The story was "Slight Rebellion Off Madison," and in it Holden is a kind of teenage Everyman. "While riding on Fifth Avenue buses," Salinger wrote, "girls who knew Holden often thought they saw him walking past Sak's or Altman's or Lord & Taylor's, but it was usually somebody else." Holden is a study in ordinariness, as evidenced by the events documented in the story. He comes home from prep school; kisses his mother; meets his girlfriend, Sally Hayes, for a drink and a night on the town dancing; tells Sally he loves her in the taxi just before she tells him she loves him; and goes with her the next night to see the Lunts in *O Mistress Mine* on Broadway. This is just the sort of life East Side WASPs raised their children to lead, and from all indications Holden is going to do his part to carry on the lifestyle. It's implied he will finish prep school, go to college, marry Sally Hayes, get a respectable job, buy an appropriate apartment, and have children who will be raised to be like their parents.

Or at least that's what Holden *is supposed to do*. However, Holden is in the middle of an emotional meltdown. Over drinks, he bares his soul to Sally in a long monologue during which he confesses he hates "everything." "I hate living in New York," he says. "I hate the Fifth Avenue buses and Madison Avenue buses and getting out at the center door." That's not all, either. He hates plays, movies, even fitting sessions at Brooks Brothers. So he tells Sally he wants the two of them to leave New York, go to Vermont or "around there," and live in a cabin near a brook until the money he has—one hundred and twelve dollars—runs out. Then he'll get a job up there so they can live in the country Always the good WASP, Sally cannot begin to understand the motivation behind Holden's "slight rebellion." "You can't just *do* something like that," she tells him.

The story ends with Holden making a drunken telephone call in the middle of the night to Sally to tell her that he will join her to trim her Christmas tree as planned. Even so, there is a disturbed, and disturbing, quality to the conversation. Holden's line "Trim the tree for ya," which he repeats over and over like a mantra, has a pleading, desperate quality to it, as if he is asking Sally to give him some sign she still wants him despite what he has told her before. She says what he hopes she will say—yes, she wants him to come trim her tree—but still, that answer doesn't seem to be enough.

By inventing Holden Caulfield, Salinger had entered an arena where he would be able to produce significant fiction. Holden was that genuine article—the literary creation that speaks from the soul of the author to the heart of the reader. Salinger had to realize Holden was special because he started another story about him right away. At this rate, perhaps he would end up with a series of stories about Holden. There was one other fact Salinger knew, and it was important. As Salinger would admit years later, Holden was an autobiographical character. Holden's drunken telephone call to Sally, for example, was based on an episode Salinger himself had lived. In the future Salinger would repeatedly contend that fictitious events had to sound real to the reader. In Salinger's case, he may have ensured that authenticity by basing his characters on real people, himself among them.

Salinger wanted to do something with "Slight Rebellion Off Madison" right away. So, at his urging, Olding submitted the story to the *New Yorker*, and in November, much to Salinger's surprise, the editors accepted it, probably looking to run it right away since the story is set during the Christmas season. When he got word of the acceptance, Salinger was overjoyed. He had been eager to break into the pages of the *New Yorker*; at the amazingly young age of twenty-two, he had been successful. Elated, Salinger wrote to William Maxwell, who would be his editor for this story at the magazine. He had another story about Holden, but he was going to hold off on sending it to him, Salinger said. Instead, Salinger told Maxwell, he would try a different story on him—another one about prep-school children, an obese boy and his two sisters.

As the *New Yorker* prepared to publish "Slight Rebellion Off Madison," the Japanese attacked Pearl Harbor on December 7, 1941, and all the warnings Roosevelt had made through the years about radical nationalism growing uncontrollably in parts of Europe and Asia seemed more than justified. Within hours, Roosevelt asked Congress, and Congress agreed, to declare war on Japan. The start of war meant the editors of the *New Yorker* did not feel it was appropriate to publish—so soon after Pearl Harbor—a story about a neurotic teenage boy whose "slight rebellion" is prompted by the fact that he has become disenchanted with the life he leads as the son in a wealthy family in New York. Holden's problems were trivial compared to world developments. So the magazine's editors postponed the publication of Salinger's story. Although he would not know it at the time, the editors would not publish "Slight Rebellion Off Madison" until after the conclusion of World War II. It would be years, then, before Salinger realized his dream of seeing his work appear in the magazine he respected most.

However, Salinger had larger concerns than the question of whether the *New Yorker* was going to run his story. At twenty-two, he was prime material for military service. Earlier in 1941, he had tried to join the Army, but military doctors turned him down because he had a minor heart condition. With the United States about to enter a world war, it was only a matter of time before Salinger's heart condition would be considered negligible, making him eligible for the newly sanctioned draft.

NOTES

p. 145. In the early days ... Martha Foley: This paragraph is based on Salinger's August 8, 1940 postcard to Burnett which is at Princeton.

p. 146. By September ... turned it down: These two paragraphs are based on the September 1940 correspondence between Salinger and Burnett which is at Princeton.

p. 147. There was a presidential ... at once: *Modern Times: The World From the Twenties to the Nineties* by Paul Johnson, HarperCollins, 1994.

p. 147. In November ... Roosevelt: *In Search of J.D. Salinger* by Ian Hamilton.

p. 149. Through his agent ... turning the story down: Letters exchanged between Salinger and the staff of the *New Yorker* are in the Rare Books and Manuscript Division at the New York Public Library.

p. 149. In the summer of 1941... Oona O'Neill: This paragraph is taken from my interviews with Gloria Murray.

p. 149–150. For some years ... Debutante Number One: The information in this paragraph is taken from *O'Neill* by Arthur and Barbara Gelb (Applause Theater, 1994) as well as *Trio: The Intimate Friendship of Carol Matthau, Oona O'Neill, and Gloria Vanderbilt* by Aram Saroyan (Simon & Schuster, 1985).

p. 150 ."Oona had ... take your eyes off her": This quote comes from my interviews with Gloria Murray.

p. 150 ."He fell for her ... a writer too": *Ibid*.

p. 151. In September ... page 32": This copy of *Esquire* is in the general collection of the New York Public Library.

p. 152. The story was "Slight Rebellion"... doesn't seem to be enough: The issue of the *New Yorker* containing "Slight Rebellion Off Madison"—it's dated December 21, 1946—is in the general collection of the New York Public Library.

p. 153. As Salinger would admit ... Salinger himself had lived: This detail comes from a source who wishes not to be named.

p. 153. Salinger wanted to ... his two sisters: This paragraph is based on the Salinger–*New Yorker* letters in the Rare Books and Manuscript Division of the New York Public Library.

p. 154. Earlier in 1941 ... newly sanctioned draft *J.D. Salinger* by Warren French.

ROBERT COLES

Anna Freud and J.D. Salinger's Holden Caulfield

For many years I was lucky, indeed, to get to talk with Anna Freud, who almost single-handedly founded the discipline of child psychoanalysis. She lived in London during the last decades of her life, on Marsefield Gardens, where she saw patients who knew, many of them, that her father once lived there—as W.H. Auden put it in his memorial poem to Sigmund Freud, "an important Jew who died in exile," one more beneficiary of that capital city's cosmopolitan generosity. But she often came to "the States"—so she called the country she visited, thereby speaking as the Englishwoman she'd become. While on the American side of the Atlantic, she taught college students at Yale, medical students there, also; and of course, she worked with psychiatrists and psychoanalysts, an effort she had pursued for many years in Austria, then England.

Once, in 1975, she looked back a half a century (my tape-recorder whirling), and she recalled, really, the origins of child psychoanalysis, not to mention the consequences such a development had for parents and for teachers, for film-makers and writers: "Those were exciting days, during the first quarter of this century (and now we are headed for the last quarter!). In Vienna we began to take my father's ideas so seriously [that] we tried to apply them not only with the adults who came to see us, but with children. That was the heart of what Freud [so she sometimes called him] contributed to our thinking—he looked

From *Virginia Quarterly Review* 76, no. 2 (Spring 2000): 214–24. © 2000 by the *Virginia Quarterly Review*.

back in a [patient's] life in order to understand where it is going, and why, and in order to help change its direction. I had worked with children as a teacher, but in the 1920s I began seeing them in an office, and training or enlisting others to do so. Today the world knows of the work done by August Aicchorn with delinquents [described in *Wayward Youth*], or Erik Erikson, through his books [*Childhood and Society, Young Man Luther*] but back then we were not as (how shall I say it?) 'reputable' as we seem to have become for so many."

She went on to give an extended account of the techniques of child psychoanalysis developed in those bold, breakthrough years—and then, abruptly, unexpectedly, made mention of a book she'd recently been reading, after hearing so much of it, over and over, from her colleagues; and very important, from her students and patients, or analysands, as she often called them: "I've been told for years about this *Catcher in the Rye*, the book, the novel with that title—I think of it, of course, as a story being told: a person is ready to catch people, save them, rescue them from some trouble they've gotten themselves into. The 'catcher' is named Holden Caulfield, we all know—but I wonder whether the story doesn't tell us about the story-teller [J.D. Salinger], though I don't like it when we in psychoanalysis do this, make guesses that turn out to be wild guesses! This young man, Holden Caulfield, is so vividly brought to the attention of the reader that it's hard not to connect him with his creator—more so, for me at least, than [is the case with] other characters, in fiction.

"I got to know this Holden Caulfield by hearsay before I met him as a reader. My analytic patients spoke of him sometimes as if they'd actually met him; they used his words, his way of speaking. They laughed as if he had made them laugh, because of what he'd said, and how he looked at things. I began to realize that they had taken him into their minds, and hugged him— they spoke, now, not only his words in the book (quotations from it) but his words become their own words (deeply felt, urgently and emphatically expressed). There were moments when I had to be the perennially and predictably pedantic listener, ever anxious, to pin down what has been spoken, call it by a [psychoanalytic] name, fit it into my 'interpretative scheme,' you could call it. I would ask a young man or a young woman who it was just speaking—him, or her, or Holden! Well, I'd hear 'me,' but it didn't take long for the young one, the youth, the teenager, to have some second thoughts! They'd be silent; they'd mull the matter over—and I wasn't surprised, again and again, to hear a quite sensible person, not out of his mind, or her mind (not 'psychotic,' as we put it in staff conferences) speaking of this Holden Caulfield as though they'd spent a lot of time with him, and now had taken up, as their very own, his favorite words, his likes and dislikes, his 'attitude,' one college student, just starting out, once termed it.

"When I asked the student, a very bright one (as he expected I would) what he meant by the word, 'attitude,' I was given a lecture that took up virtually the entire [analytic] hour, to the point that I was reprimanding myself afterwards for giving the young fellow all he needed to avoid [discussing] the important reasons he'd come to see me! But then, I smiled to myself—I realized that what I'd learned about Holden, *his* 'attitude,' was what this young man wanted to understand about himself. why he was so 'skeptical' (his chosen word), why he didn't give people the benefit of the doubt, why he kept to himself, because he was inclined to 'look for trouble' when he met people, was with them (his room-mates, those sitting near him in the cafeteria or in a lecture hall or seminar room). I asked him, naturally, what 'trouble' he was expecting; and he hesitated for a long time, and told me he couldn't easily 'come up with any,' not to mention do so then and there on my analytic couch! He knew I'd press for examples—and then a plaintive excuse: he wanted to swear, as Holden would, but he was worried that I'd be offended, so his tongue was tied!"

In fact, sitting there with Miss Freud, I knew well what Holden had prompted that young man to want to say, to think about, remember, as he spoke his mind, gave his comments, or his "free associations," as they came to him: all the "crap" in this life, all the "goddamn" acts we observe, the statements we hear. (Now I'm using quotation marks to distance myself from those words, even as I didn't choose to mention them in front of the august, illustrious older woman with whom I was talking, and even as she was not about to get specific, speak those words as belonging to a patient, to his favorite novelist.) A moment of awkward silence—whereupon, Miss Freud, true to form, hastened to remind both of us that "there is something to be learned from this book and what it says to those who bring it into their mental life." I am quick to nod, but not all that taken with the phrase "mental life." What I feel like saying is that Salinger's slurs and swear words are not original, but are shocking, because worked so vigorously, adroitly into his lively, arresting, thoroughly enticing, embracing narration—his constant interest in addressing his reader as a "you," and his constant desire, as well, to invoke a moral (yes!) "attitude," to provoke thereby our complacent, maybe to some extent compromised, sense of who we are, what we have done (or left undone).

There is a lot of "crap" in this "phony" world, a "goddamn" lot, so I wanted to say, linking arms thereby with Holden, and with any number of young analysands seen in this century by the likes of Miss Freud, and me and my shrink-buddies, so I hear my thoughts aver, their mode of expression deteriorating and becoming unavailable to my vocal chords. As if she saw my lips shut tight, and figured out the give-away reason, Miss Freud observed

tersely: "Holden Caulfield says what is forbidden us to say." I both agree
enthusiastically (another obliging nod) and feel uneasy—well, more irritated
than I want to reveal with words or bodily gestures. But I do hear myself
thinking, "What the hell!"—and then I try to speak by making a critic's
summary: "Salinger has Holden cut through a lot of cant—the 'phoniness' he
spots all the time." I'm being heard, but myself hear nothing. I see those eyes
concentrating on mine, the face that holds them as impassive as ever, the
figure so imposing. I hear my voice treasuring, nourishing that word
"phoniness"—as if I had myself become Holden. I want to run down the field
with that word, as he did, raise that voice of mine, refer to all the "phonies"
in the world, escalate to the "frauds"; but I feel my hands holding the arms
of the chair that is holding me, and quickly my reflexes deliver the goods: in
a carefully modulated voice I comment on a novelist's distinctive capability,
his repeated intention—"he cuts through a lot of cant, Salinger does." Then,
as if there is any doubt, I summon a story's protagonist as the important
moral witness: "Holden has a sharp eye for the hypocrisy and duplicity of
everyday life."

Now I am gulping, feeling nervous. Those two tell-tale words,
"everyday life," which in Miss Freud's mind, in mine, in just about anyone's
who has read Sigmund Freud's writing, have a familiar ring—I'm tempted to
summon them as a part of a derivative five-word aside: "the Phoniness of
Everyday Life." In my mind I had played with a celebrated book's title, come
up with a precis of sorts for a celebrated novel—Freud and Salinger's Holden
become joined as the observers of their fellow human beings.

Miss Freud moves us on, moves by my tongue-tied restiveness and her
own struggles with Salinger's created youth, whom she now wants to
approach in an appreciative manner, responsive strictly on her terms: "I think
this Holden Caulfield is very much with us, because he is very much—well,
he is the one who wrote of him." She is evidently aware that she has made in
that sentence a rather sweeping interpretation—her pause in the middle of
the assertion signaled as much, the "well" a cautionary indication that she
was going to take a leap. Then, inevitably for a psychoanalyst who had
distinguished herself by her reluctance to be yet another reductionist
interpreter, ever prepared (gladly, triumphantly) to explain away people and
events through recourse to psychological paradigms, theories, the time had
come for a proper acknowledgment of uncertainty's prevalent importance:
"We can never know where a writer's life has been set aside, in the pursuit of
a talent's expression."

I am moved, impressed—well (to use a word) brought up short by that
renunciation, so poignantly declared (with a characteristic mix of simplicity,
formality, and with a penetrating idiosyncrasy of affirmation). So much for

all too many explanatory or interpretive essays wrought by literary critics, biographers, psychoanalysts—the constant need to explain, unravel, account for, get to a definitive bottom of a life, a work of art. In a few seconds (almost as if she is attending her own remarks, being given pleased pause, even wonder-filled pause by them) Miss Freud tactfully moves away from the person of Salinger, from his achievement as a novelist, to the safer and surer ground of her own working experience, and out of it, her memory's sharply instructive lessons: "I've had young analysands speak to me [in her office] as if they were Holden Caulfield, and I needed badly to pay attention to them, to him through them! 'Alright,' I say to them, 'tell me what Holden wants me to know!' It's come to that, actually, a few times; I've joined with them indirectly or implicitly, in turning Holden into a real-life person—as if *The Catcher in the Rye* is a work of biography, rather than fiction. Not that fiction doesn't get us as close to the truth as biography! My father once told me when I was teaching literature [as a young woman in Vienna] that novels are the fantasies of talented people; and he did not mean to show a lack of admiration or respect with those words—quite the contrary." Now a notable silence; the speaker lowers her head ever so slightly, if significantly—as if to pay proper respect to a most talented person whose remarks about "talented people" had just been put on the record. We try to affirm our high regard for Freud by continuing to take the novel we've been discussing seriously, with no lapse into a dismissive discussion of psychopathology. "All of us have our extended spells of fantasy," Miss Freud observes, as if we'd best keep in mind a context, of sorts, for both Holden and his creator. I fear I then slipped, pointed out how often the word "depressed" got used when Holden felt the need to characterize his state of mind. I tell Miss Freud (as if to disown any inclination on my part to call Holden "sick," an all too obvious reflexive posture for me and my kind) about the critics who have not only noted Holden's way of describing himself, but counted the number of times he uses the word "depressed," more than a dozen instances. Her response was lengthy and animated: "Of course this man was 'depressed' at times and said so to himself—though I bet if anyone had called him that, spoke the very words he'd used in his thinking about himself at certain moments, then we'd hear quite something else: an angry refutation, or a surly dismissal conveyed in an angry facial grimace! As I read the novel, I stopped a few times when I came to the word 'depressed,' and I had to think that here was another adolescent who reserved the right to call himself what he wanted—but wouldn't tolerate you or me taking such a liberty, or a critic who was observing him!"

With that remark, Miss Freud showed a second's grimace on her own face, as if she was thinking back through years of difficult, demanding clinical work—so I thought as I wondered what she would say next, and wondered, too, what I might add to her words, which had, actually, in their sum, given me considerably more to consider than I'd guessed would be the case when they first began to be given voice by the one who wanted me to hear them. Suddenly, a sigh, and then a speaker's stiffened resolve: "We have to be sympathetic to our Holdens, but I'm not sure they want that from us—I mean, they are suspicious of just about every adult they know (starting with their parents, of course, and then their teachers!) and so they're ready for all grownups who come their way, certainly including us, whose offices they enter with several chips on their shoulders! I recall a young lad I saw (he had just turned fourteen) and every exchange we had was—oh, I felt we were both working ourselves through a mine-field: he was always prepared to be *doubtful*, even *scornful*, and certainly, *mistrustful*. I wrote those three words down for myself—they echoed through my mind as we tried to converse, session after session, and I tried to understand what was causing his quite evident (and loudly declared) annoyance with people he met at school. I thought of him (of those words!) as I read of Holden—read his remarks about himself and his schoolmates and teachers. Finally, after one especially tense discussion with that lad, I let go of myself, I think it fair to say: I guess I gave him a piece of my mind! I said that I believe we hurt ourselves, bring ourselves down, when we strike out at others all the time, dismiss them with our sharp words or not very friendly judgments, that go unexpressed, but give shape to our looks of contempt, disdain. (By the way, I'm not sure Holden would ever have let anyone speak that way to him!)

"In any event, I kept asking myself this question: why did that lad keep returning to me in my thoughts when I met Holden Caulfield, courtesy of Mr. Salinger? In time I reminded myself (I realized!) that Holden has been very much in the thoughts of many of the adolescents I've seen [in analysis]—he's known in England as well as here [the United States] and when he comes up [in psychoanalytic sessions] I have thought to myself yes, I know this Holden Caulfield very well, indeed; he's everyone's adolescent boy (or young man); he's trying to figure out what's important, who's important (to him!) and why; he's also trying to figure out himself, and learn what causes his moodiness, and his loneliness—a big order for anyone, even those of us who haven't been adolescents for a few decades!"

She stops there to smile wryly—a side of her I always appreciated, very much admired: her singular willingness to align herself with her patients, narrow the psychological distance between herself and them, avoid the emotional and moral smugness that all too commonly threatens, even envelops, some of us who observe others, try to engage with them in an office at home, or under the sponsorship of a clinic. Amid a few seconds of silence,

I dare pose questions about Holden Caulfield, about Miss Freud's patients, about my own, and not least, about my students who, again and again, in courses and classrooms, have made mention of that "lad," as I'd just heard him quaintly called. I want to know, especially, the reason for Holden's appeal to so many different youths; but I also want to talk about some students of mine who are inattentive to him, find him uninteresting—or as I've heard him described, "a big bore," or a "pain in the neck."

Now Anna Freud noticeably perks up—and has me struck hard, stunned, by a certain forceful intensity of dislike, some of it couched, if I may use that word, in psychoanalytic speculation, theory: "I'm always being asked what I think about Holden Caulfield, once I admit I've read the book that tells of him—after being told of him by the young patient who has just asked me! I don't dare say that he's a bit bossy and impudent and brash—that he's smitten with himself, a victim of abundant narcissism, some of it out of control, driving him to be self-indulgent, to attribute that [kind of behavior] to others, rather than see it squarely in himself. It is as if, for some young people, for a time, that character in that novel has been a talisman—he signified some elusive truth about what life means, and if you keep talking about him, you'll heal your mind, settle your mind, with his help, because he's been there, where you are, presently: the voice of experience who therefore is a wise advisor. So, the point is to overlook in him what you don't want to acknowledge about yourself—a privileged vanity constantly at work. Remember, he's seeing a psychoanalyst, in a sanitarium, and he calls himself 'sick,' at the end of the book (as I had to notice and haven't forgotten!) when he is looking ahead, but still unsure where he's going and for what reason. Of course he'll elicit the interest of his young readers, who have flocked to him—often at the behest of their teachers, who spend so much of their time working with young people beset by worries and confusions, and I should add, plenty of anger and bitterness: life's disappointments that come their way, for all the means their parents possess. The more I hear about Holden, the more I think of those who have enjoyed his company—and that is where I must let the matter rest: that he and his fans belong to the same club!"

With that comment a natural break in her flow of speech, spoken with a good deal of energy, if not emotion. I wait a few seconds, wonder what to say, but want her to continue. Her use of the word "club" is intriguing, for sure. Finally, I make bold to ask her about that word—get up the courage to use it for my own purposes: "Can anyone join that club?"

I've tried to be suggestive, provocative—stress the theme of exclusivity implicit in that way of putting things. Miss Freud quickly turns the discussion over to me: "What do *you* think—I'm not sure I know; I was only thinking of the closeness some young people I've known feel toward this fictional hero of theirs, who lives, at least for a while, in their imagination."

I let my mind have its say by addressing a memory: "I used *Catcher in the Rye* in teaching with high schoolers, down South, before I worked it into college courses up North. My wife, Jane, was a high school teacher, and we both asked a group of high school students, white and black, to read that book in Atlanta, Georgia. Soon we were sorting out the enthusiasm and interest of some, the indifference and outright annoyance of others—to the point that we were, each of us, surprised and puzzled. A black youth, memorably, told us: 'This guy [Holden], he be sweet on himself, all the time, and he be sour on everyone else.' Jane asked for more, and received a tart, pointed amplification: 'He be full of himself, he drinks up everything he sees and he hears, and makes it all his property—like our minister will say, it's grist for the mill he's got going, this Holden.'"

To that, Anna Freud nodded vigorously, smiled quite appreciatively. She responded initially with her own muted reservations about Holden, then more of her frank disapproval—to the point that I felt that I was yet again being offered a teacher's, a moralist's reprimand: "I believe the issue is not so much Holden's anger and melancholy [I had been using those two words] but I repeat, the narcissism—that's the key: what in our profession we'd call a 'narcissistic personality disorder.' He's quick to turn on others, and he gives no one the benefit of the doubt, and he's always bringing everything back to himself ('self-referential' as we'd say in a clinical conference). I hesitate to overdraw the case, but there is a certain self-assurance in this young man that slips over—becomes arrogance. One young man I was seeing [in analysis] told me his friends called him 'cocky' all the time, and then he went on to associate himself with Holden Caulfield, whose name was a commonplace of my work for a while but as you point out, there are many young people who haven't heard of him, and if he were brought to their attention they'd yawn, or look for someone else to consider interesting!"

We were getting near matters of class, of race, as they give shape to our likes and dislikes: Holden Caulfield and his Pencey Prep School, its fancy white world, readily embraced by certain of Miss Freud's patients, by a few of mine, or by my students, some of them—one or two well-to-do African-Americans, by the way: class within race. In a sense, *The Catcher in the Rye* was a prefiguration of our contemporary psychoanalytic discussion of narcissism (as Anna Freud years ago anticipated) and of the historian Christopher Lasch's book, *The Culture of Narcissism*, which summoned theoretical ideas Sigmund Freud had in mind as he attempted to understand how individuals get on with others, summoning what anticipations or apprehensions, and why. Miss Freud, in her own way, had regarded Holden as an aspect of J.D. Salinger's thinking, if not his preoccupations. She stressed several times the "significance of brotherhood" in *Catcher*, as she once or twice chose to abbreviate the novel's title, for the sake of speaking for casual convenience—though she was never altogether at a remove from interpretive reflection both serious and formal: Holden is (or is to be) a catcher; he is Caulfield—or as she put it, "calling others in the field of his life, aiming to hold them." Immediately, with some charming shyness, even nervousness, she pulled back, apologized for her "critical excess" (would that the rest of us who teach and write be given to such second thoughts, I once more caught myself thinking—the embarrassment of one's boastfulness!). Still, like Holden and like his creator and like those who are entranced by them (and by their own possibilities as they get affirmed, asserted in life) Anna Freud hopes to find coherence, give it words that "catch" the attention of others, "hold" them decisively, whatever field they "call" their own, whatever product (whether "rye" or wryness as a point of view) being grown there: "Holden and his brothers and their sister Phoebe, with their 'discontents,' as my father put it—they all seek and welcome our attention, our membership. I think Mr. Salinger had them in mind for us before he planned his famous novel—they catch us, as he was caught by the idea, the story!" Years later, after Miss Freud's death, I would stumble on a short story J.D. Salinger wrote in the middle of the Second World War, long before his first novel was published—a story that he has never allowed to appear in a book's collection of his fiction. "The Last Day of the Last Furlough" saw the light of day in *The Saturday Evening Post*, way before (July 15, 1944) its author began his writing career at *The New Yorker*. One Vincent Caulfield, a corporal, is soon to go off and fight in battle—and tells this to a sergeant friend: "No good, Sergeant. My brother Holden is missing. The letter came while I was at home." A few lines on, we learn this about Holden from his brother: "I used to bump into him at the old Joe College Club on Eighteenth and Third in New York. A beer joint for college lids and prep school kids. I'd go there just looking for him, Christmas and Easter vacations when he was home. I'd drag my date through the joint, looking for him, and I'd find him way in the back. The noisiest, tightest kid in the place...."

Thus it was for Holden early in his literary career: exclaiming loud and clear his objections, sprinkling them, no doubt, with words such as "goddamn" and "crap," putting the "drag" on us readers, with the result that we become like the "date" his brother Vincent had in the story—fellow seekers eager to spot "phonies," their "phoniness," and so doing, inch ourselves away a bit from this life's seemingly ever-present, sometimes shady ambiguities.

CARL FREEDMAN

Memories of Holden Caulfield— and of Miss Greenwood

Two years ago, the fiftieth anniversary of J.D. Salinger's *The Catcher in the Rye* took place. The book is almost exactly the same age I am. To be precise, it's about three months younger: I appeared in April 1951, the novel—after a much longer gestation period—in July. Inevitably, a good many essays about it have recently been published, and, though they indicate little consensus about the exact meaning or value of the novel, they do generally agree that it is still, in some sense, an extraordinary text. At the height of Salinger's reputation—the 1950s and 1960s—his was in many ways the dominant voice in contemporary American fiction, despite his slender output, and it was not unusual for him to be discussed in tones that suggested a genius almost on the order of Shakespeare's or Tolstoy's to be at stake. His stature has long since assumed much more modest proportions. Few, I suppose, would maintain now that *The Catcher in the Rye* belongs in the absolute first rank of the modern novel: on a level, that is, with Conrad's *Nostromo* (1904) or Lawrence's *Women in Love* (1920) or Joyce's *Ulysses* (1922) or Faulkner's *Absalom, Absalom!* (1936) or Pynchon's *Gravity's Rainbow* (1973). Yet if it is, in this strict sense, a work of the second rank, it is also a novel that possesses a remarkable hold on its readers, or at least on a good many of them. There are more than a few of us for whom *The Catcher in the Rye* still feels less like a canonical book than like a personal experience, and one of the

From *Southern Review* 39, no. 2 (2003 Spring): 401–17. © 2003 by Louisiana State University.

most powerful of our lives. Though I earn a living chiefly by producing
materialist criticism of literary texts (on the page and in the classroom), I
think of this text mainly as a part—a phase, really—of my personal history,
and of its protagonist as someone I know, or once knew: attitudes that do not
necessarily exclude a properly critical approach but that by no means
inevitably make for one either. Accordingly, though what follows will
certainly have its critical moments, it is at least as much a memoir as a critical
essay, a memoir of the Holden Caulfield I knew and of an earlier self, both
of whom are now long in the past but also still with me.

But this must also be a memoir of Miss Greenwood. No, I do not mean
Sylvia Plath's Esther Greenwood, protagonist of *The Bell Jar* (1963) and the
most memorable, perhaps, of all the many fictional characters conceived
under the direct influence of Holden Caulfield. The real Miss Greenwood
was my eighth-grade English teacher and my first teacher who was also, in
some important way, a friend. Not that I had gotten along badly with my
earlier teachers—quite the contrary. But before Miss Greenwood a teacher
was no more to be counted as a friend than was a parent, a doctor, or a rabbi.
Teachers were all just adults, authority figures, and one took it for granted
that they inhabited a world different from one's own. Miss Greenwood,
somehow, was different. Doubtless this was at least partly because she was
quite young herself, no more than a year or so out of college. It is a somewhat
staggering thought that, during the time I am remembering, she was thus
only slightly older than the seniors I teach today, and younger than nearly all
of my graduate students. It is even more staggering to think that, if she and
I were to meet today, we would be, for most practical purposes, about the
same age. In the eighth grade, of course, the gulf was much wider—and yet
bridgeable in a way that the age gulf between an adult and me had never
quite been before.

I still have before me a fairly clear mental image of Miss Greenwood.
She was thin, of about average height, with brown hair cut relatively short
and a pleasant, freckled face. Her looks were not those of a bombshell or
head-turner, but I expect that a fair number of men would have found her—
I expect that a fair number of men *did* find her—attractive, and increasingly
attractive as they got to know her better. But you would probably have had
to be in love with her to call her beautiful. I was in love with her, though it
is a love that I recognized as such only many years later. I am pretty sure that,
at the time, I never consciously thought of Miss Greenwood in a romantic or
even a sexual way, and in retrospect that seems a curious omission. After all,
I was a horny, virginal fourteen-year-old boy, and I was preoccupied with sex
in that intense, yearning way typical of my age and gender; but, as far as I can
recall, the guest stars in my lustful fantasies tended to be either female

classmates my own age or else generically "good-looking" women whose images were based on models and movie stars. Why not Miss Greenwood? She was pretty enough for the role. Perhaps I just respected her too much. Perhaps it was just that, in those more innocent days, the idea of "doing anything" with Miss Greenwood was literally beyond (conscious) comprehension.

In retrospect, however, it seems clear that nothing short of sexual love could have driven me to do what I frequently did during the eighth grade: namely, to *stay* in the school building after the final bell had rung, to use some of those precious hours of freedom between the end of school and dinner at home to talk with a teacher whose class I had been required to attend earlier in the day. Miss Greenwood was often in her classroom for a while after classes had ended, doing various chores—cleaning blackboards, arranging papers, and the like—and I got in the habit of dropping by. I would help her to the extent I could, and we would chat about various things. Some of these talks were brief—no more than ten or fifteen ales—but others went on for an hour or even more. My house was within walking distance of the school, but sometimes, especially after one of our longer chats, Miss Greenwood would give me a lift home in the used, battered Volkswagen bug that she had recently purchased and about whose mechanical soundness she was, as I remember, a bit nervous. She took some consolation in the relatively low number on the odometer, and was mildly alarmed when I told her that odometer readings could be faked. Our relations were by no means completely informal. It was always clear that we were teacher and pupil, and certainly I never called her anything except "Miss Greenwood" (with the result that today I am not sure of her first name, though I once knew it well— Mary, perhaps?). But we were definitely friends.

Our conversations were mainly about two of our strongest common interests, politics and literature, which, as it happens, are the two main fields about which I write professionally today. We probably talked more about politics than about literature. The school year was 1964–65, and we shared happiness and relief that, in the presidential election, Lyndon Johnson defeated Barry Goldwater so resoundingly, though Miss Greenwood, I believe, was somewhat discreet about her political preferences (doubtless a prudent habit for any schoolteacher, but especially wise since the school principal was widely thought to be a rather unbalanced right-winger). I think the first political bet that I ever made—and won—in my life was with Miss Greenwood. In January 1965, Hubert Humphrey was inaugurated as vice-president and so had to give up his seat in the Senate, where he had been the Democratic whip. Several senators competed to succeed him, with the frontrunners generally agreed to be John Pastore of Rhode Island and

Russell Long of Louisiana. Miss Greenwood liked Pasture's chances—a choice she shared with most journalistic pundits and by no means a stupid one, for Pasture's political profile resembled Humphrey's own, and his northeastern liberalism seemed in tune with the (very brief) moment of triumph that American liberalism was then enjoying. But I already knew a fair bit about how the Senate worked, and I reckoned that the southerners— still the dominant force in that body, despite the huge defeat they had recently suffered when the Civil Rights Act of 1964 was passed—would prove strong enough to win the post for one of their own. As indeed they did.

Long's victory brought him a position for which he never displayed much aptitude and which he lost to Edward Kennedy four years later. But it brought me the copy that I still possess of Salinger's fourth (and, as things now seem to have turned out, last) book, the one that collected the long stories, "Raise High the Roof Beam, Carpenters" and "Seymour—An Introduction." The volume was already out in hardcover, and Miss Greenwood and I agreed that the loser of the bet would buy the winner a copy of the paperback as soon as it appeared. It was a logical choice, for there was nothing we shared more intensely than our common admiration for Salinger. I think that I vaguely knew who Salinger was even before meeting Miss Greenwood—I browsed through the current paperbacks frequently, and those Salinger paperbacks, with their covers nearly blank save for title and author, were hard to miss—but I had never read his work until Miss Greenwood recommended *The Catcher in the Rye* to me. I didn't realize at the time how typical an enthusiasm for Salinger was among intelligent college students of her generation, nor did it occur to me that, in urging me to read *The Catcher in the Rye*, Miss Greenwood was running something of a risk. Salinger's novel was one of three strictly banned throughout our public school system (Aldous Huxley's *Brave New World* [1932] and George Orwell's *Nineteen Eighty-four* [1949] were the others); and, though recommending it to a single student in an after-school chat was not, presumably, a transgression on the order of assigning it to a whole class, I'm sure she could have gotten into some trouble if, for instance, my parents had been the sort to make a fuss. Looking back, I suspect that, out of college and living on her own in a new city, Miss Greenwood was missing companions with whom she could discuss her favorite writer, and so she took a chance on me.

Her recommendation was about as successful as a recommendation can be. The book just knocked me out, as Holden himself would say. Today it seems clear to me that, technically, the main source of the novel's overwhelming power is its almost unparalleled mastery of voice. Except for *Huckleberry Finn* (1884)—often enough proposed as the chief precursor text of *The Catcher in the Rye*—there is not a novel in American literature, perhaps not a novel in the world, that more convincingly invents and sustains a young colloquial voice, page after page after page, with virtually not a single false note, and while managing to avoid both sentimentality and condescension on the part of the unseen author. If it is difficult to believe that Holden Caulfield is "just" a literary fabrication, it's because the reader seems to hear an entirely real human being talking to him or her for more than two hundred pages without interruption. But at the age of fourteen, of course, I was less struck by Salinger's technique than by the reality that his technique appeared to convey. Simply put, Holden seemed absolutely right to me—in some ways the rightest human being I had ever encountered. His world was basically similar to my own—never mind the differences between an upper-class northeasterner in the late 1940s and a middle-class southerner in the mid-1960s—and, at two or three years older than me, he was just young enough to be a peer and just enough older to seem automatically savvier and more worldly wise. Again and again Holden hit off exactly what a morass of mendacity the world had prepared for children in the process of leaving childhood behind; again and again he articulated, with painful but exuberant and wonderful accuracy, the essential inauthenticity of bourgeois American society that I myself was just beginning to be able to name.

Take Holden's roommate Stradlater, for instance: crude, obtuse, brash, outgoing, handsome, athletic, and, Holden believes, one of the few boys at Pencey Prep who actually succeeds in "giving the time" to the girls that he dates. I knew the type, and I resented the all-but-universal envy and admiration that the type attracted from his fellows. Who but Holden would have had the clear-sightedness and courage to dismiss him simply as "a stupid bastard"? And who, really knowing the type, could deny that Holden was exactly right? Or take Mr. Spencer, the history teacher who pompously and uselessly lectures Holden about his future: "Life *is* a game, boy. Life *is* a game that one plays according to the rules." I heard this sort of thing all the time, and Holden knew exactly what it was worth: "Game, my ass. Some game. If you get on the side where all the hot-shots are, then it's a game, all right—I'll admit that. But if you get on the *other* side, where there aren't any hot-shots, then what's a game about it? Nothing. No game."

Or take "this guy Ossenburger," the wealthy mortician and Pencey alumnus after whom Holden's dorm is named:

> The first football game of the year, he came up to school in this big goddam Cadillac, and we all had to stand up in the grandstand and give him a locomotive—that's a cheer. Then, the next morning, in chapel, he made a speech that lasted about ten hours. He started off with about fifty corny jokes, just to show us what a regular guy

he was. Very big deal. Then he started telling us how he was never ashamed, when he was in some kind of trouble or something, to get right down on his knees and pray to God. He told us we should always pray to God—talk to Him and all—wherever we were. He told us we ought to think of Jesus as our buddy and all. He said *he* talked to Jesus all the time. Even when he was driving his car. That killed me. I can just see the big phony bastard shifting into first gear and asking Jesus to send him a few more stiffs.

Though at the age of fourteen I had never even set eyes on a school precisely similar to Pencey, this passage seemed to sum up practically every school assembly I had ever been forced to attend; and future assemblies were made a little more bearable for knowing that at least one other person saw them for exactly what they were.

Sometimes it seemed to me that there was almost no variety of phony that Holden had not managed to spot and expose, from the insufferably pretentious pseudo-intellectual Carl Luce, an old schoolmate with whom he has an extended conversation in a bar, to the young naval officer ("His name was Commander Blop or something") he meets briefly in Ernie's nightclub: "He was one of those guys that think they're being a pansy if they don't break around forty of your fingers when they shake hands with you. God, I hate that stuff." Though most of Holden's insights are delivered in this ad hoc manner, there are a few more synoptic passages. Perhaps the best is the summary of Pencey he offers to Sally Hayes, herself an excruciating phony—the sort who appears much more intelligent than she is because she knows "quite a lot about the theater and plays and literature and all that stuff" and whom Holden finds harder to shake than most phonies because she is physically very attractive and usually willing to make out with him.

> "You ought to go to a boys' school sometime. Try it sometime," I said. "It's full of phonies, and all you do is study so that you can learn enough to be smart enough to be able to buy a goddam Cadillac some day, and you have to keep making believe you give a damn if the football team loses, and all you do is talk about girls and liquor and sex all day, and everybody sticks together in these dirty little goddam cliques. The guys that are on the basketball team stick together, the Catholics stick together, the goddam intellectuals stick together, the guys that play bridge stick together. Even the guys that belong to the goddam Book-of-the-*Month* Club stick together. If you try to have a little intelligent—"

Sally is technically correct, as Holden himself agrees, when she interrupts him to object, "Lots of boys get more out of school than *that*." But no matter—Holden has Pencey, and the world, dead to rights.

Holden's wisdom seemed all the more impressive to me because there is no trace of superiority about it. He is never the detached, self-sufficient bystander, coolly and ironically observing life from its foyer; instead, he is passionate and disappointed, always newly indignant at every fresh instance of phoniness that life offers. It is also true that he is therefore extremely unhappy—an aspect of the book that I rather glossed over in my first few readings. I was able to see that Holden almost never seems to be having a good time, but I was not particularly unhappy myself—allowing for the fact that hardly any fourteen-year-old can be unambiguously called happy—and I hesitated to attribute to such a powerfully kindred spirit the extreme degree of psychic misery that now seems to me one of the principal features of Holden's character. Or to put it another way: The almost unerring acuteness of Holden's insights, and the superb colloquial vigor with which he could express them, seemed to make for a kind of intellectual high spirits that I could not, at the age of fourteen, easily reconcile with underlying pain. To see phonies so clearly could not exactly be a recipe for happiness in a world where phonies were so numerous, but surely, I felt, truth itself had its own consolations.

Not everyone has felt such a deep affinity with Holden as I did. Some readers—most prominently Mary McCarthy—believe that Holden is too harsh in his judgments of others, that he is too much the pitiless phony-spotter. "I was surrounded by jerks," says Holden of his fellow patrons at Ernie's, and for some this sentence sums up almost the entirety of Holden's world view. Miss Greenwood to some extent held this opinion. Indeed, one of the things that slightly divided us in our shared passion far Salinger was that for me, then as now, Salinger was first and foremost the author of the *Catcher in the Rye*; whereas Miss Greenwood preferred his stories about the Glass family. Looking back, I suspect that this difference of opinion was largely a tendered one. Holden's outlook is intensely masculine (though never macho), and I suppose that from the other side of the gender divide it might well often seem suffocatingly masculine. But this point never occurred to me at the time, and I doubt it did to Miss Greenwood either. The problem with Holden, she once said to me, is just that you get the idea he probably wouldn't like you very much—whereas Buddy Glass, Holden's successor as Salinger's principal narrator and alter ego, was Miss Greenwood's idea of a very nice guy indeed.

I now think that Holden's supposed pitilessness in judging others has been greatly exaggerated. It has become conventional to say that he likes nobody except his three siblings; and, since one of them, his younger brother Allie, is dead, and since another, his older brother D.B., seems, as an evidently successful Hollywood screenwriter, to be in danger of becoming a bit of a phony himself, only his kid sister Phoebe ("himself in miniature or in glory," as McCarthy insisted) would be left as an unambiguously Good Person, a certified nonphony, in the land of the living. But in fact Holden likes quite a lot of people: people of both sexes and of various ages, and chance acquaintances as well as old friends. He immensely likes Jane Gallagher, sort of his girlfriend but not exactly, who always kept her kings in the back row whenever they played checkers. He equally likes his old English teacher Mr. Antolini, even though he is understandably disconcerted when Mr. Antolini makes what appears to be a homosexual pass at him. He likes the nuns he meets in a sandwich bar, and he likes Mrs. Morrow, the mother of a classmate, whom he meets on a train. He even likes Selma Thurmer, the daughter of the headmaster at Pencey, despite her big nose and her falsies and her fingernails bitten bloody. He likes children in general, and so tries to rub out dirty words scrawled where children might see them; and, of course, he fantasizes about being the catcher in the rye, spending every day keeping children safely in the field of rye and away from the cliff's edge. He likes the ducks in the Central Park lagoon, and worries about what happens to them when the pond freezes solid in winter. Furthermore, Holden (unlike the Hemingway heroes with whom McCarthy so unjustly compares him) usually manages a good deal of concrete human sympathy even for those whom he cannot bring himself to like: his obnoxious, pimple-squeezing schoolmate Ackley, for instance, and Sunny, the prostitute who cheats him out of five dollars. His encounter with the latter makes for one of the book's most memorable scenes. At the end of a very long, very lonely, and frequently horny evening, Holden accepts a pimp's offer to send a whore to his hotel room. But when Sunny (who is "[n]o old bag," just as the pimp Maurice promises) actually arrives, Holden is so overcome with sadness at the thought of her life that his enthusiasm for losing his virginity evaporates into thin air and he offers to pay Sunny full price for just a few minutes of conversation.

In the eighth grade it did not occur to me to point out this deeply sensitive and compassionate side of Holden's character in reply to Miss Greenwood's criticism of him as too astringently judgmental. Nonetheless, her (perhaps not wholly intentional but clear enough) implication—that Holden might not like *me*—bothered me very little. It was not so much that I disagreed with her suggestion as that it somehow seemed beside the point. Maybe Holden wouldn't necessarily like me, but so what? Holden was me. And indeed, Holden by no means expresses invariable liking for himself throughout the long monologue that constitutes the novel. Though most readers have, I think, failed to notice the fact, he frequently confesses to acts of phoniness on his own part. Precept, as Samuel Johnson said, may be very sincere even when practice is very imperfect, and the fact that Holden—as sturdy a moralist, in his own way, as Dr. Johnson—is capable of self-criticism, that he can recognize his own involvement in the whole system of phoniness from which he recoils so bitterly, only made (and makes) him all the more admirable and all the more right in my eyes.

Whatever Holden might have thought of me, though, Miss Greenwood had an explanation for why I liked Holden and *The Catcher in the Rye* so much more than her own favorite, Buddy Glass, and the stories centered on his family. She once commented that people closer to her own age—people in their late teens, I believe she meant—often liked *The Catcher in the Rye* because people that age often felt rebellious toward society (this conversation took place, remember, just as the 1960s was coming into focus as a political and cultural era). She suggested that I myself was feeling that kind of rebelliousness, at an earlier age than was typical. At the time, I recall, I felt slightly uncertain as to exactly what Miss Greenwood's attitude toward my supposed rebelliousness was, though I took her remark as basically flattering, if only for the precocity it implied. Today, especially in view of the fact that I did not, at that point overtly fit the usual profile of the school rebel—I had never, by the eighth grade, detonated firecrackers in the school bathroom, or brought a subversive petition to class, or smoked marijuana, or even grown my hair long—hers must surely be counted as a pretty shrewd, prescient judgment of a fourteen-year-old boy who grew up to become a Marxist literary critic.

But it must also be pointed out that Holden himself is not really a rebel. True enough, his acute penetration into the life of his society could in principle supply the basis for rebellion, but Holden is never able to take the step from diagnosis to action, or even to serious planning. The only action he ever even contemplates is a strategy not of rebellion but of withdrawal: He imagines leaving civilization (like Huck Finn at the end of Mark Twain's novel, though in Holden's America the frontier has been long closed) and living somewhere out west in a cabin on the edge of the woods, pretending to be a deaf mute in order to avoid conversations with phonies. Even this is pure fantasizing, as Holden at heart always knows. Not only is Holden not a rebel, but (like Hamlet, who is in many ways almost as much Holden's predecessor as Huck is) he even has great difficulty acting meaningfully in *any* way. Etymologically, the opposite of an actor is a patient—someone who is acted upon—and it is no accident that a patient is precisely what Holden is during the time present of the novel. It is also significant that, though everyone knows that Holden tells his story from some sort of medical institution ("this crumby place," as he calls it), there has been considerable disagreement among readers as to exactly what sort of hospital it is and why Holden is there. Is it because he is threatened by tuberculosis and needs a long rest in a sanatorium? Or because he has suffered some sort of mental collapse and requires psychiatric help? The source of the confusion is that Salinger definitely allows both explanations. Holden is a mess, physically and psychologically.

Holden, then, might be seen as basically pathetic, someone who, despite all his advantages (intelligence, eloquence, evident good looks, family money), is essentially incapable of coping with life—hence his removal not to an isolated Thoreauvian cabin where he can practice Emersonian self-reliance, but to an expensive private hospital where a professionally trained staff is on call twenty-four hours a day to tend to his physical and emotional weaknesses. This was not, needless to say, an interpretation that occurred to me during my first reading of the novel, or my second, or even my third. But by about the fourth reading—undertaken when I was eighteen or nineteen, and so about as much older than Holden as I had been younger when in Miss Greenwood's class—I did begin to see Holden less as a hero or a kindred spirit than as a pathetic weakling. I remember some feeling of loss when I began to view him in this way, but on the whole I welcomed my changed perception: It seemed to me a more adult perception, and I considered the fact that I could now look down on Holden to be a sign of my own increasing maturity. One of the advantages of middle age, however, is that it often allows us to see how much more wisdom there usually is in even the most callow idealism of adolescence than in the superior "knowingness" of young adulthood. Yes, Holden is defeated by life, at least temporarily, and we don't know what path he will take "after" the end of the novel. He might begin to act on the insight that Mr. Antolini (quoting the psychoanalyst Wilhelm Stekel) tries to convey to him—"The mark of the immature man is that he wants to die nobly for a cause, while the mark of the mature man is that he wants to live humbly for one"—though it is also conceivable that he will gradually abandon his revulsion from phoniness and learn to "adjust" better to the latter. The incontestable point is that Holden's defeat is an honorable one, and honorable defeats are in the scheme of things more valuable than most victories. I think that I was right, at the age of fourteen, to gloss over the pain and weakness in Holden's character, for at that stage of life I probably couldn't have taken the full pressure of those things and still properly appreciated just how right Holden is.

Proust suggests somewhere that the "first edition" of a book ought to mean the edition in which one first happened to read it, and it may seem that

I am now advocating a somewhat similar privileging of the first reading, at least insofar as my own first reading of *The Catcher in the Rye* is concerned. Though I do indeed maintain the essential validity of my original pro-Holden and indeed "Holdencentric" interpretation (it is noteworthy that Holden dominates his text as relatively few great characters other than Hamlet and Huck Finn have done), I am not actually proposing an emulation of Peter Pan. Growing up can have its virtues. When I first read the book, I gave little thought to the historical contexts of Holden's character, because for me Holden's "context" was simply life itself, life as I knew it. But as a professional critic and teacher, I now insist that a more specific and rigorous analysis of context can enhance rather than diminish one's appreciation of Holden.

One such context, for example, is the Second World War. As part of the revival of interest in America's last "good war" that has in recent years played such a prominent role in American popular culture, the notion that *The Catcher in the Rye* is in some sense about that war—that it is, as Louis Menand suggested in a fiftieth-anniversary essay published in the *New Yorker*, more a book of the 1940s than the 1950s—has gained a certain currency. It has some biographical plausibility. Like several of his characters—D.B. Caulfield, Seymour Glass, the unnamed American soldier who narrates "For Esmé—with Love and Squalor"—Salinger did serve in the war. He landed on Utah Beach during the fifth hour of the Normandy invasion and in the following months took part in some of the fiercest combat of the twentieth century; his daughter Margaret (author of a fascinating and remarkably even-tempered memoir called *Dream Catcher* [2000]) has said that he was among the first American soldiers to enter a liberated Nazi concentration camp. As a result of his combat experience he suffered something like a nervous breakdown—but only after the German army had surrendered—and, again according to his daughter, has remained forever after possessed by memories of the war and by a sense of his own identity as a soldier. It is often said that the truest and most sincere pacifists are combat veterans, and there may well be a direct connection between Salinger's experience of war at its most ferocious and Holden's description of himself as "a pacifist, if you want to know the truth."

But there are no combat scenes in *The Catcher in the Rye*. A brief mention of D.B.'s military service is the most explicit indication the novel gives that World War II even took place. But perhaps it is the professional writer D.B. who himself supplies the best clue to reading the book as a war novel. Holden well remembers the occasion on which Allie suggests to D.B. that at least one advantage of D.B.'s time in the army must be that it gave him a good deal of material about which to write; D.B. replies by asking Allie to compare Rupert Brooke with Emily Dickinson and then to say who ranks as the greater war poet. The correct answer, as Allie sees at once, is of course Emily Dickinson. If Dickinson is indeed the great poet of the American Civil War—and if, for that matter, Virginia Woolf's *Mrs. Dalloway* (1925), with its unforgettable portrait of Septimus Smith, is one of the great World War I novels—then in much the same way *The Catcher in the Rye* can be read as a record of the war against Hitler. One way to express the gap between Holden's shrewd perceptions and his pathetic inability to act effectively is to say that he (again like Hamlet) just takes everything a little too hard. Wealthy and privileged as his background may be, Holden's world is every bit as bad as he says it is; but nothing plainly in it, not even Allie's death from leukemia, *quite* accounts for the extreme degree of pain and loneliness and psychic dislocation that often seems to lie just beyond Holden's awesome powers of self-expression. Life appears to have a kind of wrongness for Holden that neither he nor Salinger can ever completely verbalize, and it may be that this wrongness is finally to be identified with the inexpressible barbarism of the Second World War.

Doubtless what is at issue here is not only the war in general but the Holocaust in particular, and at this point a war-centered reading of the novel may shade into an ethnic one. Again biography seems pertinent. Salinger's own ethnic make-up—of Jewish background on his father's side and Irish Catholic background on his mother's, just like the seven Glass children—was pretty unusual in his generation, and he is said to have felt severely dislocated by his mixed heritage, especially as regards his being, yet not being, Jewish. One can easily understand that, under these circumstances—and especially given the fact that during the 1920s, the 1930s, and well into the 1940s, anti-Semitism existed in the United States at levels that are practically unimaginable today—the annihilation of European Jewry was bound to be a deeply complex and traumatic event for him, especially after seeing some of the machinery of extermination with his own eyes: "You never really get the smell of burning flesh out of your nose entirely, no matter how long you live," he told Margaret. A further complexity was that he evidently had a tense, distant relationship with his father (who vainly wished that young Jerry would join the family business, a prosperous firm that imported kosher meats and cheeses), but a warm, loving one with his mother, to whom *The Catcher in the Rye* is dedicated: a situation perhaps reflected in Salinger's giving Holden an Irish surname and a home address not on the (stereotypically Jewish) Upper West Side of Manhattan, where he himself was raised, but on the (stereotypically Gentile) East Side—while also, however, supplying a note of Jewishness in the name of the Caulfields' next-door neighbors, the Dicksteins.

The context of war and ethnicity—the two categories intimately and complexly linked by the mediating term of the Holocaust—thus enters the novel as a determinate absence. We do not get overt scenes of combat or extermination, but instead something like the negative imprint of the unspeakable physical violence visited upon the world during the decade or so prior to 1951, the period during which Salinger worked, on and off, toward the completion of his novel. This context may well illuminate Holden's sadness and mental instability, though it hardly says much about his intelligence and sensitivity. Another context, however, and one that illuminates both these sides of his character, is presented far more explicitly: the context of class relations under capitalism, which constitute a different kind of violence.

Though Holden is constantly talking about the injuries of class, this dimension of the book has been astonishingly—or maybe not so astonishingly—ignored by journalistic and academic Salinger critics, as Richard and Carol Ohmann show in "A Case Study in Canon Formation: Reviewers, Critics, and *The Catcher in the Rye*" (perhaps the single most perceptive critical treatment of the novel to date, at least insofar as my own— fairly extensive though far from exhaustive—reading of the secondary literature goes). Class, of course, has been the great taboo subject in American discourse for more than half a century, a taboo so strong that it extends, to some degree, even into the overtly "progressive" circles of institutionalized cultural studies, where elaborate attention to race and gender is taken for granted. Still, it seems extraordinary that Salinger criticism has been able so thoroughly to erase a subject with which Salinger himself deals so overtly and so often.

Consider, for instance, Mr. Haas, the headmaster at Holden's old prep school Elkton Hills, who bears the remarkable distinction of being, in Holden's opinion, "the phoniest bastard I ever met in my life." Mr. Haas's general practice is to ingratiate himself as much as possible with the parents of his pupils, and he normally turns on as much charm as he can. But he does make exceptions:

> I mean if a boy's mother was sort of fat or corny-looking or something, and if somebody's father was one of those guys that wear those suits with very big shoulders and corny black-and-white shoes, then old Haas would just shake hands with them and give them a phony smile and then he'd go talk, for maybe a half an *hour*, with somebody else's parents. I can't stand that stuff. It drives me crazy. It makes me so depressed I go crazy.

Holden understands that, in the American upper bourgeoisie at the middle of the twentieth century, a fashionable suit and pair of shoes are *de rigueur* for a man, as a trim, elegant body is for a woman. He understands, too, that Haas cares nothing for his pupils or their parents as individuals: He is interested only in toadying up to those who unambiguously appear to be members in good standing of the class with which he identifies and toward which, probably, he aspires. Or consider—again—the successful businessman Ossenburger, who has amassed a fortune through a chain of cut-rate mortuaries ("these undertaking parlors all over the country that you could get members of your family buried for about five bucks apiece"). Holden has not, perhaps, read his Max Weber as carefully as he might have, and so fails, to remark that Ossenburger's speech suggests the links between capitalist acquisitiveness and Protestant spirituality as clearly as any Weberian sociologist could wish. But he does plainly see that Ossenburger is considered important enough at Pencey to rate a cheer at the football game and a speech in the chapel simply and solely because of his ability to throw large sums of money around: "[H]e gave Pencey a pile of dough, and they named our wing after him." Holden also possesses a shrewd sense of the routine fraudulence that so typically underlies capitalist success in modern America: "You should see old Ossenburger. He probably just shoves them [i.e., the remains of his customers] in a sack and dumps them in the river."

Haas and Ossenburger, then, are especially odious because of the relative purity, so to speak, with which they incarnate the market-based relations of the capitalist class structure. Conversely, the nuns that Holden meets at the sandwich bar are admirable not so much for their religious vocation (Holden admits to being "sort of an atheist"), but because they have chosen to live outside the class system to the maximum extent feasible. It is not merely that they spend their lives teaching school and collecting money for charity. Holden, after all, has known plenty of phony teachers, and charity can be practiced by those of his own high-bourgeois background— his mother, for instance, and his aunt (who is "pretty charitable—she does a lot of Red Cross work and all"), and Sally Hayes's mother—but when such women perform good works it is with no renunciation, or even qualification, of their privileged place in the socioeconomic hierarchy. Holden's aunt may help out the Red Cross, but "when she does anything charitable she's always very well-dressed and has lipstick on and all that crap. I couldn't picture her doing anything for charity if she had to wear black clothes and no lipstick while she was doing it"—that is, if she had to abandon, even temporarily, the uniform of her class position. As for Sally's mother, she (like her daughter) craves attention as a spoiled child does, and "[t]he only way *she* could go around with a basket collecting dough would be if everybody kissed her ass for her when they made a contribution." Otherwise, "[s]he'd get bored. She mould hand in her basket and then go someplace swanky for lunch." But the nuns are genuinely different: "That's what I liked about those nuns. You could tell, for one thing, that they never went anywhere swanky for lunch." Holden immediately adds that he is saddened by the nuns' inability to enjoy the swankiness that is routine for his own people—he does not sentimentalize the poverty they have chosen—but at the same time their integrity remains an inspiration in a world so heavily populated by those obsessed with scrambling up, or staying on top of, the class ladder.

Even before striking up a conversation with the nuns (who turn out to be moving from a convent in Chicago to one in New York), Holden notices that they have with them a pair of cheap suitcases, "the ones that aren't genuine leather or anything," and this observation provokes what is perhaps the most remarkable meditation on class in the novel. Holden thinks back to his roommate at Elkton Hills, Dick Slagle, who, like the nuns, had cheap suitcases, whereas Holden's own "came from Mark Cross, and they were genuine cowhide and all that crap, and I guess they cost quite a pretty penny." Holden finds Dick to be smart and funny, and the two are capable of having a good time together. But their relationship is soon poisoned by class. Dick is resentful and envious of the superior class position that the Mark Cross suitcases symbolize: He ridicules Holden suitcases as "bourgeois" (an adjective he then extends to Holden's fountain pen and other possessions) while also pretending to other people that the Mark Cross suitcases really belong to him. Holden is baffled as to what to do. He tries stuffing his suitcases out of sight under his bed, and is perfectly willing to throw them away or even to trade suitcases with Dick, if doing so will save the friendship. But nothing avails, and within two months both boys ask to be moved. Holden sadly sums up the lesson:

> The thing is, it's really hard to be roommates with people if your suitcases are much better than theirs—if yours are really *good* ones and theirs aren't. You think if they're intelligent and all, the other person, and have a good sense of humor, that they don't give a damn whose suitcases are better, but they do. They really do. It's one of the reasons why I roomed with a stupid bastard like Stradlater. At least his suitcases were as good as mine.

On personal grounds, Holden likes and admires Dick, and despises Stradlater, but such purely personal factors are finally less powerful than the social realities of class.

So the reality Holden confronts—the reality whose phoniness he so acutely diagnoses—is not "the human condition" or "the pains of adolescence" or any of the other ahistorical clichés that have dominated

Salinger criticism; it is, rather, the specific historical conjuncture of a particular time and place. What I find especially remarkable—and this is a point that even the Ohmanns, to whose excellent analysis I am much indebted, do not, I think, sufficiently emphasize—is the extent to which Holden, while perched near the top of capitalist America's class hierarchy, is nonetheless capable of understanding how much misery class relations cause. *The Catcher in the Rye* is about as far from being a proletarian novel as a novel can be, and it would sound odd to describe Salinger as a political writer. But the novel demonstrates that the standpoint of the proletariat is not the only one from which the injustices of capitalism can be glimpsed, and Holden's situation irresistibly suggests an impeccably Marxist point: namely, that any comprehensive system of oppression corrupts the quality of life for *everyone*, even for those who materially gain the most from it. In the eighth grade, of course, I was hardly capable of constructing a class analysis of a work of literature—though I strongly suspect (especially in view of Miss Greenwood's evident prescience as regards my political tendencies) that the sheer *rootedness* of Holden's outlook, the historical concreteness of his insights, did subliminally contribute to my spontaneous sense that Holden saw things as they really were. In any case, today this concreteness helps to confirm my sense that I was always justified in seeing Holden as simply right, and, though in chronological age he is only a few years older than my own daughter is now, there are important ways in which he remains for me a kindred spirit and even a hero. Miss Greenwood was clearly a far-seeing teacher—but could she have guessed anything like the actual impact on me of being introduced to J.D. Salinger?

And what, you may ask, became of Miss Greenwood herself? I have almost no idea. Not long after she taught me, she got married—becoming, after the all-but-universal fashion of the time, Mrs. Walker—and soon after that she left the school, probably because she and her new husband moved out of town. She is most likely a grandmother today—yet another staggering thought. I am tempted to try to get in touch with her, though it is not clear to me that this is feasible. How much, after all, do I have to go on? One possible—and very common—first name, two common Anglo-Saxon surnames, and the certain knowledge that, for a brief time in the mid-1960s, she taught English at Leroy Martin Junior High School in Raleigh, North Carolina. The evidence is scant, and the trail very cold. Still, I suppose a professional detective could do the job, and, given the resources of the telephone and the Internet, even an amateur might have a reasonable shot. But, beyond the question of whether the thing could be done, there is also the question of whether it would be a good idea. Such reunions sometimes produce much pleasure and even joy—such, indeed, has been my own personal experience—but one hears that sometimes they yield little but disappointment and embarrassment. It is possible that, in the aging grandmother I now imagine Miss Greenwood to be, I would plainly see traces of the skinny kid just out of college who once so enchanted my much younger self. But it is also possible that her whole manner and personality would seem utterly different and unfamiliar to me, whether because of actual changes in her, or because of flaws in my adolescent perceptions of more than three and a half decades ago, or because of the tricks that memory can play. Perhaps she would not even remember me except after detailed prompting, or—most humiliating possibility of all—not even *with* such prompting. So I remain undecided about trying to see Miss Greenwood again. One of the most startling and disconcerting things about living in a world with other human beings is the thousand and one ways they have of turning out to be different from what one had thought or assumed or expected or remembered them to be. The Miss Greenwood of this memoir may or may not (still) exist. But—and this is, of course, one of the most magical things about art—I am quite certain that for me Holden Caulfield will always, *always*, be there.

Character Profile

Holden Caulfield is a teenage boy rebelling against the hypocrisy of the world around him, refusing to conform to its expectations, and who is forever fantasizing about a highly romanticized utopian venue in which he can find solace and happiness. *The Catcher in the Rye*, in which he is the exclusive narrator, charts a series of episodes that take place during the course of approximately two days and is the story of the events leading up to his emotional breakdown and hospitalization in some unspecified mental health facility. As he tells us from the outset, his rejection of the established code at Pencey Prep, as evidenced in the school's advertisement, becomes his prototypical stance to all adult authorities and institutions. "'Since 1888 we have been molding boys into splendid, clear-thinking young men.'" The novel provides, in a very straightforward manner, a realistic expression of some of the most terrifying fears and anxieties experienced by its adolescent protagonist—essentially a simultaneous fear of, and preoccupation with, death, change and the anticipated responsibilities of adult sexuality. Thus, it is not surprising that Holden literally carries memories around in his suitcase or his great fondness for museums, where nothing ever changes and memories are safely stored. At the Natural History Museum, Holden enjoys looking at the dioramas which depict a romantic perspective on the Indians. "The best thing, though, in that museum was that everything always stayed right where it was. Nobody'd move.... and that squaw with the naked bosom would still be weaving that same blanket." And, true to his character, Holden's preoccupation with sex is manifested in all of his observations, even when he gazes at the inanimate Indian woman.

While the events which take place and the description of other people's response to him mandate a psychological interpretation of a troubled and frightened adolescent on the threshold of manhood, Holden also feels disenfranchised from the privileged social circle he is born into and the hypocrisy of the larger society of New York City in the early 1950's. Thus, *The Catcher in the Rye* is also a period piece, representative of the socio-economic and cultural concerns of post World War II America and is equally relevant to an understanding of Holden's personality because he observes phoniness and hypocrisy everywhere he turns. Finally, to the extent that J.D. Salinger is weaving literary references and allusions into Holden's narrative, a further dimension to Caulfield's character alleviates what would otherwise be a thoroughly depressing story. Indeed, as will be shown, Holden's literary interests are really the only vehicle for self-expression and communication with others, and, further, provide a rather touching sensitivity to an otherwise jaded and alienated selfhood. That literary sensibility is a highly "romantic" one, influenced by specific books which Holden mentions, and perhaps some which he has not told us about, a vivid imagination given to flights of fantasy, and, for all of his sexual bravado, a chivalrous attitude towards women. "The girls I like best are the ones I never feel much like kidding."

Holden Caulfield's crises begin with his having just been informed that he is being expelled from school because he is flunking all his subjects except English. However, though his departure is imminent, his remaining hours at Pencey are eventful, highly dramatic, and preoccupied with disgust for the hypocrisy and deceitfulness which surrounds him, a theme which is pervasive throughout *The Catcher in the Rye*. The first traumatic confrontation occurs when he must take leave of old Spencer and his wife, his history teacher who flunked him because he "knew absolutely nothing." Their meeting is torturous and filled with minute details of Holden's disgust. "But I just couldn't hang around there any longer, the way we were on opposite ends of the pole, and the way he kept missing the bed whenever he chucked something at it, and his sad old bathroom with his chest showing, and that grippy smell of Vicks Nose Drops all over the place." Indeed, this observation is vintage Holden Caulfield, for he will be telling the reader repeatedly exactly why, in the most minute detail, he is repulsed by the world around him, save for a few very notable exceptions.

Following his farewell to Spencer, Holden returns to empty his dorm room in the Ossenburger Memorial Wing (named after a proud alumnus who grew rich in the undertaking business) and is thankful to find himself alone while all the others are at a football game. This idyllic solitude provides a few moments of reflection in which Holden tells us that he enjoys reading books of true literary merit. "I read a lot of classical books, like *The Return of the Native* and all, and I like them, and I read a lot of war books and mysteries and all, but they don't knock me out too much." Following this literary meditation, Holden gives us his impression of some of his schoolmates. He finds Robert Ackley revolting to look at, with an equally distasteful personality. "His teeth were always mossy-looking, and his ears were always dirty as hell, but he was always cleaning his fingernails." But when he finds out that his roommate, Stradlater, has a date with a Jane Gallagher, Holden becomes extremely anxious that she will be seduced—Jane was a childhood friend whom he remembers very fondly. "It made me so nervous I nearly went crazy. I already told you what a sexy bastard Stradlater was." Holden wishes he could protect Jane from his unscrupulous roommate. Ironically, despite Holden's hostility towards Stradlater and his grave concerns about his date with Jane, he agrees to write a descriptive composition for him. Holden finds inspiration in thinking about his deceased brother Allie, whom he misses very much. Apparently, Allie wrote poetry on his baseball mitt, and it becomes the descriptive topic for the composition. "I happened to have it with me in my suitcase, so I got it out and copied down the poems that were written on it.... Besides, I sort of liked writing about it." Nevertheless, when the ungrateful Stradlater returns to his room, refusing to discuss the date and dissatisfied with Holden's essay, a fistfight ensues, and Holden takes a real beating. The act of fighting with Stradlater can be read as a literary analogue, namely that of a chivalrous knight in a medieval romance, placing himself in danger for a lady's honor. It is also significant that Holden will later remark that he knows Jane Gallagher like a book. "I knew her like a book.... I really did. I mean, besides checkers, she was quite fond of all athletic sports.... I really got to know her quite intimately." Following his fight with Stradlater, Holden decides to leave Pencey that very night, ahead of schedule, a preemptive gesture by one who is fearful of an uncertain future, most especially his parent's reaction to his failure.

Holden embarks on the next episode of his journey home when he decides to take a hotel room in New York City before facing his parents. It is a relatively brief interlude fraught with real danger and a critical time during which his fears and doubts of his own sexuality are repeatedly accentuated in a series of encounters with strangers. Indeed, one of the critical encounters during his hotel stay will lead to a potentially life-threatening confrontation with a prostitute and her violent pimp. Following his arrival in New York, Holden checks into the Edmont Hotel, an establishment "lousy with perverts," and then ventures out into the urban jungle where he meets a wide spectrum of society. In the hotel nightclub, the Lavender Room, Holden meets three girls "around thirty or so" whom he thinks of as "witches" and who evoke a profound sadness in him. "And that business about getting up early to see the first show at Radio City Music hall depressed me.... I'd've bought the whole three of them a *hundred* drinks if only they hadn't told me that."

As Holden makes his way back to his room, he meets Maurice, the elevator operator who offers to send a prostitute to his room for a supposed set fee. The events that soon unfold are both anxious and humorous when Sunny (the hooker) knocks on Holden's door. Before she arrives, Holden is extremely nervous as he recalls his previous, unconsummated sexual encounters with girls. "If you want to know the truth, I'm a virgin.... Anyway, something always happens. I came quite close to doing it a couple of times, though." Thus, it is no surprise that Holden does not avail himself of Sunny's proffered services. For Holden, the entire scenario becomes lurid and intensely lonely. "I felt more depressed than sexy.... She was depressing. Her green dress hanging in the closet and all." In his many extreme apprehensions about sexual experience, Holden indeed presents himself as one who prefers the safety of unrequited love. However, his original "contract" with Maurice proves invalid as prostitute and pimp try to extort more money from him. Fortunately, Holden survives the beating he receives from Maurice.

The following morning, Holden meets two nuns at a coffee shop. He becomes engaged in conversation with them when he learns that they are school teachers newly arrived from Chicago. Holden takes an immediate liking to them, especially to the one who is an English teacher, though he is also quite embarrassed when she mentions *Romeo & Juliet*, a play which, among other things, is about forbidden love between two young lovers. "I mean that play gets pretty sexy in some parts, and she was a nun and all, but she *asked* me, so I discussed it with her for a while." A short while later, he will think back positively about the nuns and how they are without social pretense. "That's what I liked about those nuns. You could tell, for one thing, they never went anywhere swanky for lunch."

The final critical encounters take place after Holden checks out of the hotel and resolves to visit his younger sister, Phoebe, a child whom his fantasies have transformed into the perfect adult—a woman who will listen to what he has to say and never pass judgment. There is also an implicit sexuality in his idyllic perception of his sister. However, since Holden is not ready to make his presence known to his parents, his initial return home is done surreptitiously, under cover of darkness, with the meeting taking place in Phoebe's bedroom. "She put her arms around my neck and all. She's very affectionate. I mean she's quite affectionate. Sometimes she's even *too* affectionate." After emerging from the closet (he is forced to hide when his parents get home earlier than expected), Holden resolves to look up his former English teacher, Mr. Antolini, who is now a professor of English at NYU. Though he is readily welcomed by the Antolinis, despite the fact that it is the middle of the night, Holden is left traumatized by what he considers a homosexual advance by his former teacher. The last bastions of refuge, having unraveled before his eyes, lead tragically to a nervous breakdown and his institutionalization in a mental health facility.

Contributors

HAROLD BLOOM is Sterling Professor of the Humanities at Yale University. He is the author of over 20 books, including *Shelley's Mythmaking* (1959), *The Visionary Company* (1961), *Blake's Apocalypse* (1963), *Yeats* (1970), *A Map of Misreading* (1975), *Kabbalah and Criticism* (1975), *Agon: Toward a Theory of Revisionism* (1982), *The American Religion* (1992), *The Western Canon* (1994), and *Omens of Millennium: The Gnosis of Angels, Dreams, and Resurrection* (1996). *The Anxiety of Influence* (1973) sets forth Professor Bloom's provocative theory of the literary relationships between the great writers and their predecessors. His most recent books include *Shakespeare: The Invention of the Human* (1998), a 1998 National Book Award finalist, *How to Read and Why* (2000), *Genius: A Mosaic of One Hundred Exemplary Creative Minds* (2002), *Hamlet: Poem Unlimited* (2003), and *Where Shall Wisdom be Found* (2004). In 1999, Professor Bloom received the prestigious American Academy of Arts and Letters Gold Medal for Criticism, and in 2002 he received the Catalonia International Prize.

WILLIAM T. NOON taught English at Fordham University and is the author of *Joyce and Aquinas* (1957); "Bard of the Shapeless Cosmopolis: James Joyce" (1965) and "The Religious Position of James Joyce" (1969).

LEVI A. OLAN was a renowned theologian and was made Rabbi Emeritus in 1970 at Temple Emanu-El in Dallas, Texas; served on the Board of Regents of the University of Texas from 1963 to 1969 and was President of the Central Conference of American Rabbis from 1967–69. He is the author of numerous works, including *Prophetic Faith and the Secular Age* (1982); "The Stone Which the Modern Builders Rejected" (1960); and *The Palestinian National Covenant:* (1968).

JAMES BRYAN has published several essays on Salinger's short fiction, as well as essays on William Dean Howells, Ernest Hemingway, and Sherwood Anderson.

WARREN FRENCH is the author of *John Steinbeck's Fiction Revisted* (1994); *The San Francisco Poetry Renaissance, 1955–1960* (1991); and *The Social Novel at the End of an Era* (1966).

SANDRA WHIPPLE SPANIER has been an Associate Professor of English at Penn State. She is the author of *Kay Boyle, Artist and Activist* (1986) and a contributing editor of *American fiction, American Myth: Essays* by Philip Young (2000) and *Process: A Novel* by Kay Boyle (2001).

EDWIN HAVILAND MILLER is Professor Emeritus at New York University. He is the author of *Salem Is My Dwelling Place: A Life of Nathaniel Hawthorne* (1991); Melville (1975); contributing editor of The Artistic legacy of Walt Whitman; a tribute to Gay Wilson Allen 1970) and editor of the six-volume *Correspondence of Walt Whitman* (1961–77).

MARY SUZANNE SCHRIBER is the author of *Writing Home: American Women Abroad, 1830–1920* (1997); *Gender and the Writer's Imagination: From Cooper to Wharton* (1987) and editor of *Telling Travels: Selected Writings by Nineteenth-Century American Women Abroad* (1995).

A. ROBERT LEE is the author of *Designs of Blackness: Mappings in the Literature and Culture of Afro-America* (1998) and *Black American Fiction Since Richard Wright* (1983); and editor of numerous books, including *The Beat Generation Writers* (1995).

JOYCE ROWE has been an Assistant Professor of English at Fordham University. She is the author of *Equivocal Endings in Classic American Novels: The Scarlet Letter, Adventures of Huckleberry Finn, The Ambassadors, The Great Gatsby* (1988) and "Social History and the Politics of Manhood in Melville's *Redburn*" (1993).

PAUL ALEXANDER is the author of *Boulevard of Broken Dreams: The Life, Times, and Legend of James Dean* (1994); *Death and Disaster: The Rise of the*

Warhol Empire and the Race for Andy's Millions (1994); and *Rough Magic: A Biography of Sylvia Plath* (1991).

ROBERT COLES is a child psychiatrist and has been a Professor of Psychiatry and Medical Humanities at Harvard University. He is the author of numerous books, including *Children of Crisis: A Study of Courage and Fear* (1967); *The Secular Mind* (1997); *Anna Freud: The Dream of Psychoanalysis* (1991); *That Red Wheelbarrow: Selected Literary Essays* (1988); and *Irony in the Mind's Life: Essays on Novels by James Agee, Elizabeth Bowen, and George Eliot* (1974).

CARL FREEDMAN has been an Associate Professor of English at Louisiana State University. He is the author of *Critical Theory and Science Fiction* (2000) and *The Incomplete Projects: Marxism, Modernity, and the Politics of Culture* (2002).

Bibliography

Bank, Stanley. "A Literary Hero for Adolescents: The Adolescent." *English Journal* 58(1969): 1013–20.

Baumbach, Jonathan. "The Saint as a Young Man: A Reappraisal of *The Catcher in the Rye*." *Modern Language Quarterly* vol. 25, no. 4 (December 1964): 461–72.

Belcher, William F. and James W. Lee, ed. *J.D. Salinger and the Critics*. Belmont, California: Wadsworth Publishing Co., 1962.

Bell, Barbara. 'Holden Caulfield in Doc Martens': The Catcher in the Rye and My So-Called Life." From *Studies in Popular Culture* 19, no. 1 (October 1996): 47–57.

Bloom, Harold, ed. *Holden Caulfield*. New York: Chelsea House Publishers, 1990.

Branch, Edgar. "Mark Twain and J.D. Salinger: A Study in Literary Continuity." *American Quarterly* IX (1957): 144–85.

Bryan, James. "The Psychological Structure of *The Catcher in the Rye*." *PMLA* 89, no. 5 (1974): 1065–74.

Cohen, Hubert I. "'A Woeful Agony Which Forced Me to Begin My Tale': *The Catcher in the Rye*." *Modern Fiction Studies* (1966-67): 355–66.

Edwards, Duane. "Holden Caulfield: 'Don't Ever Tell Anybody Anything.'" *ELH* 44, no. 3 (Fall 1977): 554–65.

Goldhurst, William. "The Hyphenated Ham Sandwich of Ernest Hemingway and J.D. Salinger: A Study in Literary Continuity." *Fitzgerald/Hemingway Annual* (1970): 136–50.

Hainsworth, J.D. "Maturity in J.D. Salinger's *The Catcher in the Rye*." *English Studies* 48(1967): 426–31.

Hamilton, Ian. *In Search of J.D. Salinger*. New York: Random House, 1988.

Hamilton, Kenneth. *J.D. Salinger: A Critical Essay*. Grand Rapids, MI: Eerdmans, 1967.

Huber, R. J. "Adlerian Theory and Its Application to *The Catcher in the Rye* - Holden Caulfield." From *Psychological Perspectives on Literature: Freudian Dissidents and Non-Freudians: Casebook*. Edited by Joseph Natoli. Hamden, Connecticut: Archon (1984): 43–52.

Kaplan, Charles. "Holden and Huck: Odysseys of Youth." *College English* XVIII (1956): 76–80.

Laser, Martin and Norman Fruman, eds. *Studies in J.D. Salinger: Reviews, Essays, and Critiques of* The Catcher in the Rye *and Other Fiction*. New York: Odyssey Press, 1963.

Lettis, Richard. "Holden Caulfield: Salinger's 'Ironic Amalgam.'" *American Notes and Queries* 15 (1976): 43–45.

Lewis, Jonathan P. "All That David Copperfield Kind of Crap: Holden Caulfield's Rejection of Grand Narratives." *Notes on Contemporary Literature* 32, no. 4 (Sept. 2002): 3–5.

Luedtke, Luther S. "J.D. Salinger and Robert Burns: *The Catcher in the Rye*." *Modern French Studies* 16 (1970): 198–201.

Lundquist, James. *J.D. Salinger*. New York: Ungar, 1979.

Menand, Louis. "Holden at Fifty: *The Catcher in the Rye* and What It Spawned." From *New Yorker* 77, no. 29 (October 1, 2001): 82–87.

Miller, James E., Jr. "*Catcher* in and out of History." *Critical Inquiry* 3 (1977): 599–603.

Nadel, Alan. "Rhetoric, Sanity, and the Cold War: The Significance of Holden Caulfield's Testimony." *The Centennial Review* 34, no. 4 (Fall 1988): 361–71.

Ohmann, Carol and Richard Ohmann. "Reviewers, Critics and *The Catcher in the Rye*." *Critical Inquiry* 3 (1977): 15–37.

Pinsker, Sanford. *The Catcher in the Rye: Innocence Under Pressure*. New York: Twayne Publishers; Toronto: Maxwell Macmillan Canada; New York: Maxwell Macmillan International, 1993.

———. "*Catcher in the Rye* and All: Is the Age of Formative Books Over?" *The Georgia Review* 50, no. 4 (1986): 953–67.

Roemer, Danielle M. "The Personal Narrative and Salinger's *Catcher in the Rye*." *Western Folklore* 51, no. 1 (January 1992): 5–10.

Rosen, Gerald. "A Retrospective Look at *The Catcher in the Rye*." *American Quarterly* 24 (1977): 547–62.

Salzberg, Joel, ed. *Critical Essays on Salinger's* The Catcher in the Rye. Boston: G.K. Hall, 1990.

Salzman, Jack, ed. *New Essays on The Catcher in the Rye.* New York: Cambridge University Press, 1991.

Seng, Peter J. "The Fallen Idol: The Immature World of Holden Caulfield." *College English* 23, no. 3 (December 1961): 203–09.

Steed, J.P., ed. *The Catcher in the Rye: New Essays.* New York: Peter Lang, 2002.

Steinle, Pamela Hunt. *In Cold Fear*: The Catcher in the Rye: *Censorship Controversies and Postwar American Character.* Columbus, Ohio: Ohio State University Press, 2000.

Strauch, Carl F. "Kings in the Back Row: Meaning through Structure—A Reading of Salinger's *The Catcher in the Rye.*" *Wisconsin Studies in Contemporary Literature* 2 (1961): 5–30.

Vanderbilt, Kermit. "Symbolic Resolution in *The Catcher in the Rye*: The Cap, the Carrousel and the American West." *Western Humanities Review* 17 (1963): 271–77.

Wells, Arvin R. "Huck Finn and Holden Caulfield: The Situation of the Hero." *Ohio University Review* (1960): 31–42.

Whitfield, Stephen J. "Cherished and Cursed: Toward a Social History of *The Catcher in the Rye.*" *New England Quarterly* vol. 70, no. 4 (December 1997): 567–600.

Acknowledgments

"Three Young Men in Rebellion" by William T. Noon. From *Thought* 38, (1963): 559–577. © 1963 by Fordham University Press. Reprinted by permission.

"The Voice of the Lonesome: Alienation from Huck Finn to Holden Caulfield" by Levi A. Olan. From *Southwest Review* XLVIII, No. 2 (Spring 1963): 143–150. © 1963 by *Southwest Review*. Reprinted by permission.

"The Psychological Structure of *The Catcher in the Rye*" by James Bryan. From *PMLA* 89, no. 5 (October 1974): 1065–74. © 1974 by The Modern Language Association of America. Reprinted by permission.

"The Artist as a Very Nervous Young Man" by Warren French. From *J.D. Salinger*. Boston: G.K. Hall & Co. (1976): 102–29. © 1976 by G.K. Hall & Co. Reprinted by permission of The Gale Group.

"Hemingway's 'The Last Good Country' and *The Catcher in the Rye*: More Than a Family Resemblance" by Sandra Whipple Spanier. From *Studies in Short Fiction* 19, no. 1 (Winter 1982): 35–43. © 1982 by Newberry College. Reprinted by permission.

"In Memoriam: Allie Caulfield in *The Catcher in the Rye*" by Edwin Haviland Miller. From *Mosaic* 15, no. 1 (Winter 1982): 129–140. © 1982 by Mosaic. Reprinted by permission.

"Holden Caulfield, C'est Moi" by Mary Suzanne Schriber. From *Critical Essays on Salinger's The Catcher in the Rye*. Edited by Joel Salzberg. Boston: G.K. Hall & Co. (1990): 226–37. © 1990 by G.K. Hall. Reprinted by permission of The Gale Group.

"Flunking Everything Else Except English Anyway": Holden Caulfield, Author" by A. Robert Lee. From *Critical Essays on Salinger's The Catcher in the Rye*. Edited by Joel Salzberg. Boston: G.K. Hall & Co. (1990): 226–37. © 1990 by G.K. Hall. Reprinted by permission of The Gale Group.

"Holden Caulfield and American Protest" by Joyce Rowe. From *New Essays on The Catcher in the Rye*. Edited by Jack Salzman. New York: Cambridge University Press (1991): 77–95. © 1991 by Cambridge University Press. Reprinted with permission of Cambridge University Press.

"Inventing Holden Caulfield" by Paul Alexander. From *Salinger: A Biography*. Los Angeles: Renaissance Books (1999): 63–77. © 1999 by Paul Alexander. Reprinted by permission.

"Anna Freud and J.D. Salinger's Holden Caulfield" by Robert Coles. From *Virginia Quarterly Review* 76, no. 2 (Spring 2000): 214–24. © 2000 by the *Virginia Quarterly Review*. Reprinted by permission.

"Memories of Holden Caulfield—and of Miss Greenwood" by Carl Freedman. From *Southern Review* 39, no. 2 (2003 Spring): 401–17. © 2003 by Louisiana State University. Reprinted by permission.

Index